Tropicalizations

Reencounters with Colonialism:
New Perspectives on the Americas

editors (all of Dartmouth College)

Mary C. Kelley, AMERICAN HISTORY
Agnes Lugo-Ortiz, LATIN AMERICAN STUDIES
Donald Pease, AMERICAN LITERATURE
Ivy Schweitzer, AMERICAN LITERATURE
Diana Taylor, LATIN AMERICAN AND LATINO STUDIES

Frances R. Aparicio and Susana Chávez-Silverman, eds.
Tropicalizations: Transcultural Representations of Latinidad

Michelle Burnham
Captivity and Sentiment: Cultural Exchange in American Literature, 1682–1861

Colin G. Calloway, ed.
After King Philip's War: Presence and Persistence in Indian New England

Tropicalizations

Transcultural Representations of Latinidad

Edited by Frances R. Aparicio and Susana Chávez-Silverman

Dartmouth College
Published by University Press of New England
Hanover and London

Dartmouth College
Published by University Press of New England, Hanover, NH 03755
© 1997 by Trustees of Dartmouth College
Printed in the United States of America
5 4 3 2 1
CIP data appear at the end of the book

"The Latino Imaginary: Dimensions of Community and Identity" by Juan Flores was originally published in *Polifonia salvaje: Ensayos de cultura y política en las postmodernidad*, I. Rivera Nieves and C. Gil, eds. (San Juan, P.R.: Editorial Postdata, 1995).

"On Sub-versive Signifiers: U.S. Latina/o Writers Tropicalize English" by Frances R. Aparicio appeared in different form in *American Literature* 66, no. 4 (December 1994): 795–801.

Contents

I. Tropical Refractions: *Latinidad* under the Dominant Gaze

II. In the Heat of the Night: Sexuality (South) of the Border

III. Relocating Hegemony: Tropicalizing Cuba from the United States

Acknowledgments

My love and gratitude to Gabriela and Camila for their patience and under-standing. Now they find the "tropics" in many spaces I would not have guessed. To Julio, for his love and unconditional support, *te doy las gracias*. And, of course, to Susana Chávez-Silverman, for daring to mix work and friendship in a most productive way!

F.R.A.

I am grateful to Peter R. Rainville for his editorial assistance with this book in its early manuscript stage, and for his patience and support throughout this lengthy project. Thanks also to my son, Etienne Joseph Strauss, for his enthu-siasm for the project, even when it (often) impinged on his computer time. I am grateful to my research assistant Marissa Muñoz for her assistance with the book in its final stages.

To my friend and colleague Frances R. Aparicio, I extend heartfelt thanks for her perseverence with this book and for nearly two decades of encourage-ment and support for this and all my intellectual endeavors (academic or not). We share a true collaboration vitally necessary and all too rare in academia. I would also like to thank the contributors for their essays and their patience, as well as the staff at the University Press of New England, especially series edi-tor Diana Taylor.

S.C.-S.

Frances R. Aparicio and
Susana Chávez-Silverman

Introduction

The term *tropicalization* was used by U.S. Puerto Rican poet Víctor Hernández Cruz in his eponymous collection published in 1976. Intimately linked to the concept of "transculturation" coined by Cuban anthropologist Fernando Ortiz, tropicalization, like its counterpart, has been employed in highly diverse contexts, often departing in substantial ways, both semantically and ideologically, from its original use. Drawing on the value of transculturation as the dynamic, mutual influence that a subordinate and a dominant culture effect upon each other in the "contact zones" (Pratt) of colonial encounters, this volume constitutes itself as a space for discursive dialogism in which both dominant and marginal subjectivities (Anglo, Latin American, and U.S. Latino/a) are at once given voice and constantly relativized in an analysis that attempts to transcend the old binary of self/other.[1]

Clearly indebted to Said's "orientalism," the etymological correlative within the Latino context would be "tropicalism," the system of ideological fictions (Said 321) with which the dominant (Anglo and European) cultures trope Latin American and U.S. Latino/a identities and cultures. The tropics have, of course, been scripted in Europe and the United States over twenty years ago by Levi Strauss's important book *Tristes Tropiques.* Moreover, since the turn of the nineteenth century, Anglo-American fiction writers, artists, journalists, and poets have represented the countries and cultures "south of the border" in textualizations that have, in the main, reified the political, economic, and cultural hegemony of the "neighbor to the north." In order to account for the overarching discursive patterns inherent in these hegemonic *tropicalizations*, the notion of tropicality, overdetermined for the Caribbean, must be extended to embrace México, Latin America, and, in more radical and innovative ways, the United States. In other words, our focus is perhaps better characterized as geocultural rather than narrowly geophysical.

1

In contrast to the unidirectional thrust implicit in Said's theory of orientalism, in which the Arab world is represented under the dominant western gaze, constructed by European discourses exclusively (and thus deprived of agency with regard to its own history and collective cultural identity), the conceptual framework of *tropicalizations*—its plural form and multiple subject locations proposed in this volume—allows us to include, as Silvia Spitta observes about transculturation, "the dynamics of the colony from the space and the perspective of the colonized" (Spitta, in this volume). Rejecting, however, as John Beverley does in "Writing in Reverse: On the Project of the Latin American Subaltern Studies Group," the earlier use of transculturation (informed by Angel Rama) as a model that "continues to privilege a fundamentally literary notion of the actual or potential representational adequacy of intellectuals and elite culture in relation to the subaltern" (Beverly 273), we conceptualize *tropicalizations* precisely as a tool that foregrounds the transformative cultural agency of the subaltern subject. In addition, Pratt's concept of the "contact zone," that is, "social spaces where cultures meet, clash, and grapple with each other often in contexts of highly asymmetrical relations of power" (Pratt 34), also informs our postcolonial reading and writing of *tropicalizations*.

Given the potential for semantic ambiguities in the term *tropicalizations*, even as we have distinguished it from the term in the singular—*tropicalization*—which would analogously follow from Said's *orientalism,* it is crucial that we define it further, also locating it in relation to earlier studies dealing with the influence of Latin America in the United States. As old as this term may be (it was used by Spanish *cronistas* upon their arrival in the so-called New World), it is still being defined and rewritten, notably by the essays in this volume.

Celeste Olalquiaga's *Megalopolis* (1992) and Frederick B. Pike's monumental study *The United States and Latin America: Myths and Stereotypes of Civilization and Nature* (1992) speak about the "latinization of the United States" (Olalquiaga 76) and "the Latin Americanization of America" (Pike 352) respectively. Although these terms suggest very different meanings, neither is congruent with our conceptualization of *tropicalizations*. Mapping these two approaches will allow us to situate our project within current scholarly and ideological frameworks.

Olalquiaga defines the "latinization of the United States" as "a process whereby U.S. culture and daily practices become increasingly permeated by elements of Latin American culture imported by Spanish-speaking immigrants from Central and South America as well as the Caribbean" (Olalquiaga 76). This process is one of three instances of cultural transformation involving Latin America and the United States. The other two, "the formation of hybrid cultures such as the Chicano and the Nuyorican" (76), and what Olalquiaga calls "the pop recycling of U.S. icons of both Latin America and U.S. culture itself at the moment of postindustrialization," a sort of "postmodern parody" (76), appear very different from the first type of cultural transformation.

Latinization proper is exemplified by the appropriation and reformulation of cultural icons such as food and clothing, language, popular music (the recycling of instruments, rhythms, and pop songs in "world beat" music), film, and religious iconography. Latinization is limited to reformulations of cultural icons by the dominant sector: it is, thus, synonymous with commodification. While Olalquiaga realizes, for instance, that the appropriation of Latin American food and clothing in the United States reifies the binary of "American" versus "ethnic" (77), she does not problematize the neocolonial gestures of a mainstream society that appropriates and co-opts subordinate cultural productions. In this context, Olalquiaga tacitly condones the dominant culture that constantly mines subordinate cultures for novel ideas, as Russell Ferguson puts it, constituting itself thus as the "invisible center" that cannibalizes the Third World other (Ferguson et al. 11).

Informed by a transculturative model that privileges the intellectual voice and is thus "complicit in the construction and maintenance of subalternity," as John Beverley would sustain (Beverly 273), Olalquiaga's examination of Chicano and Nuyorican agency in the latinization of the United States unfortunately conflates both sectors into a homogeneous group and virtually erases and silences the impact of Chicanos/as and U.S. Puerto Ricans in contemporary revisions of North American cultural identity and history. For Olalquiaga, both Chicano and Nuyorican cultures are "hybrid cultures" (Olalquiaga 80) that tend

to pull toward a more traditional setting, to the nostalgia for the homeland that characterizes first-generation immigrants. This nostalgia permeates the second- generation in the form of highly ethnocentric values—or resistance to them, an adamant denial of the legacy—and a family-centered behavior that, coupled with inadequate housing, education, and job opportunities, promote the isolation they should fight against. (80)

Basic contradictions underlie Olalquiaga's argument regarding Latino immigrants. If she earlier located latinization precisely in those "elements . . . imported by Spanish-speaking immigrants" (76), here she censures these "first-generation immigrants" for their tendency towards tradition and nostalgia. Perhaps rather than a flawed argument this is a strategy used to erase the power of Chicanos/as and Nuyoricans as political and cultural subjects (this is supported by the self/other construction reflected in her use of the third person in the quote above). For the author of *Megalopolis*, latinization is exclusively a "top-down" phenomenon, effected through the power and agency of the Anglo mainstream, not by the cultural agency of the Latino communities.

In the context of postmodern theory, Olalquiaga is certainly not alone in imbuing nostalgia with reactionary values. What theorists achieve in their dismissal of nostalgia is the depoliticization of the neocolonial status of U.S. Latinos by focusing on the individual (as Richard Rodríguez, the quintessential "Hispanic" apologist, does in his *Hunger of Memory*, for example)—memory, nostalgia, the "emotional" (Rodríguez 77)—as the exclusive repository of tradition and locus of cultural change. By ignoring the colonial history of both groups—the different political and cultural problematics that inform their current cultural heterogeneity—some cultural theorists neutralize the radical gestures of Chicano/a and U.S. Puerto Rican writers, artists, and cultural workers in the ongoing process of revising U.S. cultural history.

Contesting these interpretations, in "The Latino Imaginary: Dimensions of Community and Identity," Juan Flores foregrounds how "[f]rom a Latino perspective, analysis is guided above all by lived experience and historical memory, factors which tend to be relegated by the dominant approach as either inaccessible or inconsequential," possibly referring to studies such as Olalquiaga's, which dismiss the political and cultural significance of historical memory for colonized peoples such as U.S. Latinos/as.

After Olalquiaga mentions just three Nuyorican artists and musicians who mix traditional and modern elements in their work, she concludes her troubling analysis of Chicano and Nuyorican cultures with the following observation: "it is important to note that it has been precisely this nostalgia that has kept the majority of Latino communities from developing the parodic distance characteristic of the third type of acculturation" (Olalquiaga 81).

The third type of cultural transformation, the "postmodern parody" (82), is privileged over the previous two examples. This type of "pop recycling" involves turning "inside out the Latin American stereotypes produced by the United States and the postindustrial iconography thought to be primarily from the First World" (82). Olalquiaga illustrates this by focusing on Brazilian carnival floats, thus displacing these so-called postmodern practices from the U.S. Latino sphere. She indeed employs the term "tropicalization" in the context of this postmodern parody, suggesting that this category is the only effective one, for it "heightens the perception of [the] impersonality and consumptiveness [*sic*] [of high tech culture] without a trace of demagogy" (84). It can only follow, then, that the cultural productions of U.S. Latinos are inherently, fatally "demagogic" when they privilege the power and authority of the colonized subject.

In this discussion, Olalquiaga renders invisible the postmodern parodies of Chicanos/as and Nuyoricans. The works of performance artists such as John Leguizamo, Culture Clash, Guillermo Verdecchia, Luis Alfaro, Chicano Secret Service, Marga Gómez, Mónica Palacios and others, along with what we call the re-tropicalizing gestures of countless writers—Tato Laviera, Víctor Hernández Cruz, Pedro Pietri, Gloria Anzaldúa, Cherríe Moraga, Alicia Gaspar de Alba, and even Alurista and early Chicano writers from the Movimiento—have shown that the "turning inside out" of stereotypes has been a constant strategy among these two cultural groups.

The words of John Leguizamo and Guillermo Gómez-Peña, two decidedly non-nostalgic immigrants (the former is a second-generation Colombian-American, the latter a first-generation "Chicalango," as he puts it, born in Mexico), eloquently and decisively give the lie to Olalquiaga's analyses. In the introduction to the recently published script of his performance piece "Mambo Mouth," Leguizamo writes:

Some reviewers and members of the press insinuated that I was perpetuating stereotypes rather than lambasting them . . . In creating "Mambo Mouth," I felt that mocking the Latin community was one of the most radical ways to empower it . . . Like Latin itself, "Mambo Mouth" is harsh, graphic, funny—and at the same time tragic, desperate, painfully raw. No stereotype could contain the pressure of all those explosive, conflicting emotions. (Leguizamo 16)

In fact, according to Homi K. Bhabha, Leguizamo is right on. In a symposium for a special issue of *Art in America*, Bhabha writes: "Mimicry can be subversive: you use the language of the master in an alloyed form . . . to deflect the dominating ideologies being imposed on you" ("Art and National Identity" 82).

As if speaking directly to Olalquiaga and her postmodern "acculturation," in a piece called "Documented/Undocumented," Gómez-Peña writes: "We should clear up this matter once and for all: We (Latinos in the United States) don't want to be a mere ingredient of the melting pot" (Gómez-Peña 41). In "The Multicultural Paradigm," he writes:

We are undetermined "objects of desire" within a meta-landscape of Mac Fajitas, La Bamba crazes, MTV border rock, Pepsi ads in Spanish, and Chicano art without thorns . . . the contemporary art world needs and desires the spiritual and aesthetic models of Latino culture without having to experience our political outrage and cultural contradictions . . . our art is described as "colorful," "passionate," "mysterious," "exuberant," "baroque," etc., all euphemistic terms for irrationalism and primitivism. (51)

Finally, describing the above-mentioned process of domestication and articulating succintly his own "turning inside out" project, Gómez-Peña states: "These mechanisms of mythification generate semantic interference and obstruct true intercultural dialogue. To make border art implies to reveal and subvert said mechanisms" (40). By privileging the Latin American (Brazilian) subject and one particular artistic strategy (the so-called postmodern parody), Olalquiaga's theorizing on the latinization of the United States excludes and nullifies the cultural agency and transformations within a long tradition of re-writing by Chicanos/as and U.S. Puerto Ricans during the last thirty years. Olalquiaga's erasure of these two cultural sectors in her analysis of latinization illustrates how cultural studies unwittingly can exclude the very voices and subjects the scholar claims to "speak about."

In his recent and timely study, Frederick B. Pike traces in painstaking detail the historical development of the bipolar and bidirectional stereotyping that occurs from North to South and vice versa. Pike discusses a certain cultural permeability in both the North and Latin American contexts: "Latin Americans by the end of the 20th century have undergone a significant degree of Americanization. Meantime . . . the U.S. has been in many ways Latin Americanized, transformed into a land whose citizens flaunt in abundance the very worst traits that stereotypes throught the years imputed to Latin Americans" (Pike xvii).

What Pike addresses in a later chapter is the historical irony of the process by which the United States has become like the stereotyped Latin America. The recent social ills of increasing poverty giving way to a First World/Third World dichotomy in our own cities, the recent instances of political corruption in the government (Watergate, the Iran-Contra affair) that have led to cynicism among the populace, the failing economy and increasing national debt, social problems such as increasing random violence and drug trafficking, use, and abuse, an ineffectual educational system, the corruption of the free enterprise system—these are all examples evoked by Pike. This phenomenon, then, is not synonymous with Olalquiaga's "latinization" or with *tropicalizations* as we propose it here.

Pike does offer a valuable analysis of how the Self—the United States—has become its Other. This sort of iconic, negative "Latin Americanization" is the result of the ways in which the United States has displaced and transferred its own problems and internal social realities onto the Other south of the border. This is related, in particular, to the inability of so-called "Americans" "to part with the myth [of American exceptionalism]" (357–58), thus creating an "ongoing psychological and environmental distress in the domestic sphere" as well as [poisoning] "the environment of foreign relations with projects to refine and perfect Others—sometimes sincere and sometimes a fig leaf to cover naked self-interest" (357–58).

Indeed, Pike's "Latin Americanization" of the United States is reduced to the assumption that the social ills embodied south of the border—poverty, political corruption, the national debt, lawlessness, drugs, and loose morality, among others—have simply come home to roost (352–58). As we will see later, Pike's analysis informs our own definition of "hegemonic tropicalization," a process closely tied to the political and economic interests of the U.S. government, the media, and multinationals. While dominant discourses have displaced these "ills" onto Latin America, their very presence in the United States points to the ever-growing economic disparities between social classes that have resulted from the restructuring of the workplace (i.e., corporate downsizing), from free-trade agreements, and from the globalization of productivity.

While the use of the phrase "Latin Americanization" to convey the negative realities and symptoms of U.S. society is not necessarily Pike's own, his adopting the phrase indeed replicates and reinscribes the very constructs that he has traced throughout history. Pike's uncritical use of this phrase, along with his insistence on "America" to refer to the U.S., points up our own implication, as scholars, in the potential of discourse to represent and perpetuate asymmetrical relations of power. Although we can appreciate Pike's foregrounding the perniciousness of North American negative stereotyping of Latin America and Latin Americans in his massive book, his final paragraph constitutes a disappointingly trivializing coda which only reifies both the stereotypes and the structures that he has so painstakingly articulated throughout his study:

As the old saying goes, it takes two to tango; and the North-South partners who grudgingly share a hemisphere seldom make it out together onto the dance floor. Occasionally, though, as in the Good Neighbor days, they do manage to dance. Even then their movements, as in the classic tango, demonstrate a love-hate relationship. But this is what brings spark and drama to their dance. It's a dance of love and hate, of death, and maybe rebirth, pitting civilization against nature, with both partners disagreeing as to who assumes which role . . . It's a fascinating spectacle and almost as good as a happy one with which to end this book. (365)[2]

Pike's hemispheric, geophysical study, the vast continent, the complex web of historical interrelations of the two regions detailed through almost 400 pages, is reduced, finally, to the overdetermined sentimentality and sensuality of two petulant, fiery individuals dancing that most stereotypically hypereroticized Latin dance: the tango. Pike lards his allegory with plenty of old chestnuts: "as the saying goes," "it takes two to tango," "spark and drama," etc., and concludes by freeze-framing it into a "spectacle," "almost as good," he tells us, as the fairy-tale happy ending. Pike ironically seems to end up purveying the "mythical views" that, according to Guillermo Gómez-Peña, "only help to perpetuate the colonizing notions of the South as a wild and exotic preindustrial universe ever waiting to be discovered, enjoyed, and purchased by the entrepreneurial eye of the North" (Gómes-Peña 51).

For us, then, *Tropicalizations* takes on the challenge of constant vigilance and self-critique, aware of the binarisms and discursive traps that are not only structural but also deeply ideological in their repercussions.

I. Tropical Refractions: Latinidad under the Dominant Gaze

To *tropicalize*, as we define it, means to trope, to imbue a particular space, geography, group, or nation with a set of traits, images, and values. These intersecting discourses are distributed among official texts, history, literature, and the media, thus circulating these ideological constructs throughout various levels of the receptor society. To tropicalize from a privileged, First World location is undoubtedly a hegemonic move. In "Selling Nations," Brian Wallis writes that "Orientalism is a political fiction, a mythic idea of the East based on Western projections of fear. [It] is a deformed representation sustained through the misappropriation of the signs of foreignness, often entailing suppressions and exclusions" (Wallis 88). Analogously, the sort of *tropicalization* we are considering here would be a mythic idea of *latinidad* based on Anglo (or dominant) projections of fear. It is intricately connected to the history of political, economic, and ideological agendas of governments and of social institutions. Furthermore, these inscriptions facilitate the popular acceptance and justification of imperialist interventions, invasions, and wars, as the volume's opening essay, Beatriz Urraca's "A Textbook of Americanism: Richard Harding Davis's *Soldiers of Fortune*," proposes about the impact of Davis's novels on popular support for the Spanish-American War. By reproducing the image of a fragmented (fictional) Central American nation, a country in chaos and disarray, Davis justifies the need for U.S. intervention in Cuba and the Caribbean and "cements the illusion of the [U.S.'s] own post–Civil War unity." More recent instances of U.S. intervention in Latin America make manifest the strong political interests of the U.S. globally, interests that—as Pike has pointed out—were masked by reproducing negative images, by *tropicalizing*, in effect, the target countries and their leaders.

These *hegemonic tropicalizations*, instances in a long history of Western representations of the exotic, primitive Other, are deployed through particular discursive strategies. In her recent book *English Is Broken Here: Notes on Cultural Fusion in the Americas* (1995), artist and cultural critic Coco Fusco discusses the "literal" manner in which most Anglo and European spectators interpreted the "Couple in the Cage" exhibit. Fusco's and Gómez-Peña's performance—and audience reactions to it—powerfully illustrates how "human exhibitions dramatize the colonial unconscious of American society" (Fusco 47), which considers itself a model of democracy and represses its neocolonial guilt, displacing colonial phenomena onto so-called developing nations. The refusal to acknowledge (neo)colonial practices within the United States, as Fusco points out in the chapter "Who's Doin' the Twist?," is analogous to "the resistance of white artists, intellectuals and global cultural consumers to interrogate the power relations implicit in these [cultural] exchanges"

(66). Artists and writers from dominant sectors often appropriate images, symbols, and material elements of subaltern cultures, invoking creative "freedom" and the license to use and manipulate cross-cultural materials to augment their artistic repertoire. However, Coco Fusco insists that "more than freedom," it is "power" that continues to inform the "pitifully undemocratic" ways in which "the distribution of cultural goods and wealth" takes place in the Americas (77).

The essays in this first section foreground the complexities and power dynamics underlying Anglo-American representations of Latin America. In her essay on Richard Harding Davis, cited above, Beatriz Urraca demonstrates the ways in which the United States colonizes Latin America by establishing "Anglo Saxon homogeneity" throughout these countries. As Urraca suggests, the response of readers to Davis's *Soldiers of Fortune* evinced the blurring of fiction and history that was part and parcel of naturalizing the dominant textualizations proposed by Davis. Stephen Benz's "Through the Tropical Looking Glass: The Motif of Resistance in U.S. Literature on Central America," identifies the theme of resistance among writers such as Paul Theroux, Joan Didion, and others whose narratives about the tropics (and Central America in particular) textualize a simultaneous attraction and repulsion toward these cultures—a tension between fixation and disavowal, to use Homi Bhabha's phrase—in which the assumptions of narrators from dominant sectors are "tested" by the tropics. Debra Castillo's "The Tropics of the Imagination: 'Quetzalcoatl and All That,'" offers a lucid analysis of the tensions inherent in this contact with the southern "other," cultural encounters fraught with contradiction, with attraction and repulsion toward these cultures, which Castillo exposes as "vexed dis/positions" on the part of the imperialist subject.

Stephen Benz also examines a systematic discursive strategy, which predominates in hegemonic tropicalizations by U.S. authors, whereby the Latin American land is scripted as positive but its people are represented negatively. Analogous to representations of the western frontier in the history of the United States, artistic, literary, and cinematic representations of Latin America as a landscape evacuated of its human communities constitute a chilling objective correlative for the economic and political interests of an imperial power such as the United States. Writing Latin Americans out of the script, so to speak, is similar to representing them as primitive savages: in either case, whether scripted as lack or excess, *latinoamericanos* are dispossessed of their potential for economic, political, and cultural agency.

In the visual arts, Katherine Emma Manthorne's *Tropical Renaissance: North American Artists Exploring Latin America* offers a detailed and informative analysis of the ways in which the gaze of North American painters of Latin American landscapes was historically and politically conditioned—drawn—by "geographical myths" (10) about the land "south of the border." One of these myths privileges the taxonomy of flora and fauna over the recognition of the land's inhabitants. This discursive strategy—still current in tourist propaganda that depicts Mexican or Caribbean beaches invitingly deserted, laid out, laid bare under the gaze of the Anglo visitor—prevailed also in the Disney film *Three Caballeros*. Indeed, Disney's pivotal influence, since the '40's, in imprinting and translating *latinidad* (or *otredad*, cf. *Aladdin* and *Pocahontas*) for the Anglo consumer audience continues undiminished.

II. In the Heat of the Night: Sexuality (South) of the Border

The essays in this section analyze, among other topics, a powerful and pervasive variant of *hegemonic tropicalization*—omnipresent not only in literature but also in the popular media—that circulates and exploits gender-based myths and stereotypes about Latin American and Latino/a sexuality. In her essay "Tropicolada: Inside the U.S. Latino/a Gender B(l)ender," Susana Chávez-Silverman explores the circulation and deconstruction of representations of Latina subjectivity and its encoding as tropical, exotic, hyper-eroticized sexuality in a variety of aesthetic texts. From appropriative—and potentially exploitative—representations of Latinas in Kate Braverman's acclaimed second novel, *Palm Latitudes* (1988), and Sandra Cisneros's self-tropicalizing poetic speaker in *Loose Woman* (1995), Chávez-Silverman moves through Guillermo Gómez-Peña's radically contestatory yet virtually woman-erasing *borderology* to the Chicana lesbian *borderotics* textualized in Alicia Gaspar de Alba's poetry collection *Beggar on the Córdoba Bridge*.

These *hegemonic tropicalizations* are not the exclusive domain of First World writers, as Debra A. Castillo's and David Román's essays show. Latin American, Caribbean, and U.S. Latino/a communities are not internally homogeneous, and asymmetries of power are also evident in the representational gestures of subaltern subjects who write about and "other" those with even less power and social status. For *tropicalizing the other* can also be part of the project of Latin American writers from the center, as the figure of Mario Vargas Llosa illustrates in his representation of the indigenous subjects of the Amazon in "El hablador." By characterizing Vargas Llosa as a hegemonic writer, Castillo demonstrates how, in the Peruvian case, the intellectual "images" an Other as a way of reconsolidating a power that has been fragmented or historically threatened. In this sense, Castillo begins to unsettle the center/margin binary that our volume as a whole attempts to destabilize.

In "Tropical Fruit," by foregrounding the figure of the Latino "gay" man, David Román illustrates how "one system of counter-hegemonic practice ends up duplicating an equally troubling system of exclusion, both narrative and material." In Allende's *Of Love and Shadows*, Mario serves as a derivative figure to the protagonist—heterosexual lovers—and their revolutionary cause.

By having Mario facilitate the couple's escape but never fully developing him as a character—*disappearing* him after he performs his pivotal role in the narrative—Allende recuperates heterosexuality as the dominant paradigm. Similarly, Harry/Harriet in Michelle Cliff's *No Telephone to Heaven* and Dell in Paul Monette's *Afterlife* serve as the fulcrum for radical and revolutionary consciousness, yet their sexual difference ultimately is contained by literary representations that persist in eroticizing and exoticizing them.

In *Hybrid Cultures*, Nestor García Canclini calls for a recognition of "oblique powers," that is, the cultural reorganization of power which obliges cultural critics to analyze "the political consequences of moving from a vertical and bipolar conceptualization to one that is decentered, multidetermined, of sociopolitical relations" (García Canclini 323). While García Canclini's discussion focuses on the ways in which high and popular cultures have merged and on the contributions of cultural semiotics that allow us to recognize the power of audiences to construct their own meanings in their role as receptors, it reminds us of the constant need to relativize power, thus moving beyond the self/other paradigm. We agree with García Canclini that such a stance poses risks, mostly those of minimizing the pernicious effects of social, state, and media institutions in perpetuating social, racial, and gender differences. These are risks that in the '90s we cannot afford to forget.

It falls precisely to cultural critics—and to subaltern scholars with particular urgency—to be ever vigilant about the ways that Latino and Latina critics like ourselves also participate in the reinscription of boundaries and power differentiations. Silvia Spitta's essay warns that Cuban-American critics may "inadvertently reproduce or parodically engage" the same Western constructs about the Caribbean that have plagued its history. In her discussion of Cuban-American re-writing of Fernando Ortiz's concept of "transculturation," Spitta analyzes how pre-eminent critics Pérez Firmat and Benítez Rojo have we(l)dded "transculturation" to notions of assimilation while simultaneously developing "a theory of the bicultural U.S. minority subject." Spitta's close reading of Pérez Firmat's highly parodic deployment of Latin-lover discourse—which he internalizes to throw back at both the Anglo and the feminist reader—exposes the risks of these re-appropriations, many of which, as Chávez-Silverman also shows, ultimately lead to literal interpretations by the intercultural reader/ spectator of "uncritical self-tropicalizations" resulting in the commodification of the Latino/a body and of Latin America as a body politic.[3]

III. Relocating Hegemony: Tropicalizing Cuba from the United States

The notion of *tropicalizing from* is key to understanding how writing subjects position and re-position themselves inside and outside their objects of inquiry.

For Cubans in the United States—writers, scholars, immigrants—Cuba has remained the central object of their gaze. As the essays by María Teresa Marrero and Silvia Spitta reveal, to tropicalize Cuba from within the United States implies a distance from home that is historical, racial, political, generational, and based on class. Representations of Cuba and of Cuban identity by Cuban-Americans in the United States suggest a desire to recover that country and the home culture lost to the Cuban Revolution. As Marrero indicates in "Historical and Literary Santería: Unveiling Gender and Identity in U.S. Cuban Literature," Caucasian Cuban writers like Cristina García construct representations of Santería in ways that whitewash and deform the African-based elements of these rites. The racially informed reconstruction of Santería in García's *Dreaming in Cuban* constitutes an important example of how Cuban-Americans tropicalize Cuban culture from their own positions. Spitta, in "Transculturation, the Caribbean, and the Cuban-American Imaginary," critiques Antonio Benítez Rojo's nostalgic reconstruction of the Caribbean islands as both essentializing and eroticizing.

IV. Si(gh)ting *Latinidad:* Tropicalized Cultural Locations

A different, more radical sort of *tropicalization* emerges from the cultural productions, political struggles, and oppositional strategies deployed by some U.S. Latinos/as. The margins that bell hooks evokes as "sites of radical possibilities" are the locations from which these *re-tropicalizing* tendencies are surfacing. Guillermo Gómez-Peña's "border art," John Leguizamo, performer of the sensational "Mambo Mouth" and the more recent "Spic-O-Rama," Marga Gómez's one-woman "Latina Lezbo" monologues, and many other Latino/a writers and performers are standing the dominant culture's stereotypes and images on their heads from the margins, resemanticizing them, in García Canclini's words (*Transforming Modernity*), from hegemonic tools into discursive weapons of resistance.

Yet this is no mere discursive inversion. It is the embodiment of a larger instance of *transculturation*—also described by John Beverley and the Latin American Subaltern Studies Group as "transculturation from below" (Beverly 283)—by which subaltern Latino and Latina subjects and communities struggle to attain power and cultural authority in the circulation of cultural discourses. This struggle for discourse—for symbolic hegemony—is, certainly, also a struggle for social, economic, and cultural power. Latino/a cultures in the United States have achieved a modicum of visibility as a result of the Civil Rights movement. However, during the '80s and '90s, Latinos/as are witnessing systematic counterattacks on the part of the U.S. nation-state that are seriously undermining our previous political gains. The nationwide

"English-only" movement and legislation, Proposition 187 and the so-called "California Civil Rights Initiative" in California, and in California and Texas the dismantling of Affirmative Action in higher education are the most egregious recent examples of the resistance of the State, in part, to the *latinization* of the United States, to the visible empowerment of Latino and Latina voices in the debates over U.S. culture and identity.

The contested nature of discourse and particularly of labels as they have been used to imagine Latinos in the United States is the subject of Juan Flores's "The Latino Imaginary: Dimensions of Community and Identity." The author also distinguishes among three principal modes of defining the U.S. Latino community: the demographic, the analytic, and the imaginary. In response to studies that undermine the Latino/a subject's own conceptualization of self and community, Flores argues for the need to distinguish between the imposition of a "Hispanic" or even a "Latino" label from the outside and Latinos' own imagined identity as social movements and cultural agency continue to characterize their resistance and oppositionality to the colonized conditions that have informed their cultural displacements. The dynamic process of newly constructing subjectivity is evident in cultural practices and social movements such as *las casitas*, music, hybrid language, poetry, and art. Thus, Flores highlights the overlapping textures of both hegemonic and re-tropicalizing currents in the circulation of discourse about Latino identity.

In contrast to certain very specific *re-tropicalized* cultural locations (such as the *casitas* in New York's Bronx), Miami stands out as a tropical city par excellence, both in its public image as a Caribbean paradise and as tropical pandemonium a la *Miami Vice,* a city steeped in violence, chaos, and fear. Tropical Miami, then, is not necessarily the product of Latino resistance and cultural transformation but more the result of publicity, economic self-interest, and public relations. Miami is the epitome of the tropics in the United States. Yet these tropics, as read by Juan León in "Tropical Overexposure: Miami's 'Sophisticated Tropics' and the *Balsero*," manifest the complexities and contradictions of an urban construct that plays on its tropicality and *latinidad* as a tourist attraction, yet whose cultural attitudes and social policies towards immigrants from Latin America and the Caribbean reveal the very same fear and resistance—examined by Benz and Castillo—underlying *hegemonic tropicalizations* of Latin America.

It is urgent, then, that we dialogize studies on representation, power, and identity as they pertain to Latin(o) American geocultural spheres. As Frances R. Aparicio concludes in "On Sub-Versive Signifiers: Tropicalizing Language in the United States," it is essential to map "the historical attempts of the [Latino] communities to take into their own hands the transformation of their own circumstances," be they physical—as in the case of the *casitas* in the Bronx—or linguistic, educational, social, or political. Víctor Hernández

Cruz's narrative poem "The Man Who Came to the Last Floor," according to Aparicio, allegorizes the utopian inversion of Latino subordinate power in U.S. society. A Puerto Rican man throwing mango seeds from the top floor signifies a displacement of cultural power, an inversion of the exotic cultural Other, and a reconceptualization of English as the "pure" official language of the United States, as the concept of "sub-versive signifiers" proposes. Hernández Cruz's poem—and by extension much of his *oeuvre*—textualizes both actual and potential transformations by Latinos/as of the U.S. cultural topography. While for many, everyday survival in the geocultural borderlands, now perhaps more than ever, continues to be an existence of pain and powerlessness, many Latino/a cultural productions are becoming incorporated into the U.S. mainstream (García Canclini, *Culturas híbridas,* 291). This mainstreaming, made possible in part by the access to education and power gained as a result of the Civil Rights movement, also serves as a gatekeeping mechanism by which the dominant sector mediates and contains the political power of these self-representations.

In this context, the presence of "fruit" in this volume is not coincidental. David Román uses the term as a metaphoric codeword to refer to the representation of the "gay" Latino male in novels of resistance. Víctor Hernández Cruz's poem, in Frances R. Aparicio's interpretation, allegorizes the ideological, economic, and cultural symbolism that fruit evokes in cultural and gender politics. From Fernández de Oviedo's exoticizing colonial representation of the *piña* to Carmen Miranda's fruit-laden *sombrero,* through Pablo Neruda's famous anti-imperialist poem "La United Fruit Co." and García Márquez's magical realist evocation of the banana workers' strike in *One Hundred Years of Solitude* to the commercial campaign by Chiquita Brands to introduce the mango in the daily diets of Anglo-Americans, fruit has been an all-important symbolic—and literal—site of contestation between dominant, imperial cultures and Latin(o) America.

Conclusion

Tropicalizations seeks to contribute a polydirectional and multivocal approach to the politics of representation, seeking to avoid the pervading binarism in the field and the colonial gaze that essentializes and fetishizes subaltern cultures and privileges dominant ones. The essays in this volume position and reposition center and margin, subject and object, self and other in an ideological and discursive polyphony that, we hope, subverts and undermines these dualities, rendering them porous rather than dogmatic and antithetical. Thus, Latino Studies appears in the interstices of North and Latin American literatures and cultures, mediating between them, positioned as neither center nor margin.

We agree with Henry Louis Gates, Jr., that the "ritualized invocation of otherness is losing its capacity to engender new forms of knowledge" (Gates 299), and thus our attempt has been to inscribe Anglo, U.S. Latino/a and Latin American subjects as self as well as other, margin and center, or as neither. This volume conceives of itself as an interdisciplinary, cross-cultural dialogue around the changing dynamics of (at least) two major cultures in the Americas, exploring the transformations that have resulted both from the disturbing distance between them and from their mutual proximity.

Notes

1. We are indebted to the two evaluators for the University Press of New England, whose careful readings and incisive commentaries were indispensable for our revisions of this Introduction. Our conceptualization of the term *latinidad,* to which David Román and Alberto Sandoval allude in their recent essay, "Caught in the Web: Latinidad, AIDS, and Allegory in *Kiss of the Spider Woman, the Musical"* (*American Literature*, 67:3 [September 1995]: 580 n. 5), is at once in concert and in (fruit-ful) tension with Román and Sandoval's. Whereas we concur with Román and Sandoval that "[Latinidad] stands in direct relation to the term *Latino"* and we admire and support their stated project to "begin a much needed contextualization of theatrical representations of Latinidad" (558), we do not agree with some of their conclusions. Following the influential work of Chon Noriega, especially his important essay in *Jump Cut,* "El Hilo Latino: Representation, Identity, and National Culture" (1993), Román and Sandoval assert: "Just as *Latino* emerged as a term for self-identification to protest the U.S. Government–imposed census term *Hispanic, Latinidad* emerges as a term out to agitate the imposed imperialist notion of *Hispanic* culture (or *Hispanidad)"* (588). They continue: "the basis of its own [latinidad's] ideological construction and sustenance, however, is never overtly challenged. No need, then, to belabor the point that Latinidad does not distinguish between the various races, ethnicities, national origins, languages, and cultures housed under its label, or that the term slyly and comfortably homogenizes gender" (588). Our notion of *latinidad* is contestatory and contested, fluid, and relational, most easily conceived of along with our idea of *tropicalizations.* Just as we describe a bi-directional impulse in the plural form *tropicalizations,* so *latinidad,* for us, cannot be contained as a "type of organic understanding and appreciation of all things Latino," or even "a critical shorthand valorizing seemingly authentic cultural practices that challenge both colonial and imperialist U.S. ideologies in North and South America" (588). *Latinidad* has been, perhaps, and may still be, in some circles, synonymous with these descriptions, but for us it is more complex. We also utilize the term, for example, to describe the sets of images and attributes superimposed onto both Latin American and U.S. Latino subjects from the dominant sector—the object, therefore, of what we describe in this introduction as *hegemonic tropicalization.*

Our volume, as an intervention within and about *latinidad*, attempts precisely to "overtly challenge" "the basis of [latinidad's] own ideological construction and sustenance," problematizing the monolingualism, ethnocentrism, sexism, and homophobia present in the dominant Anglo as well as traditional Latin American and Latino cultures: the presence of Chávez-Silverman's, Marrero's, Aparicio's, Flores's, and Román's own essays in this volume poignantly give pause to some of the less hopeful conclusions about *latinidad* expressed in "Caught in the Web."

2. The descriptive imagery Pike settles on to conclude his study closely resembles the scenario Gustavo Pérez Firmat presents to his reader in the introduction to his 1990 edited volume *Do the Americas Have a Common Literature?* Unfortunately, as in Olalquiaga's postmodern analysis of "latinization," Pérez Firmat recycles these familiar dichotomies in hip, eroto-theoretical fashion, in order that they may serve here, he says, "as something of a critical model" (1). One does not have to read too deeply between the lines to recognize the selfsame "myths and stereotypes" Pike's book purported to unravel and which he, too, like Pérez Firmat, falls back on in his book's final paragraph.

3. Overall, the feminization of Latin America constitutes another discursive strategy in the overarching patterns of *hegemonic tropicalizations* by dominant sectors and by the so-called First World. This is clearly evident in Disney's *The Three Caballeros* as well as in subsequent filmic representations of "south of the border"; in the history of political cartoons about Latin America (cf. John Johnson); and in myriad discursive images that circulate in popular culture. For studies of this and related tendencies, see, for example, Young's *Colonial Desire: Hybridity in Theory, Culture, and Race* (1995), Donaldson's *Decolonizing Feminisms: Race, Gender, and Empire-Building* (1992), Coser's *Bridging the Americas* (1994), and especially Williamson's "Woman Is an Island: Femininity and Colonisation" in *Turning It On: A Reader in Women and Media* (1996).

Works Cited

Beverley, John. "Writing in Reverse: On the Project of the Latin American Subaltern Studies Group," *Subaltern Studies in the Americas, dispositio* XIX/46 (1994): 271–88.

Bhabha, Homi. "The Other Question: Difference, Discrimination, and the Discourse of Colonialism." In *Out There,* edited by Russell Ferguson et al., 71–88.

———. "Art and National Identity: A Critics' Symposium." *Art in America* (Sept. 1991), 80–83, 142–43).

Coser, Stelamaris. *Bridging the Americas: The Literature of Toni Morrison, Paule Marshall, and Gayl Jones.* Philadelphia: Temple University Press, 1995.

Donaldson, Laura E. *Decolonizing Feminisms: Race, Gender, and Empire Building.* Chapel Hill: University of North Carolina Press, 1992.

Ferguson, Russell, Martha Gever, Trinh T. Minh-ha, and Cornel West, eds. *Out There:*

Marginalization and Contemporary Cultures. New York: New Museum of Contemporary Art; Cambridge, Mass.: MIT Press, 1990.

Fusco, Coco. *English Is Broken Here: Notes on Cultural Fusion in the Americas*. New York: New Press, 1995.

García Canclini, Néstor. *Culturas híbridas: estrategias para entrar y salir de la modernidad*. México: Editorial Grijalbo, 1990.

———. *Transforming Modernity: Popular Culture in Mexico*. Translated by Lydia Lozano. Austin: The University of Texas Press, 1993.

———. *Hybrid Cultures*. Translated by Christopher L. Chiappari and Silvia L. López. Minneapolis and London: University of Minnesota Press, 1995.

Gates, Henry Louis, Jr. " 'Ethnic and Minority' Studies." In *Introduction to Scholarship in Modern Languages and Literatures*, edited by Joseph Gibaldi, 228–302. New York: Modern Language Association of America, 1992.

Gómez-Peña, Guillermo. *Warrior for Gringostroika*. Saint Paul, Minn.: Greywolf Press, 1993.

Leguizamo, John. *Mambo Mouth*. New York: Bantam Books, 1993.

Levi-Strauss, Claude. *Tristes Tropiques*. Translated by John and Doreen Weightman. New York: Atheneum, 1974.

Manthorne, Katherine Emma. *Tropical Renaissance: North American Artists Exploring Latin America, 1839–1879*. Washington and London: Smithsonian Institution Press, 1989.

Noriega, Chon. "El Hilo Latino: Representation, Identity, and National Culture" *Jump Cut* 38 (1993): 45–50.

Olalquiaga, Celeste. *Megalopolis: Contemporary Cultural Sensibilities*. Minneapolis: University of Minnesota Press, 1992.

Ortiz, Fernando. *Contrapunteo cubano del tabaco y el azúcar*. La Habana: J. Montero, 1940.

Pérez Firmat, Gustavo, ed. *Do the Americas Have a Common Literature?* Durham and London: Duke University Press, 1990.

Pike, Frederick. *The United States and Latin America: Myths and Stereotypes of Civilization and Nature*. Austin: University of Texas Press, 1992.

Pratt, Mary Louise. "Arts of the Contact Zone." *Profession* 91. New York: Modern Language Association (1991), 33–40.

Rodríguez, Richard. *Hunger of Memory*. New York: Bantam Books, 1982.

Said, Edward. *Orientalism*. New York: Vintage Books, 1979.

Wallis, Brian. "Selling Nations." *Art in America* (Sept. 1991): 84–91.

Williamson, Judith. "Woman Is an Island: Feminity and Colonization." In *Turning It On: A Reader in Women and Media*, edited by Helen Baehr and Ann Gray. London: Arnold, 1996.

Young, Robert J. C. *Colonial Desire: Hybridity in Theory, Culture, and Race*. London and New York: Routledge, 1995.

I

Tropical Refractions:
Latinidad **under the Dominant Gaze**

Beatriz Urraca

A Textbook of Americanism: Richard Harding Davis's *Soldiers of Fortune*

> [T]he United States of America—bounded on the north by the North Pole; on the south by the Antarctic Region; on the east by the first chapter of the Book of Genesis and on the west by the Day of Judgment . . . The Supreme Ruler of the Universe . . . has marked out the line this nation must follow and our duty must be done. America is destined to become the Light of the world.
> —Arthur Bird, *Looking Forward* (1899)

When Richard Harding Davis died in 1916, ex-President Theodore Roosevelt wrote in *Scribner's Magazine*: "He was as good an American as ever lived and his heart flamed against cruelty and injustice. His writings form a text-book of Americanism which all our people would do well to read at the present time" (Roosevelt, "Davis and the Rough Riders" 89). Davis's biographers disagree on the nature of the personal relationship between these two men, which dates from the late 1890s when Davis, then a correspondent for William Randolph Hearst's *New York Journal*, was reporting the Spanish-American War from the vantage point afforded by his attachment to the Rough Riders. The mutual admiration between Davis and Roosevelt is indicative of their engagement in a common project of exuberant nationalism in which writing, history, and politics intersect in order to redefine U.S. national identity primarily through the terms of its new role as a world power and its relationship with the rest of the western hemisphere.

Davis, the son of writer Rebecca Harding Davis, was born in Philadelphia in 1864. He began his journalistic career in Philadelphia and later moved to work for several New York newspapers. He traveled extensively in and reported from Mexico, Central America, Cuba, and other Caribbean countries, which eventually became the backdrop for his travel books, novels, and dramas. In this study, I will discuss the function of his work, especially his 1897 novel *Soldiers of Fortune*, in the textualization of Latin America for the U.S. imagination, in the fictionalization of the Monroe Doctrine, and in the construction of what Roosevelt called "Americanism" as a symbol of U.S. national identity in a hemispheric context. In the 1840s, the United States became a model of success to be imitated by the emergent southern republics; at that time, however, the U.S. notion of Americanism was still a question of asserting cultural independence from Europe and, at least for intellectuals, rarely involved a consciousness of Latin America's role in New World relations. In the following five decades, contacts between the Anglo-Saxon and Hispanic cultures increased, both through the westward expansion of the United States on the North American subcontinent and its increased political and economic interests in the Caribbean and Central America. Because of these historical developments, the nineteenth century drew to a close with a greater mutual awareness between the Americas, often expressed in terms of fear or defiance on the Latin American side and of power and superiority on the U.S. side.

The meaning of Americanism was also modified. While it retained the connotations of political and cultural independence from Europe that lay behind the formulation of the Monroe Doctrine in 1823 and Emerson's essay "The American Scholar" in 1837, Roosevelt's notion of Americanism, as defined in his speeches and writings of the 1890s, was also "broad adhesion to the whole nation," conceived as a monolithic entity in contrast to the anarchy and fragmentation of a South America he considered "a squabbling multitude of revolution-ridden States, not one of which stands even in the second rank as a power" (Roosevelt, *American Ideals* 19–26). National identity for the United States was—and continues to be—a function of existing in between two worlds: Europe and the other America.

Roosevelt's definition of Americanism against both Europe and Latin America was also consistent with his commitment to the Monroe Doctrine. To this would-be President, his country was like a woman in need of a defender "to stand up manfully for her when her honor and influence are at stake in a dispute with a foreign power" (241), and the Monroe Doctrine was the weapon to protect her against her potential enemies. This kind of gendered rhetoric exalting maleness and the "strenuous life" was also present in José Martí's calls for "una respuesta unánime y viril" [a virile and unanimous response] on the part of Latin America as a form of resistance to the advance of the U.S. empire (Martí, *Nuestra América* 48).[1] The original text of President Monroe's 1823 address reflects an intent to preserve the uniqueness of the American republican

system and to prevent European powers from extending their colonial possessions in the New World:

> The political system of the allied powers is essentially different in this respect from that
> of America . . . It is impossible that the allied powers should extend their political sys-
> tem to any portion of either continent without endangering our peace and happiness;
> nor can any one believe that our Southern brethren, if left to themselves, would adopt it
> of their own accord. It is equally impossible, therefore, that we should behold such in-
> terposition, in any form, with indifference. (Showman 13–14)

However, after Monroe's administration, the Doctrine had gained increasing
acceptance as a justification of U.S. interference in Latin America's internal
affairs. This interpretation culminated with the Roosevelt Corollary of 1904,
which declared that

> chronic wrong-doing, or an impotence which results in a general loosening of the ties
> of civilized society, may in America, as elsewhere, ultimately require intervention by
> some civilized nation, and, in the Western Hemisphere, the adherence of the United
> States to the Monroe Doctrine may force the United States, however reluctantly, in
> flagrant cases of such wrong-doing or impotence, to the exercise of an international po-
> lice power. (Showman 34)

The Monroe Doctrine ultimately drove a wedge in U.S.–Latin American
relations. The southern republics interpreted it as a gesture promising U.S.
protection against European encroachment on their territory; when these expectations went repeatedly unfulfilled (Perkins 54, 63), and the unilateral
character of the Doctrine was established, what was regarded in the South as
a possible instrument of unification became a provocation and a cause for resentment (Selser 24; Fabela 11–12; Whitaker 37). I agree, however, with
Richard Collin's assertion that the idea of a unified western hemisphere was
always an illusion (Collin 5). As Lester Langley writes, "For the United States
the Monroe Doctrine ultimately assumed the lofty status of first principle of
the nation's foreign policy; for Latin America it became the distortion of the
Bolivarian dream by an acquisitive United States" (Langley 52). The reactions
varied from country to country. Toward the end of the nineteenth century, just
as the United States was paying closer attention to Latin America, Argentina
began to tighten its ties with Europe and to reject North American influence. In
the 1880s, Irigoyen and Alberdi, among others, voiced alarm at U.S. expansionism (McGann 105, 97). But Argentina was too far away to have cause for
real concern. As President Pellegrini wrote, "the Yankee empire will have as
its bounds the *aurora borealis* in the north, the equator in the south, the rising
sun in the east, and the immensity of the west. Lucky for us they are stopping
for the present at the equator" (quoted in McGann 187).

Mexico, the Caribbean, and Central America fared differently. Their geographical proximity placed them in danger of real aggression. By the end of the century, with the end of western expansion in North America, Manifest Destiny was redirected toward noncontiguous territories and new forms of empire, including "infinite expansion without colonial annexation, total control through the abdication of political rule, [and] the disembodiment of national power from geographical boundaries" (Kaplan, "Romancing the Empire" 671). Indeed, contemporary historians are exploring the similarities between frontier-building and empire-building and viewing turn-of-the-century imperialism as a special type of frontier expansionism (Nugent). Because Richard Harding Davis's novel deals with situations reminiscent of events taking place in Cuba at the time, it will be important, throughout this study, to juxtapose his views with the discourse of Cuban and Central American intellectuals who felt directly affected by the political effects of the ideology Davis's work espoused.

The changes in the history of the Monroe Doctrine force us to consider the United States' use of the term "America" in the light of the reactions which began to arise toward the end of the century. From early on, both Anglo- and Spanish-Americans associated the exclusive appropriation of the term by the United States with the Monroe Doctrine: "The United States have a proper name by which all the world knows and calls them. The proper name of the country is America . . . the fact is significant, and foretells for the people of the United States a continental destiny, as is also foreshadowed in the so-called 'Monroe Doctrine'" (Brownson 63). Though written in 1865, these words had the same force at the turn of the century when, more than ever, "America" was erected as a potent, virile U.S. empire. In one of the first Latin American books written about the Monroe Doctrine, the Cuban historian José María Céspedes maintained that it was necessary to read between the lines of the President's address, and that "America for the Americans" actually meant "América para los americanos del Norte" [America for North Americans] (Céspedes 218). Later on, when commenting on Secretary of State Frelinghuysen's 1882 assertion that the decision about American affairs rested with America, the Mexican scholar Isidro Fabela asked:

Al decir América, ¿se refería a los Estados Unidos? Parece ser que sí, pues es de observarse que cuando los estadounidenses hablan de América, casi siempre designan con este término a los Estados Unidos. Como si las veinte repúblicas restantes no constituyeran la mayor parte de América, o como si todas ellas pertenecieran a Estados Unidos. (Fabela 172)

[When he said America, was he referring to the United States? It seems so, for it must be observed that when the people of the United States speak of America, they almost always designate the United States with that term. As if the other twenty republics did not constitute the largest part of America, or as if they all belonged to the United States.]

Thus the greater mutual awareness did not bring the Americas closer. "America" became an increasingly divisive term, counteracted by José Martí's coinage of "our" America (1891) and José Enrique Rodó's exposition of the seemingly irreconcilable differences between the two major American cultures in *Ariel* (1900).

It was in this political climate, and alluding directly to these issues, that *Soldiers of Fortune* was published. The novel's protagonist, Robert Clay, is an engineer hired by Mr. Langham, a wealthy entrepreneur, to extract ore from the mines he owns in an imaginary Central American country called Olancho and to transport it to the United States. A military attempt to overthrow the current President, Mr. Alvarez, and restore control of the mines to the government of Olancho, disrupts Langham's plans. Clay single-handedly restores freedom and democracy to the country, thus preserving the economic interests of his employer, whose daughter he marries. At the end, Clay returns to the United States with his bride and becomes a member of the social elite to which the Langhams belong.

Many of Davis's works are unilaterally concerned with how the United States perceives its southern neighbors, and his treatment of Hispanic culture contains flaws that betray his lack of thorough knowledge of the language and culture (Porter 560–61). But this was not a problem for his audience, who always found more interest in his life than in his work, even though *Soldiers of Fortune* was an enormous literary success and was eventually turned into a play and a movie.[2]

The critical approaches to Richard Harding Davis have been dominated by the assumption that the history of the period developed as though following a script prearranged by him. It has been suggested that "the Rough Riders were an incarnation of Richard's conception of soldiers" (Langford 198), that "the Spanish-American War might best be described by saying that it could have occurred in one of Richard's novels" (Langford 193), and that "the war then looming was merely an elaboration of Davis's *Soldiers of Fortune*" (Hyde 97). Frederic Hyde credits this novel with having directly influenced United States–Latin American relations:

The disdain shown in it for members of the Latin race probably had something to do with the fact that American troops, when they landed in Cuba, soon decided their allies, the Cuban insurgents, were "worthless." And *Soldiers of Fortune*, as much as any novel of its time, seems to have prepared the way for that North American exploitation of the so-called "banana republics" which in the first years of the 20th Century was to sow seeds of distrust for "Yankee imperialism." (134–35)

My own approach takes its point of departure from the premise that the representation of identity and otherness in *Soldiers of Fortune* reflects the practices described by Edward Said as "Orientalizing":

The value, efficacy, strength, apparent veracity of a written statement about the Orient therefore relies very little, and cannot instrumentally depend, on the Orient as such. On the contrary, the written statement is a presence to the reader by virtue of its having excluded, displaced, made supererogatory any such *real thing* as "the Orient." (Said 21)

Said's theory refers primarily to underlying cultural assumptions in works about the "Orient"; Davis himself consciously nourished the presumption that the Latin American reality had taken a backseat to his fiction. When he visited Central America in 1895 he had already written *Soldiers of Fortune*, though it would not be published until 1897, and in his letters home he expressed his surprise "to find how true my novel was to what really exists here" (C. B. Davis 143). On his return to Cuba in 1897, he described the island as the setting of *Soldiers of Fortune* and related his visit to various imaginary places mentioned in the book. "It is just like the description in that remarkable novel of mine," he wrote to his mother (195). And, while covering the Spanish-American War in 1898, he discovered that the heroic feats he narrated in his fiction presented a more readily acceptable vision of U.S. heroism than the performance of the army, which he described as amateurish (246).

At the same time, during his extensive and frequent travels, Davis dismissed the opportunity to obtain firsthand knowledge of Latin America in favor of previous literary descriptions of it. He said he shunned direct contact with the people of the countries he visited, though he frequently blamed this on Latin Americans' distrust and unwelcoming attitude towards North Americans (145). Rather than describing his experiences to his family, he referred them to previous readings: "It is pretty much as you imagine it is from what you have read, that covers it, and I have discovered nothing new by coming to see it. I only verify what others have seen" (143). His fiction drew upon and reinforced pre-existing literary stereotypes, offering "the sayings of others about the other" (de Certeau 68) to his U.S. audience as a filter for the understanding of Spanish America and, at the same time—echoing Roosevelt's definition of Americanism—creating an image of the United States as a powerful, virile, unified nation that depended on those contrasting stereotypes to be believable. Davis's validation of his experience in Latin America through the authority of previous writings by himself and others places his own work in dialogue with western literary tradition about the Oriental, the primitive, and the barbarian; at the same time, his experience of writing translates and mediates the extra-textual reality, subordinating its existence to the fiction, and ultimately seeking to obliterate it. As Said writes, "It seems a common human failing to prefer the schematic authority of a text to the disorientations of direct encounters with the human" (Said 93). Yet while what Said describes is the traveler's "disappointment that the modern Orient is not at all like the texts" (100), in Davis's letters we find a disappointment precisely in the fact that the other America *is* the texts. Mutual contact between the Americas has always been mediated by a textual barrier through which representations of Latin America have penetrated the U.S. imagination as the exotic spot for vacations and shopping sprees or the dangerous region of illegal drugs and chronic revolutions, only at the expense of being silenced, and having national differences suppressed. In the early 1880s, José Martí, then living in the United States, had noticed an increasing respect for Latin America in the press, and a diminished number of allusions to the political instability of countries that were beginning to arise from social strife through hard work and technological progress (Martí, *Nuestra América* 12). Davis's work gave new validity to those stereotypes, proclaiming that any advancement made in Latin America had been brought about by U.S. expertise.

For Edward Said, "such texts can *create* not only knowledge but also the reality they appear to describe" (Said 94). Davis's story goes further: Olancho, the setting of *Soldiers of Fortune*, is literally an imaginary country, a conscious attempt to create the Latin America that best conformed to his own preconceptions and that best served the political ideology he supported. Much of the attention *Soldiers of Fortune* received was directed toward proving the real basis for the fiction, which in turn sought to validate it as history (Edeson; Porter). Similarly, in nineteenth-century Latin America "they went so far as considering narrative to *be* history; and several issued calls to literary action as part of the nation-building campaign . . . All this assumes that literature has the capacity to intervene in history, to help construct it" (Sommer 9–10). But as Doris Sommer also points out, this was possible because Latin American fiction and politics were inseparable, as the writers often were also politicians and even presidents (4–5); in the United States, where the two tend to be divorced, the task of connecting national imaginings to political realities has traditionally fallen to the journalist, and *Soldiers of Fortune* was the most successful novel of a very well-known one. Its serialization in newspapers, together with Davis's other non-fiction works on Latin American themes—*Three Gringos in Venezuela and Central America* (1896), *Cuba in War Time* (1897), and *The Cuban and Porto Rican Campaigns* (1898)—probably contributed to the blurring of the line between fiction and history.[3]

Much has been written about the geographical basis for *Soldiers of Fortune* and its characters' real-life counterparts. Weimer is based on the American Consul in Cuba, Otto E. Reimer, and MacWilliams on David Kirkpatrick, the engineer of the Juragua Iron Company (Osborn and Phillips 50). W. H. Porter provides a map and a detailed description of the locale, which he identifies as a faithful reproduction, inverted, of the territory from Santiago to Siboney in the island of Cuba. Fairfax Downey tells of how during the Spanish-American War it was suggested that a copy of *Soldiers of Fortune* be given to every member of the Fifth Army Corps, so accurately were the scenes of the novel taken from that country, and ventures that "Davis was about to campaign in one of his own fiction settings" (Downey 151).

But the imaginary country of *Soldiers of Fortune* also has a "generic" quality that allows it to stand for any place in Latin America—to Davis, there were no meaningful differences between one country and another. In his letters home from Central America he recorded the monotony of the region: "we will probably . . . not visit another Republic. We have all travelled too much to care to duplicate, and that is what we would be doing by remaining longer in Central America" (C. B. Davis 147). Similarly, those characters in *Soldiers of Fortune* who are familiar with Latin America are bored with it; the rest are ignorant. The novel opens with a scene in which two ladies are talking about Robert Clay, who is said to have been "in New Mexico, or Old Mexico, I don't remember which" (R. H. Davis, *Soldiers of Fortune* 1).[4] Mr. Langham describes Olancho to his daughter as "one of those little republics down there" (25). The place is predictable and uninteresting to those who are more familiar with the region: "King knew what the capital would be like before he entered it, from his experience of other South American cities" (103). As they did for Davis himself, his characters' preconceptions blind them to the authenticity of experience.

According to William Ellis, "It was common in the nineteenth century to see one's national culture as unique and to contrast it to the rest of the world (often seen as an undifferentiated mass)" (Ellis 98). Yet in Davis's work the United States is also undifferentiated. Thus the novel glosses over the differences among Latin American nations at the same time as it makes its case for Anglo-Saxon homogeneity in the United States, a monolithic vision of citizenship that clashes with the cultural reality of the North American social body. The images were effective for political reasons: as Perkins suggests, "The American people . . . have believed, and they have frequently been told by their leaders, that their government was the most democratic, their institutions the most perfect, in the world" (Perkins 1). The persuasive power of Davis's book lies in its reinforcement of these tenets of North American national identity; the allegory of U.S. hemispheric control embodied in the strong, handsome, virile hero of *Soldiers of Fortune* was as seductive as the eroticism that dominated the plots of nineteenth-century Latin American national novels (Sommer 31).

Roosevelt's practice of defining U.S. Americanism in opposition to "a contemptible knot of struggling nationalities" (Roosevelt *American Ideals* 3) was typical of the period and coincided with Davis's project. The fragmentation and instability of the socially and politically divided Latin America depicted in Davis's fiction provided the United States with a powerful contrast to cement the illusion of its own post–Civil War unity and strength at a time when the country

was not nearly as unified a colossus as it appeared. Congress represented a vast sea of separate American local interests, and until the 1890s the president was a relatively weak political figure who superintended the division of national party spoils in a nation that had little foreign policy and little interest in foreign affairs. (Collin xi)

In addition, by showing how a strong North American figure could easily bring law and order to war-torn Olancho, Davis's novel reassured readers of the imaginary political stability and racial homogeneity of their country, populated and governed by a "civilized" white majority. The work reinforced North American exceptionalism, embodied in what Nicolás Shumway has termed the "guiding fictions" which "give individuals a sense of nation" (Shumway xi): the Monroe Doctrine, the Declaration of Independence, the Constitution, Manifest Destiny, and the Civil War.

Davis's fictional and travel writings respond to his impression that Latin America by itself could never be appealing to a U.S. audience unless the story involved North Americans:

Up to date I think the trip will make a good story but it will have to be a personal one about the three of us for the country as it stands is uninteresting to the general reader for the reason that it *duplicates* itself in everything. But with our photographs and a humorous story, it ought to be worth reading and I have picked enough curious things to make it of some value. (C. B. Davis 155)

Like the travel book that resulted from these experiences, *Soldiers of Fortune* depends on the Anglo-Saxon hero for its success, grounded in the author's complicity with readers of his own culture whose assumptions about North American superiority and Latin American inferiority are not challenged. The novel is ultimately about Robert Clay and his friends; Olancho is seen through Clay's eyes, and the Olanchoans are secondary characters who speak in the same register as Clay does, a unitary language that stands in direct opposition to what Bakhtin terms "heteroglossia," and which effectively silences native voices and suppresses their difference. Yet, as Bakhtin argues,

[E]ven when heteroglossia remains outside the novel, when the novelist comes forward with his own unitary and fully affirming language (without any distancing, refraction or qualifications) he knows that such language is not self-evident and is not in itself incontestable, that it is uttered in a heteroglot environment, that such a language must be championed, purified, defended, motivated . . . for this discourse cannot forget or ignore, either through naiveté or by design, the heteroglossia that surrounds it. (Bakhtin 332)

For this reason, it would be unjustifiable to read Davis without reference to the contemporary Latin American, particularly Caribbean, voices also engaged in the discourse that constructed the new hemispheric relationships.

Contrast is what shapes self-definition: the barbarian, the savage, and the primitive all contribute to interpreting one's own identity by negation. Yet the self, as Said's argument implies, is inevitably imagined through its own invention of the other. *Soldiers of Fortune* fictionalizes both, interpreting the other America exclusively through the mediation of the United States and thus effectively denying its existence as an autonomous reality. Olancho's exoticism and simplicity astonish first-time travelers "with the fierce, hot tropics of their sister continent" (R. H. Davis, *Soldiers of Fortune* 102). As a knowledgeable guide, Clay escorts the Langhams through "what was most characteristic and picturesque" (103), "entertaining" (104), and "quaint" (105), in a country that seems to exist solely as a spectacle for the gaze of the North American visitor. In his role of guide, Clay gives his audience a simplified, easy-to-assimilate version of Olancho:

"It's a very beautiful country for the *pueblo*," was Clay's comment. "Different parts of the same tree furnish them with food, shelter, and clothing, and the sun gives them fuel, and the Government changes so often that they can always dodge the tax-collector." (101)

Olancho is packaged in the glittery, enticing rhetoric of tropical exoticism: "a land of romance and adventure, of guitars and latticed windows, of warm brilliant days and gorgeous silent nights, under purple heavens and white stars" (85), the perfect background—but nothing more—for the Anglo-Saxon hero's chivalrous feats and love conquests. For Davis, Latin America was a land of wealth and beauty, but also of laziness and incompetence (R. H. Davis, "William Walker" 161). He compared it to Africa, for in both continents he saw barbarism, lack of civilization (C. B. Davis 145), and a climate in which the customs of the civilized inhabitants of the temperate zone degenerated (Osborn 56). Davis thus refers us to the archetype of barbarism and primitivism, as well as to the tropes whereby Africa has traditionally been known: "a testing ground for men, a place of adventure, of rescues from danger. Then, after colonization, Africa is a place of 'work'" (Torgovnick 10). Thus Latin America must be known *by* Anglo-America, known *through* Africa; it is the new "dark" continent. Its authenticity and originality are once more denied through the Anglo-American's monolithic vision of what is different. As Marianna Torgovnick writes:

Our culture's generalized notion of the primitive is by nature and in effect inexact or composite: it conforms to no single social or geographical entity and, indeed, habitually and sometimes willfully confuses the attributes of different societies. Ethnographers tend to compare the societies they study to Western culture and to other societies that have been the object of ethnographic inquiries; even here a generalized primitive is often indirectly invoked as a way of understanding the special qualities of the group at hand. Less professional discourses often unabashedly and irresponsibly mix attributes and objects from widely separate geographical locales. (22)[5]

This process of invention of the primitive had traditionally been carried out by Europe and, after the mid-1800s, by the United States. As Edmundo O'Gorman argues in *The Invention of America*, "America was no more than a potentiality, which could be realized only by receiving and fulfilling the values and ideals of European culture" (O'Gorman 139). At the end of the nineteenth century, Latin America was once again reinvented by some of its own intellectuals in view of its prospects of becoming like the United States, and by the Northern Republic itself in view of its economic and political use for the aggrandizement of the Anglo-Saxon civilization in the New World. The process is far from over: throughout the twentieth century, the construction of Latin America has been an integral part of U.S. mainstream culture, with the difference that the global distribution of U.S. cultural products through the mass media facilitates the penetration of these images into the everyday life of the very societies they fabricate.[6]

Soldiers of Fortune was not only received as an accurate reflection of an extratextual reality, but also as playing a key role in creating that reality. Davis's fiction has been credited with shaping Latin America for the U.S. imagination (Langford x). His way of living and writing had a considerable influence on writers who followed (Hyde 116), and at a historical moment in which U.S. politics turned its attention toward Latin America, his plots and settings provided a literary means of expression that "opened a new locale for American writers, the bullets-and-bananas school of fiction" (Downey 114). His biographers and critics have credited him with shaping American attitudes and opinions toward Latin America for several decades (Langford 158; Osborn and Phillips 63; Boggs 199), and with making "an immense contribution to the fantasy of the natural superiority of the American, which halfway through the twentieth century still dominated Hollywood" (Ziff 180). Davis's fictional and journalistic writings contributed not only to North American mythmaking but, so his critics claim, had tangible effects on the election of Theodore Roosevelt to the Presidency,[7] on the nation's policymaking towards Latin America,[8] and on the North American public's readiness to see their country at war with Spain over Cuba.[9]

By locating the imagery of national self-definition outside the frontiers of the United States, *Soldiers of Fortune* displaces attention from internal conflict onto the foreign. Internal racial and political friction appears as the identifying feature of all of Latin America, whose inhabitants are uniformly described as a dark, barbarian race incapable of self-government and economic progress. Arthur Boggs's review of *Soldiers of Fortune* describes the racist aspects of the book, which assumes

> that North Americans . . . are innately superior to South Americans; that white is much better than brown or black; that most Americans are honest, resourceful, and energetic and that most Olanchoans (South Americans) are greedy, unimaginative, and lazy. (Boggs197–98)[10]

Davis had found Central American governments despotic, uncivilized, and unstable (C. B. Davis 143), their economic infrastructure in the hands of North Americans and other foreigners (R. H. Davis, *Captain Macklin* 74; Langford 156, 158; Osborn and Phillips 63). Robert Clay's adventure suggests a course of interventionist action that, like Roosevelt's 1904 Corollary to the Monroe Doctrine later proposed, would correct the Olanchoans' "chronic wrong-doing." Clay is fashioned as a Quixotic righter of wrongs, a "powder-splashed young man who set American citizens at liberty" (335) in strange lands.

Earlier in his career, Davis had been strongly anti-imperialistic, and had written in favor of the Monroe Doctrine as a moral position and not a promise to back Latin America by force of arms against European intrusion (Langford 160); later on, however, he moved to a position that advocated imperialism and supported U.S. intervention in Cuba both to protect North American business and properties, and "in the name of humanity" (quoted in Langford 184). During his first trip to Central America, he viewed the natives as incompetent for self-government and self-defense as well as for exploitation of their own national resources:

> The Central-American citizen is no more fit for a republican form of government than he is for an arctic expedition, and what he needs is to have a protectorate established over him . . . There is no more interesting question of the present day than that of what is to be done with the world's land which is lying unimproved . . . The Central-Americans are like a gang of semi-barbarians in a beautifully furnished house, of which they can understand neither its possibilities of comfort nor its use. (Quoted in Langford 157)

This is the attitude that shaped *Soldiers of Fortune*, which denies, as Amy Kaplan puts it, "national agency to the conquered" (Kaplan, "Romancing the Empire" 680). The native soldiers work the mines while a dandy's recreational yacht is easily turned into a warship and its sailors into soldiers. The Olanchoans are even incapable of doing what they do best—revolutions—properly. Clay knows that "the revolutionists will sleep late, . . . drugged with liquor and worn out with excitement"; the loyal soldiers submit to him because their natural state is a dearth of native leadership:

We have no officers. If you do not command us, there is no one else to do it. We promise that our men will follow you and give you every obedience. They have been led by foreigners before, by young Captain Stuart and Major Fergurson and Colonel Shrevington. (312)

In *Soldiers of Fortune*, Latin American backwardness and incompetence provide the perfect contrasting background for a show of North American strength and exceptionalism. The novel is a fictionalization of the political discourse of U.S. expansionism and national greatness, enacted as a reinvention of the national origins of Latin American independence. Davis admired Bolívar (C. B. Davis 164), and Clay himself claims to be "following out General Bolívar" (223), but the neglect of the Plaza Bolívar in Olancho signals the decline of the Independence ideals and forgotten heroes that were once thought by North Americans to be following the lead of George Washington:

The Plaza Bolívar stood in what had once been the centre of the fashionable life of Olancho, but the town had moved farther up the hill, and it was now far in the suburbs, its walks neglected and its turf overrun with weeds . . . Clay picked his way over the grass-grown paths to the statue of Bolívar, the hero of the sister republic of Venezuela, which still stood on its pedestal in a tangle of underbrush and hanging vines . . . "It's just the place for plotting. I hope there are no snakes." (174–75)

The fact that the town has moved away from the square and its trivialization by the hero symbolize a turning away from the ideals for which the Liberator stood. The definition of national identity involves a simultaneous process of exclusion and inclusion. The exclusion of Latin America from the ideals of Americanism has also had internal repercussions for the exclusion of the United States' nonwhite population from full participation in the nation's political life and has helped define new forms of empire that prevent the further incorporation of these populations into the Union. According to Amy Kaplan, the New American Empire was the expression of "a desire for total control disentangled from direct political annexation" (Kaplan, "Romancing the Empire" 662), and it imagined "American global power . . . as anti-imperial in nature and not territorially based, but depending on international commerce and the spread of the United States' cultural institutions" (Kaplan, "Nation, Region, and Empire" 258). Throughout the 1890s, this was the side Roosevelt took in the debate about whether the United States, after the end of western expansion, should annex noncontiguous territories: he declared that "The Monroe Doctrine may be briefly defined as forbidding European encroachment on American soil . . . The United States has not the slightest wish to establish a universal protectorate over other American States, or to become responsible for their misdeeds" (Roosevelt, *American Ideals* 230). Territorial annexation in Latin America and the Pacific was considered by Roosevelt, among others, as inconsistent with the ideals of liberty and democracy that formed the basic tenets of the North American republic. Unlike Buchanan, a staunch supporter of Manifest Destiny, he considered the colonial subjugation of people ineffective and immoral.

However, North American attitudes rejecting an overseas empire had also been formed, throughout the nineteenth century, by two other ways of reasoning. On the one hand, there was the idea that the United States "conquer[s] to set free, and every accession of territory is only an extension of civilization and liberty" (Horsman 286). On the other, there was a political racialism that found its expression in the reluctance of Anglo-Saxon Americans to extend equal rights to nonwhites. Reginald Horsman has studied the influence of this "racial Anglo-Saxonism" in Manifest Destiny, concluding that though the United States had had designs on Cuba since the early 1800s, they objected to the incorporation of its Spanish population into the Union (Horsman 281–82). These objections, which remain in today's debate about Puerto Rico's statehood, were also present in the mid–nineteenth century after the United States' victory against Mexico (Berkhofer 155). Unlike Texas or Louisiana, "Cuba was too densely populated to be 'Americanized,' and Americanization consisted not in changing institutions but in changing the racial characteristics of the population" (Horsman 283). It is a combination of these two ideologies that finally accounts for Robert Clay's rejection of the Presidency of Olancho and the restoration of Rojas, a native, in his place. Thus at a time when the United States' foreign policies were not yet firmly established, Davis's fiction developed the manner in which North American intervention and expansion was to be done in much the same way as Roosevelt's ideology constructed it in the political arena.

Much of Davis's Latin American fiction was based on variations of the historical figure of William Walker. In *Real Soldiers of Fortune* (1906), Davis wrote a sketch about this North American filibuster who, in the 1850s, became President of Nicaragua and abolished the country's anti-slavery laws.[11] Walker's flag was a five-pointed star, which symbolized his ambition to rule the five "United States of Central America." Davis grouped him with the likes of Winston Churchill, and, like the North American people who gave Walker a hero's welcome in New York, admired this figure who, though prominent as a source of his fiction, has been largely ignored in his criticism. He wrote that "at no time in its history, as during Walker's administration, was Nicaragua governed so justly, so wisely, and so well" (R. H. Davis, "William Walker" 175). For Davis, Walker's only flaw was that he advocated slavery, and in *Captain Macklin* he creates characters that follow in Walker's footsteps to correct it: while also governing Honduras more justly and wisely than the natives, the Foreign Legion "will found an empire—not the empire of slaves that Walker planned, but an empire of freed men, freed by you from their tyrants and from themselves" (R. H. Davis, *Captain Macklin* 199). According to Gregorio Selser, the armed union of the five Central American countries contributed to Walker's ousting from Nicaragua (Selser 8, 38), but in Davis's version he was checked by his own countrymen (R. H. Davis, "William Walker" 147) because his economic interests conflicted with those of entrepreneur Cornelius Vanderbilt. Though Congress turned a deaf ear, both Presidents Pierce and Buchanan initially disapproved, but ended up first tolerating, then supporting and recognizing Walker's regime (Selser 38–39).[12]

Walker, like Robert Clay and several other characters in the novel, was a soldier of fortune, a figure that upholds North American ideals and superiority condoned by, but acting independently of, the United States Government. The soldier of fortune is Davis's solution to the dilemma of North American imperialism, because it achieves the expansion of U.S. influence while dissociating its government from the dishonest aspects of his methodology. As Martí observed, "Por violencia confesada, nada tomarán. Por violencia oculta, acaso" [Through admitted violence, they will take nothing. Through hidden violence, perhaps] (Martí, *Nuestra América* 17). The Government thus escaped charges of intervention and violation of international treaties untainted, leaving the nation's dirty work and questionable wars to individuals who, like Oliver North in the Iran-Contra scandal, are hailed as heroes for actions that remain officially unsanctioned. Like Walker, Clay is hailed by the natives as "the Liberator of Olancho, as the Preserver of the Constitution, and their brother patriot" (330), but he turns down the offer of the Presidency of Olancho, a job he had previously considered he could do better than the natives (62, 205), apparently satisfied simply with having brought political order and justice to the country while securing the Langhams' economic interests. Here it may be useful to note that Roosevelt considered the merely material and commercial interests debasing to the ideal of true Americanism (Roosevelt, *American Ideals* 13); hence it was necessary for Davis, if his novel was to be consistent with this ideal, to present a positive political impact of the United States in Olancho. As a white man taking control of a Latin American revolution, Clay effects what Amy Kaplan calls a "whitewashing" of the Revolution "as an indisputably Anglo-Saxon heritage" (Kaplan, "Romancing the Empire" 682). Clay does not want Olancho, with its nonwhite native population, for himself or for the United States; instead of a five-pointed star that signals the ambition to control five nations, Olancho's five ore mountains will suffice.

The mediation of the events in the novel through the imagery of play highlights Davis's perception of the incapacity of primitive societies to take care of themselves and sets up Latin America as the ideal stage for the display of U.S.

superiority in engineering and warfare abilities while minimizing the importance and repercussions of the Latin American revolution. In *Soldiers of Fortune*, war is an easy game. The first skirmishes of the revolution are for Langham—the wealthy owner of the ore mines—the basis of an anecdote to amuse his friends at the Union club (216); for the sailors in the dandy King's yacht, an exciting opportunity to play with weapons (227); for the engineer MacWilliams, a card game in which "we took the first trick" (236). The tense military parade that precedes the outburst of the revolution is for Hope Langham, Clay's bride-to-be, "the same thing as a polo match," for her brother Ted, the reminiscence of a football match (244), and for Clay himself, a chess game, a scene in a play (245). When the revolution is fully underway, the American soldiers are "inclined to consider the whole affair as a pleasant outing" (316). The final moments are referred to as theatrical—the scene takes place in a theater—and a spectacle of gladiators (323–24). Similarly, in *Captain Macklin* the Foreign Legion's participation in the Honduran revolution is described as a comic opera (R. H. Davis, *Captain Macklin* 72) and a gamble (274). For all these reasons the North Americans are able to fight successfully with few "players"—the backing of native soldiers is significantly down-"played"—and to avoid casualties by counting on the Olanchoan admiration of their superiority at arms: "every South American thinks that every citizen of the United States is a master either of the rifle or the revolver, and Clay was counting on this superstition" (316).[13]

This kind of mediation also contributes to making the United States' involvement in the Olancho revolution appear trivial and indirect, exonerating North Americans from the consequences of violence and the accusations of imperialism; as in recent history, it is justified as an act of self-defense as well as of generosity in restoring peace and democracy abroad. When General Mendoza starts the revolution in Olancho, Hope asks Clay to intervene. His reply is modest: "You are very flattering . . . Even if I could stop him, it's not my business to do it as yet. I have to wait until he interferes with me, or my mines, or my workmen. Alvarez is the man who should stop him, but he is afraid. We cannot do anything until he makes the first move" (205). It does not take long for Clay to decide that the threat to himself and his business is sufficient, and the time comes to intervene. When he does, his motivation has changed:

They were there with arms in their hands, he said, for two reasons: the greater one, and the one which he knew actuated the native soldiers, was their desire to preserve the Constitution of the Republic . . . The second motive, he went on, was a less worthy and more selfish one. The Olancho mines, which now gave work to thousands and brought millions of dollars into the country, were coveted by Mendoza, who would, if he could, convert them into a monopoly of his government. If he remained in power all foreigners would be driven out of the country, and the soldiers would be forced to work in the mines without payment. (319)

José Martí had ridiculed the United States' pretension that a Latin American country could pose a threat to its national security (Martí: *Nuestra América* 17). As Lester Langley suggests, "Rarely were the goals that sustained the quest for national security called into question, only the means used to bring them to reality" (Langley 260). Even in our day, United States–Latin American policy follows the same dynamics, maintaining that intervention in Panama, Grenada, El Salvador, and Nicaragua responds to the necessity of self-defense as much as to interest in furthering the cause of democracy in the western hemisphere.

Politically, Olancho society is burdened by the corruption of President Alvarez, who seeks to steal the national treasure for his own personal use, and by the caudillismo of General Mendoza, who wishes to impose a military dictatorship on the country. Economically, there is no free trade, a fact which is hinted at through criticism of the low quality of Government monopoly products (104). Thus restoring liberty and democracy to Olancho goes hand in hand with an economic system that favors U.S. interests; Clay's goal in controlling the outcome of the revolution is not to duplicate the United States in Olancho—if this happened, the competition for power in the Americas would mean that the United States no longer was the strongest nation—but only to create the perfect conditions for its economic exploitation in a way that, as Martí remarked, repeats Spain's colonial despoliation (Martí, *Nuestra América* 60). Though Davis credits the native soldier-workmen with fighting for "their desire to preserve the Constitution of the Republic," which mandates that the Vice-President, Rojas, succeed the President (318), their patriotic duty is coupled with the desire to maintain the economic prosperity brought to Olancho by the North American entrepreneurs. If Mendoza won the revolution,

all foreigners would be driven out of the country, and the soldiers would be forced to work in the mines without payment. Their condition would be little better than that of the slaves in the salt mines of Siberia. Not only would they no longer be paid for their labor, but the people as a whole would cease to receive that share of the earnings of the mines which had hitherto been theirs. (319)[14]

Thus the materialistic image of Latin America as a path to riches contrasted with the notion of the United States as a nation founded on ideas. The new North American empire was more concerned with commercialism than with patriotism, as observed by Benjamin Kidd, a British traveler and writer who remarked that the United States' policies of overseas expansion, especially to Latin America, were driven by economic reasons.[15] Similarly, José Martí's descriptions of North American society highlighted, as Rodó's would a decade later, the United States' lack of a spiritual dimension and its emphasis on materialism:

[L]o que asombra allí es, el tamaño, la cantidad, el resultado súbito de la actividad humana, . . . esa movilidad, ese don de avance, ese acometimiento, ese cambio de forma, esa febril rivalidad de la riqueza . . . Otros pueblos—y nosotros entre ellos—vivimos devorados por un sublime demonio interior, que nos empuja a la persecución infatigable de un ideal de amor o gloria . . . No así aquellos espíritus tranquilos, turbados sólo por el ansia de la posesión de una fortuna. (Martí, "Coney Island" 163–64)

[What astonishes there is the size, the quantity, the sudden result of human activity, . . . that mobility, that gift for advancement, that aggressiveness, that change of shape, that feverish rivalry of wealth . . . Other peoples—and we among them—live devoured by a sublime inner demon that impulses us toward the indefatigable persecution of an ideal of love or glory . . . Not so those tranquil spirits, troubled only by the anxiety of possessing a fortune.]

While at this time Latin American nations were concerned with rectifying the errors of their short histories as independent nations, the United States set itself up as the agent of change not at home but abroad. Intervention in the Olancho revolution "corrects" history by staging a rebellion against an undemocratic regime and, in accordance with the Monroe Doctrine, by liberating its inhabitants at once from Europe's designs on their country and from their own mistakes. The main European element is the character of Madame Alvarez, the President's wife, a Spanish noblewoman plotting, separately from her husband, to become Queen of Olancho and to return the country to Spain:

She's a tremendously ambitious woman, and they do say she wants to convert the republic into a monarchy, and make her husband King, or, more properly speaking, make herself Queen. Of course that's absurd, but she is supposed to be plotting to turn Olancho into a sort of dependency of Spain, as it was long ago, and that's why she is so unpopular. (131)

Her plotting was never considered serious enough to be dangerous except to herself; her presence even ridicules her also corrupt husband, as it is considered a shame for the revolution to be started by a woman, and it highlights Davis's point that Latin Americans were incompetent to handle even their own political systems, no matter how corrupt and unjust: "And if you're a South American Dictator, you can't be squeamish about throwing your enemies into jail or shooting them for treason. The way to dictate is to dictate,—not to hide indoors all day while your wife plots for you" (206). Clay enjoys a short stint as Dictator of Olancho before a new President can be democratically elected, thus hoping not only to show Olanchoans how a proper dictator operates, but also utilizing this foreign arena as the stage for a role that would be considered inappropriate on U.S. soil.

The most action-packed parts of the novel deal with how Clay and his friends rescue Madame Alvarez from the forces of General Mendoza, who wants her dead. That Clay should devote his energies to saving a woman with whom he is not in love—in fact, he enlists his own lover, Hope Langham, in the effort—and with whose politics he does not agree either, suggests an image of a weakened, feminized Spain necessitating the charitable aid of the strong, male United States to save her from a dangerous situation created by her own hopeless thirst for colonial power. Madame Alvarez is saved, but her forced departure from Olancho is a gesture of giving up America to the sole influence of the United States.

The European presence pervades the novel in other, subtler ways, that contribute to acknowledging a link to Old World civilization while demonstrating the ways in which the United States has been able to surpass its Anglo-Saxon heritage. Stuart, President Alvarez's English bodyguard, is one such element. He is also a soldier of fortune who combines loyalty to his new country and to the old. He "has been selling his sword" for military and economic advancement (207). His death in defense of Madame Alvarez makes him a true knight-errant, a crusader who "serves her with the same sort of chivalric devotion that his ancestors felt for the woman whose ribbons they tied to their lances, and for whom they fought in the lists" (207). Stuart's glorious ending aggrandizes him in the eyes of the other characters at the same time as it links him to a remote past:

One who had known him among his own people would have seen in the attitude and in the profile of the English soldier a likeness to his ancestors of the Crusades who lay carved in stone in the village church, with their faces turned to the sky, their faithful hounds waiting at their feet, and their hands pressed upward in prayer. (263)

However, though his death is heroic, it also represents a failure to fulfill his obligation of defending the President's hearth and home. Thus while finding in the European a glorious chivalric past to imitate, the new North American knight-errant bypasses death by combining chivalry with the practical skills of engineering. During his campaigns in Europe, Clay, rather than selling arms like Burke, the novel's mercenary, had "showed the other good-for-nothings how to dig trenches" and "designed a fort" (168–69), fighting with technology instead of weapons. In Olancho, he steps in as a new "Connecticut Yankee" who brings a happy ending instead of the catastrophic destruction of Hank Morgan's utopian dream. One of the most powerful scenes in the novel, illustrated by Charles Dana Gibson, shows the vigorous, manly figure of Robert Clay carrying Stuart's small, lifeless body up the stairs. Thus North America lays down the weight of a dead old world and continues its undone work.

Benedict Anderson has argued that one of the manifestations of nationalism is people's willingness to die for their country (Anderson 129–31). But North

American patriotism outside the nation's borders makes death a wholly unnecessary, outdated sacrifice. Stuart does not die for England, but for a woman; as for Clay, "He groaned at the mockery of having found his life only to lose it now, . . . and to lose it in a silly brawl with semi-savages" (290). This also makes William Walker's death seem like a thing of the past; having surrendered to a British naval officer, he was turned over to the Hondurans along with other prisoners and executed:

[The British captain] turned over his white brothers to the mercies of half-Indian, half-negro, savages, who were not allies of Great Britain and in whose quarrels she had no interest . . . and he offered, if Walker would ask as an American citizen, to intercede for him. But Walker, with a distinct sense of loyalty to the country he had conquered, and whose people had honored him with their votes, refused to accept life from the country of his birth, the country that had injured and repudiated him. (R. H. Davis, "William Walker" 186)

Clay displays no such loyalty to Olancho. Though Davis writes admiringly of Walker's loyalty to Nicaragua, his fictional characters triumph and live. Clay belongs to a different historical moment in which imperialist patriotism requires that the righter of wrongs escape unscathed to share everlasting happiness with the heroine. What the United States brings to Olancho is a new, efficient way of fighting a revolution, one that has a minimal cost in human lives while rapidly restoring political stability without jeopardizing the nation's natural and economic resources. Indeed, one of the causes of Davis's support of the United States' intervention in Cuba was his preoccupation with the island's destruction by the native insurrections (C. B. Davis 197).

This is a historical moment in which the outright exclusion of Europe from the western hemisphere gives way to Anglo-Saxon racial solidarity. According to Kelley Griffith, Davis's imperialism "upholds three things: the inferiority of non-European cultures to United States' republicanism; the inferiority of non-European races to White Anglo-Saxons . . . ; and the belief that the United States and other 'superior' cultures should rule these 'inferior' cultures or control their businesses and natural resources" (Griffith 130). Thus certain links with Anglo-Saxon Europe are cultivated, as long as the United States' superiority remains intact. Clay cooperates with the Englishman Stuart, his friend MacWilliams identifies himself as Scotch (123), and though he disagrees with Burke, the Irish-American arms dealer, mercenary, and promoter of revolutions, Clay sets him free at the end of the novel. Although a soldier of fortune like the others, Burke is not a heroic figure, because he is unpatriotic. His Irish accent is detectable (196), and he claims to be an Irishman and thus a British subject in order to obtain the protection of Her Majesty's representative against his imprisonment by Clay: "'That's no good, either,' said Clay, shaking his head. 'You fixed your nationality, as far as this continent is concerned, in Rio harbor, when Peixoto handed you over to the British admiral, and you claimed to be an American citizen, and were sent on board the "Detroit"'" (195).

This incident places Burke in direct contrast with Clay, Stuart, and MacWilliams, all of which also have interests in Latin America, but are ultimately loyal to their own countries. Burke exemplifies the kind of anti-Americanism that Roosevelt lashed out against:

> We welcome the German or the Irishman who becomes an American. We have no use for the German or Irishman who remains such. We do not wish German-Americans and Irish-Americans who figure as such in our social and political life; we want only Americans, and, provided they are such, we do not care whether they are of native or of Irish or of German ancestry. (Roosevelt, *American Ideals* 26)

Madame Alvarez, Stuart, and Burke all end up leaving Olancho. None of them is an entirely negative character, yet they all represent aspects of Europe that no longer have a place in America. On the other hand, Robert Clay integrates North American values with a kind of high European civilization that the United States has yet to internalize. He is a rough self-made frontiersman who in his spare time has obtained a European education. He learned to appreciate European art and music, and he can talk about concerts in Vienna with the same facility as about fighting wars in Africa or building bridges in South America. He has been decorated by European statesmen, and has been better received in European society than in the United States, where he is still considered a rough and semi-civilized cowboy.

In his social refinement, Clay represents the legacy of European civilization, which is portrayed as alien to Latin American culture, and at the same time he legitimizes the United States' position of power by means of an association with the religious Puritan rhetoric of North American mission that excludes Latin America:[16]

> [T]hey don't know how to amuse themselves in a civilized way—at least not in my way. I wish I could just drop in at home about now; don't you, MacWilliams? Just about this time up in *God's country* [my emphasis] all the people are at the theatre, or they've just finished dinner and are sitting around sipping cool green mint, trickling through little lumps of ice. What I'd like . . . to do now . . . would be to sit in the front row at a comic opera, *on the aisle*. (44–45)

On another level, however, Clay represents a uniquely North American aspect of civilization. He plays the role of the engineer as civilizer, the one who continues to extend the imaginary frontier of the United States overseas:

> They were marching through an almost unknown part of Mexico, fighting Nature at every step and carrying civilization with them. They were doing better work than

soldiers, because soldiers destroy things, and these chaps were creating, and making the way straight . . . They dragged their chains through miles and miles of jungle, and over flat alkali beds and cactus, and they reared bridges across roaring cañons . . . They are the bravest soldiers of the present day, and they are the least recognized. I have forgotten their names, and you never heard them. But it seems to me the civil engineer, for all that, is the chief civilizer of our century. (12–13)

This civilizing task is carried out through the North American work ethic, which contrasts with the laziness of Latin Americans. For Robert Clay, this is so important as to influence his choice of a wife who will understand, as Alice Langham does not, that the work he has done is a more important part of himself than the personality he was born with. Alice's sister Hope, on the other hand, proves to be an adequate spectator for Clay's endeavors, because she understands and admires both his person and his work: "We do not like men because they build railroads, or because they are prime-ministers. We like them for what they are themselves. And as to your work! . . . I think it is a grand work, and a noble work, full of hardships and self-sacrifices . . . You should be very proud" (211).

It is by virtue of the North American's transformation of Olancho's beauty and abundance into economic profit that the country becomes a place of interest to U.S. audiences. And Clay's fight against a dehumanized Spanish-American general's politics of enslavement is inseparable from his battle against a humanized nature: "And beyond the house he saw his five great mountains, the knuckles of a giant hand, with its gauntlet of iron that lay shut and clenched in the face of the sea" (97).

The civilizing mission of the North American engineer consists in transforming not only nature but also human attitudes, in turning native soldiers into miners. His work, as Davis himself put it in 1914 while making the movie version of *Soldiers of Fortune* in Cuba, is not only "to make the dirt fly and clear the jungle, to build bridges, barracks, hospitals, a railroad, and an ore pier, but with diplomacy to overcome the prejudices and indolence of a people who . . . had never changed" (R. H. Davis, "Breaking into the Movies" 275). Davis depicts the Olanchoan workers as shiftless, though not innately so. When Clay discovered the ore in the mountains, he wrote to Langham about the natives' ignorance and laziness which led to such resources going unused (29); the same attributed incapacity extends to self-government or the ability to choose the right form of government. But just as Clay can extract ore from the mountains, so can he obtain good work from the natives by respecting them, paying them fairly, living in the same conditions as they do, and speaking their Spanish patois. He compares the Spanish engineers' treatment of the workers to Southern slavery: "I've more respect for these half-breeds that you've allowed to starve in this fever-bed than I have for you. You have treated them worse than they'd treat a dog, and if any of them die, it's on your heads. You have put them in a fever-camp which you have not even taken the trouble to drain" (35). By improving the workers' conditions, Clay is also able to steal their loyalty to Mendoza and win their support as soldiers in the revolution.

Of all the soldiers of fortune in the novel, MacWilliams is the only one who retains a somewhat conventional patriotic feeling toward the United States. Though at the end of the novel he resolves to follow Burke to Macedonia, MacWilliams remains the prototype of the now-extinct western frontiersman who carries his country with him wherever he goes:

He came from some little town in the West, and had learned what he knew of engineer-ing at the transit's mouth, after he had first served his apprenticeship by cutting sage-brush and driving stakes. His life had been spent in Mexico and Central America, and he spoke of the home he had not seen in ten years with the aggressive loyalty of the confirmed wanderer, and he was known to prefer and to import canned corn and canned tomatoes in preference to eating the wonderful fruits of the country, because the former came from the States and tasted to him of home. (45)

While Clay can feel at home in European cultural circles and in the tropical ad-versity of Latin America, MacWilliams remains homesick and homeless, ide-alizing the United States to the smallest detail of everyday life.

Neither Burke nor Clay share this sense of belonging. For Clay, "Captain Burke is a brave soldier and a citizen of my own or of any country" (188), though Clay himself is unrecognizable as a North American officer because he has served in several armies but never in that of the United States (335).[17] All he has in North America is "a plot in the cemetery" in Colorado, where his mother is buried (169). And yet what distinguishes Clay from Burke is pre-cisely his Americanism, his sense of what is right to fight for. The only thing that binds the two men is a racial solidarity that, in the novel's system of val-ues, supersedes patriotism.

For all that the novel attempts to present the United States as a united, whole, homogeneous nation, Clay's character also exposes the class divisions existing in the society of the time. All the soldiers of fortune are social out-casts, though Clay's European refinement prevents him, unlike MacWilliams, from resigning himself to this fact. For Clay, living in the United States again entails being accepted in circles comparable to those he frequented in Europe, an acceptance that can only be sanctioned through marriage to Hope Langham. By representing the United States abroad, the novel achieves a certain social homogenization of the nation at home. The only racial differences are between North and South America. But in North American society, Clay himself is the outsider. He and his colleagues treat the Langhams like royalty, and when he plans a dinner for the Langhams, he is "gratified that they should know him to be not altogether a barbarian" (111). MacWilliams keeps reminding Clay of these class divisions which exclude them from the Langhams' social circles (147). Clay's marriage to Hope helps him bridge the class barrier but, in distinction from the Latin American novels analyzed by Doris Sommer, this union does not bring about the kind of nation in which lovers from divided camps can be together; it only reinforces the myth that class barriers can more easily be crossed than the racial, which remain as strong within the nation as those that separate the Americas. For marriage to have worked as an allegory of racial unification, Clay would have had to marry Mme. Alvarez, the "damsel in distress" whom he rescues from danger, and the only non-Anglo-Saxon female character in the novel.

Clay's name suggests a down-to-earth character.[18] As an engineer, he is in close contact with nature; at the same time, he is able to adapt as easily to the circumstances of life of the people who work for him as to the social conventions of the ruling class. By contrast, Reggie "King" denotes aristocracy and recalls the concepts of monarchy and social inequality inherent in European society. King redeems himself by helping in Clay's fight against the insurgents, but the differences between them remain. Clay fights on land while King fights from his yacht on the sea, at a safe distance. While Clay is an engineer who extracts from the earth the natural resources that will enrich his country and advance progress, King dabbles in archaeology, an activity that makes him useless as well as exploitative, like the Spanish conquerors: "From King he drew forth tales of the buried cities he had explored, and then robbed of their ugliest idols" (109). Yet Clay wants to be an engineer by day and an aristocrat by night, moving between the two environments as easily as he changes clothes. The occasional crossing over the borders of class and gender liberates the new North American hero and heroine, even if the crossing can only be done in one direction: both Clay and Hope are comfortable in European concert halls and American jungles; Hope herself, who "should have been a boy" (82), can adapt to both the feminine world of dance-halls and the masculine world of mines and railroad-engine driving. However, Hope, as Griffith points out, returns to dependence on men following her "bout of independence" and assumes a more feminine role after her marriage to Clay (Griffith 139).

Just as the turn-of-the-century United States defined itself through its borders, so its civilizing mission was being carried out by outcasts and outsiders who sacrificed recognition in their own country in favor of a world audience for the United States' international relevance at a time when Theodore Roosevelt became the first President concerned with America's position in the world while many politicians were absorbed in domestic issues (Collin 51).[19] The new heroes of Americanism were those who did not feel at home in North America because they were doing controversial, though desirable, work. Although they extended U.S. cultural values and protected its economic interests, soldiers of fortune did not fight for their country but for themselves, for economic gain, exciting adventure, and personal heroism. The Latin American view of them was, as can be expected, different: "Estos eran filibusteros vulgares que pensaban aprovecharse del botín, y que arriesgaban sus vidas por paga y no por patriotismo. Si hubiese existido en ellos el sentimiento más noble de acrecentar el poderío de su propia nación, merecerían alguna disculpa sus actos invasores" [These were vulgar filibusters who wanted to take advantage of the loot, and who risked their lives for pay and not for patriotism. If there had existed in them the nobler sentiment of aggrandizing the power of their own nation, their invasive actions would deserve some forgiveness] (Céspedes 365). Yet their individualism was also an expression of Roosevelt's definition of Americanism: "I ask only that what every self-respecting American demands from himself and from his sons shall be demanded of the American nation as a whole" (Roosevelt, *The Strenuous Life* 1). While his actions bring freedom to Olancho, the hero of *Soldiers of Fortune* remains more interested in his employer and in his lover than in rhetorical altruism and patriotism. Thus when MacWilliams announces that he is going to liberate the Macedonians, he fails to arouse Clay's sympathy for a feeling entertained for "a quarter of an hour": "Think of them all alone down there bullied by the Sultan of Turkey, and wanting to be free and independent. That's not right. You, as an American citizen, ought to be the last person in the world to throw cold water on an undertaking like that. In the name of Liberty now?" (343–44).

The popularity of *Soldiers of Fortune* was enabled by an idealization of United States–Latin American relations that presented an extensive North American economic empire while rejecting colonial domination over the tropics. In this novel, the United States' control of Latin American resources is masked by the heroic feats of the soldier-engineer whose restoration of liberty and democracy to strife-torn Latin American countries reimagines the terms of their independence as an accomplishment of the United States. At the same time, leaving Latin America politically independent temporarily reassures the United States of the prevalence of its own exceptionalism not only against Europe, but also within the western hemisphere.

Notes

1. See Kaplan, "Romancing the Empire," for an analysis of *Soldiers of Fortune* and other novels of the period as rewritings of U.S. national identity in terms of the male body.
2. John Solensten laments the lack of "major published studies devoted exclusively to

either the journalism or the fiction" of Richard Harding Davis and the fact that some of the existing biographies present "the man as greater than the work" (Solensten 303–4); Van Wyck Brooks called Davis "one of the most influential of writers, not as a writer but as a man" (Brooks 101). A new biography of Richard Harding Davis appeared recently, portraying him in a less than ennobling light as a person and dismisses his writings as crowd-pleasing and unimportant pieces that never challenged the status quo (Lubow).

3. In addition, Davis is the author of a novel loosely based on the story of the filibuster William Walker—*Captain Macklin* (1902)—two minor plays involving Americans embroiled in Central American revolutions—*The Orator of Zepata City* (1900) and *The Dictator* (1906)—and a book of biographical sketches, of which some have Latin American themes, *Real Soldiers of Fortune* (1911).

4. Page numbers correspond to this edition of *Soldiers of Fortune* and will subsequently appear in parentheses in text.

5. I agree with Torgovnick's point, though it is unfortunate that her own book fails to meaningfully take into account the discourses of intellectuals from the "primitive" societies she discusses.

6. See Julianne Burton's essay in *Nationalisms and Sexualities* (1992) for a discussion of how Hollywood's Latin America has been received on both sides of the border.

7. "His despatches from Cuba, featuring a colonel of the Rough Riders, helped to make a President of the United States" (Downey 2); "Davis . . . ultimately helped open to him the door of the White House" (Hyde 105–6); "with Davis to chronicle their exploits for newspaper readers, the Rough Riders so captured the public imagination that their organizer, Theodore Roosevelt, returned from Cuba to find a straight path to the White House laid out for him" (Langford x–xi).

8. In an 1895 letter to his brother Charles, Davis wrote: "Several of the papers here jokingly alluded to the fact that my article on the Venezuelan boundary had inspired the President's [Cleveland's] message" on the Monroe Doctrine (C. B. Davis 170–71; Quinby 37). Cleveland's message declared: "The doctrine upon which we stand . . . is strong and sound, because its enforcement is important to our peace and safety as a nation, and is essential to the integrity of our free institutions and the tranquil maintenance of our distinctive form of government" (quoted in Perkins 189–90).

9. *Soldiers of Fortune* sparked interest in Central America and "played a role in preparing the mood of America for the conflict which loomed just ahead" (Hyde 132). Others claim that "it must have stirred American fighting blood and been an unintentional preparation for the war we were about to wage" (Knight 122). A biographer writes: "Indeed, his part in the making of history at this time should not be discounted. Considering his reports from Cuba in 1897 and his coverage of the American invasion in 1898, it might be said that without him Hearst would have been somewhat less successful in whipping up war sentiment, and it is an obvious fact that without Richard as his laureate Roosevelt the Rough Rider would not have captured the public imagination so vividly as he did" (Langford 192).

10. In his later novel *Captain Macklin*, Davis describes the Latin American population even more contemptuously as "swarthy barefooted brigands" (R. H. Davis, *Captain Macklin* 61).

11. There are varying accounts of how Walker became President of Nicaragua. Davis himself believed that he was elected (R. H. Davies, "William Walker" 175); the Nicaraguan historian Gregorio Selser states that he made himself President (Selser 38). Other U.S. sources suggest that there was a rigged election (Carr 189).

12. See also Arthur D. Howden Smith's 1926 novel *A Manifest Destiny*, a fictional account of William Walker's exploits.

13. A few years later, while reporting the Spanish-American War in Cuba, Davis dismissed it as expensive entertainment, realizing that fictional entertainment was safer: "if this is war I am of the opinion that it is a senseless wicked institution made for soldiers, lovers, and correspondents for different reasons, and for no one else in the world and it is too expensive for the others to keep it going to entertain these few gentlemen" (C. B. Davis 198). He makes a similar comment in the William Walker sketch: "with his rifle one American could account for a dozen Nicaraguans" (R. H. Davis, "William Walker" 165).

14. Showman and Judson insist that the economic motivations of the United States' policy toward Latin America were linked to this country's uses and interpretations of the Monroe Doctrine throughout the nineteenth century (Showman and Judson 23–24, 32).

15. "The people of the United States will be driven to seek the widest possible outside market for their industrial productions; they must be able to buy raw material in outside markets . . . [T]here can be little doubt that the trade of the world in the future will be largely a trade with the tropics. The tropics are naturally the most richly endowed portion of the world . . . [N]o nation can remain permanently indifferent to the condition of a country with which it has large and vital trade relations" (Kidd 116–17).

16. "Only in the United States has nationalism carried with it the Christian meaning of the sacred. Only America, of all national designations, has assumed the combined force of eschatology and chauvinism. Many other societies have defended the status quo by reference to religious values; many forms of nationalism have laid claim to a world-redeeming promise; many Christian sects have sought, in secret or open heresy, to find the sacred in the profane, and many European defenders of middle-class democracy have tried to link order and progress. But only the American Way, of all modern ideologies, has managed to circumvent the paradoxes inherent in these approaches. Of all symbols of identity, only *America* has united nationality and universality, civic and spiritual selfhood, secular and redemptive history, the country's past and paradise to be, in a single synthetic ideal" (Bercovitch 176).

17. Davis's biographers have described him as a soldier of fortune (Downey 130; Griffith 104). While reporting the Spanish-American War, Davis was offered a captaincy, which he declined. In a letter to his brother he regretted the decision, thinking of himself as the hero of his own novel: "We shall not have another war and I can always be a war correspondent in other countries but never again have a chance to serve in my own" (C. B. Davis 240).

18. It also reminds us of Henry Clay, the U.S. politician who was a staunch supporter of Latin American independence.

19. See also Roosevelt's essay "The Two Americas" (Roosevelt, *The Strenuous Life* 229–41).

Works Cited

Anderson, Benedict. *Imagined Communities: Reflections on the Origin and Spread of Nationalism.* London: Verso, 1983.

Bakhtin, M. M. *The Dialogic Imagination.* Austin, Texas: University of Texas Press, 1981.

Bercovitch, Sacvan. *The American Jeremiad.* Madison: University of Wisconsin Press, 1978.

Berkhofer, Robert F. *The White Man's Indian.* New York: Alfred A. Knopf, 1978.

Boggs, W. Arthur. "Prologue to an Unpleasant Image (A Book Review Over Sixty Years Late)." *Phylon* 24, 1 (1963): 197–200.

Brooks, Van Wyck. *The Confident Years: 1885–1915.* New York: E. P. Dutton & Co., 1955.

Brownson, Orestes A. "The Proper Name of the Country Is America (1865)." In *Manifest Destiny and the Imperialism Question*, edited by Charles L. Sanford, 61–64. New York: John Wiley & Sons, 1974.

Burton, Julianne. "Don (Juanito) Duck and the Imperial-Patriarchal Unconscious: Disney Studios, the Good Neighbor Policy, and the Packaging of Latin America." In *Nationalisms & Sexualities*, edited by P. Yaeger et al., 21–41. New York: Routledge, 1992.

Carr, Albert H. Z. *The World and William Walker.* Westport, Conn.: Greenwood Press, 1963.

Céspedes, José María. *La Doctrina de Monroe.* La Habana: Imprenta La Moderna de A. Miranda y Comp, 1893.

Collin, Richard H. *Theodore Roosevelt's Caribbean: The Panama Canal, the Monroe Doctrine, and the Latin American Context.* Baton Rouge and London: Louisiana State University Press, 1990.

Davis, Charles Belmont, ed. *Adventures and Letters of Richard Harding Davis.* New York: Scribner's, 1917.

Davis, Richard Harding. *Soldiers of Fortune.* New York: Scribner's, 1897.

———. *Captain Macklin. His Memoirs.* New York: Scribner's, 1902.

———. "William Walker, The King of the Filibusters." In *Real Soldiers of Fortune.* 147–88. New York: Scribner's, 1911.

———. "Breaking Into the Movies." *Scribner's* 55 (1914): 275–93.

de Certeau, Michel. "Montaigne's 'Of Cannibals': The Savage 'I.'" In *Heterologies: Discourse on the Other*, 67–79. Minneapolis: University of Minnesota Press, 1986.

Downey, Fairfax. *Richard Harding Davis and His Day.* New York: Scribner's, 1933.

Edeson, R. "Soldiers of Fortune Founded on Facts." *The Philadelphia Press*, 1903.

Ellis, William. *The Theory of the American Romance: An Ideology in American Intellectual History.* Ann Arbor and London: U. M. I. Research Press, 1989.

Fabela, Isidro. *Las doctrinas Monroe y Drago.* Mexico: Escuela Nacional de Ciencias Políticas y Sociales, 1957.

Griffith, Kelley E. *The Genteel Romance in American Fiction 1880–1910.* Dissertation, University of Pennsylvania, 1968.

Horsman, Reginald. *Race and Manifest Destiny: The Origins of American Racial Anglo-Saxonism.* Cambridge: Harvard University Press, 1981.

Hyde, Frederic. *American Literature and the Spanish American War*. Dissertation, University of Pennsylvania, 1963.

Kaplan, Amy. "Romancing the Empire: The Embodiment of American Masculinity in the Popular Historical Novel of the 1890s." *American Literary History* 2, 4 (1990): 659–90.

———. "Nation, Region, and Empire." In *The Columbia History of the American Novel*, edited by E. Elliott, 240–66. New York: Columbia University Press, 1991.

Kidd, B. "The United States and the Control of the Tropics (1898)." In *Manifest Destiny and the Imperialism Question*, edited by Charles L. Sanford, 110–18. New York: John Wiley & Sons, 1974.

Knight, Grant C. *The Critical Period in American Literature*. Chapel Hill and London: University of North Carolina Press, 1951.

Langford, Gerald. *The Richard Harding Davis Years: A Biography of a Mother and Son*. New York: Holt, Rinehart and Winston, 1961.

Langley, Lester D. *America and the Americas: The United States in the Western Hemisphere*. Athens and London: University of Georgia Press, 1989.

Lubow, Arthur. *The Reporter Who Would Be King*. New York: Scribner's, 1992.

Martí, José. "Coney Island." Pp. 159–68 in *Obras Completas de Martí, Vol. 27*. La Habana: Editorial Trópico, 1940.

———. *Nuestra América*. Caracas: Biblioteca Ayacucho, 1977.

McGann, Thomas F. *Argentina, the United States, and the Inter-American System, 1880–1914*. Cambridge: Harvard University Press, 1957.

Nugent, W. "Frontiers and Empires in the Late Nineteenth Century." In *Trails: Toward a New Western History*, edited by Patricia Nelson Limerick et al., 161–81. Lawrence: University Press of Kansas, 1991.

O'Gorman, Edmundo. *The Invention of America*. Bloomington: Indiana University Press, 1961.

Osborn, Scott Compton, and Robert L. Phillips, Jr. *Richard Harding Davis*. Boston: Twayne Publishers, 1978.

Perkins, Dexter. *The Monroe Doctrine 1867–1907*. Gloucester, Mass.: Peter Smith, 1966.

Porter, W. H. "Mr. Davis and the Real Olancho." *The Bookman* XV (1902): 557–61.

Quinby, H. C. *Richard Harding Davis. A Bibliography*. New York: E. P. Dutton & Co., 1924.

Roosevelt, Theodore. *The Strenuous Life*. New York: The Century Co., 1902.

———. "Davis and the Rough Riders." *Scribner's* 60 (1916): 89.

———. *American Ideals and Other Essays Social and Political*. New York: AMS Press, 1969.

Said, Edward W. *Orientalism*. New York: Random House, 1978.

Selser, Gregorio. *Nicaragua de Walker a Somoza*. Mexico: Mex-Sur Editorial, 1984.

Showman, R. K., and L. S. Judson. *The Monroe Doctrine and the Growth of Western Hemisphere Solidarity*. New York: The H. W. Wilson Co., 1941.

Shumway, Nicolás. *The Invention of Argentina*. Berkeley: University of California Press, 1991.

Smith, Arthur D. Howden. *A Manifest Destiny*. New York: Brentano's, 1926.

Solensten, John M. "The Gibson Boy: A Reassessment." *American Literary Realism 1870–1910* 4, 4 (1971): 303–12.

Sommer, Doris. *Foundational Fictions: The National Romances of Latin America.* Berkeley: University of California Press, 1991.

Torgovnick, Marianna. *Gone Primitive: Savage Intellects, Modern Lives.* Chicago: University of Chicago Press, 1990.

Whitaker, A. P. *The Western Hemisphere Idea: Its Rise and Decline.* Ithaca, N.Y.: Cornell University Press, 1954.

Ziff, Larzer. *The American 1890s: Life and Times of a Lost Generation.* Lincoln and London: University of Nebraska Press, 1966.

Stephen Benz

Through the Tropical Looking Glass: The Motif of Resistance in U.S. Literature on Central America

Herman Melville, writing in 1846, begins the American literary encounter with the tropics, an encounter we are here calling "tropicalization." Early in his first work, *Typee*, Melville anticipates his arrival in the Marquesas:

The Marquesas! What strange visions of outlandish things does the very name spirit up! Naked houris—cannibal banquets—groves of coconut—coral reefs—tattooed chiefs—and bamboo temples; sunny valleys planted with breadfruit trees—carved canoes dancing on the flashing blue waters—savage woodlands guarded by horrible idols—*heathenish rites and human sacrifices*. (Melville 5; emphasis in original)

Melville's lines provide a good introductory description of "tropicalization." As I will use it here, the term suggests that travelers or fictional characters in U.S. literature, forced out of their cultural milieu, encounter, or believe they encounter, "strange visions of outlandish things." Tropicalization, then, is a process by which the hidden axioms and assumptions of the "temperate" North American culture have been tested in some way by exposure to a tropical environment, culture, or society.

Melville's paean exemplifies several conventions typical to North American accounts of the tropics. First, and perhaps most important, Melville's Marquesas are imaginary, an invention of the colonizer's mind, much like the Orient was invented by Europeans and turned into, in Edward Said's description, "a place of romance, exotic beings, haunting memories, landscapes, remarkable experiences" (Said 5). Second, Melville's visions focus on "outlandish things," including all manner of exotica from the sensual ("naked houris") to the lurid ("cannibal banquets"). Third, for Melville's narrator, the advantageous side of the tropics is associated with nature or the land—in particular its tropical ambience. On the other hand, the baleful side of the tropics is identified exclusively with the natives and their horrible "heathenish rites."

This early representation of the tropics in U.S. literature establishes a precedent that remains remarkably consistent over time, despite changes in politics and aesthetic programs. As Marianna Torgovnick has noted in *Gone Primitive*, first encounters between cultures are usually what count most (Torgovnick 48). Such is the case in the U.S. encounter with tropical cultures. In work after work, the image of the tropics that dominates the North American imagination can be reduced to a single formula: tropical lands are desirable, but tropical people are not (though there are exceptions, especially where females are involved). Such a perception encouraged neocolonial and imperial aspirations. That a potentially bountiful land remained undeveloped and unexploited "attested to a debased people, willing to live in an indolent standoff with nature because they lacked the moral stamina to conquer it" (Pike 125). The corollary to this view was that a superior race had the right to dominate these debased peoples and their lands.

. . .

My focus here is on a particular motif that derives directly from this formula: the motif of resistance. This resistance is grounded in the First World travelers' need to protect themselves from the unsettling influences of the Third World. The motif emerges from a fundamental tension between two contrasting North American attitudes towards the tropics. On the one hand, there is a tremendous attraction to the tropics that draws Americans there with visions of an earthly paradise, fecundity, and surpassing beauty. On the other hand, there is also a fear of tropical charm (in the pejorative sense of the word) and excess that repels North Americans from these anticipated paradises, so that their sojourns turn dreary and monotonous at best or nightmarish at worst. This swift reversal is neatly summarized by the bold-lettered blurb on the paperback cover of Paul Theroux's *Mosquito Coast*: "An American family's search for paradise becomes a hellish fight for survival!"

Initially, the search for tropical exotica discovers a salubrious tropical freedom from the routine and dullness of home. But with time, the seekers' image of the tropics darkens. They experience the sinister aspects of life in the tropics and soon abandon their paradisiacal expectations. In short, the pre-journey paean transforms into a scoff, and enthusiasm yields to disparagement.

Typee provides a useful starting place, but in general, and in contrast to other U.S. writers, Melville is sympathetic to the tropics and tropical peoples, an early voice decrying the corruption that "civilization" brings to so-called primitive places and peoples. Other writers are far more disparaging. Since my interest lies in the disparagement and rejection of the tropics, I will focus on the motif of resistance as it appears in U.S. literature on Central America. North Americans have written about Central America since the 1820s. Travelers such as John Lloyd Stephens, Ephraim Squier, Helen Sanborn, and Joan Didion have attempted to produce Central America for their compatriots, while writers of fiction—including O. Henry, Richard Harding Davis, Paul Bowles, Robert Stone, and Paul Theroux—have used Central American settings as testing grounds for their North American characters. The motif of resistance constantly appears in these works. Only in very recent works, the poetry of Carolyn Forché, for example, is the motif questioned and reconsidered.

Like Melville's narrator in *Typee*, these travelers have great expectations about what they will find in the tropics. They anticipate a feminized landscape of marvels and natural wonders beyond anything to be found in the temperate climes, a place for pleasures unavailable at home. For example, Frank Holliwell, a character in Robert Stone's *A Flag for Sunrise* (1978), considers the fictional Central American country of Tecan "a seductress, *la encantada*, a perfect place of pleasure" (Stone 101).

The first U.S. text to use Central America as a setting for imaginative literature—Ephraim G. Squier's *Waikna* (1855)—voices these same desires. Squier, who visited Nicaragua on a diplomatic mission in the 1850s, published *Waikna* under the pseudonym of Samuel Bard. Subtitled "Adventures on the Mosquito Shore," the semi-fictional narrative tells of adventures during travels from Jamaica to Nicaragua and then up the Caribbean coast into Honduras, pursuing the romantic allure of the tropics. For other travelers as well, Central America promises to be "the glorious tropics" or some such paradise. Allie Fox, protagonist of Paul Theroux's *Mosquito Coast* (1982), sees Central America as a land of escape. He is hoping to flee the decadence of the United States for a place where people have room to do as they please, an extension of the American frontier. Indeed, the call of the tropics, as it has sounded through American literature, is in many ways a call toward the frontier and the libertarian attractions that the frontier held: escape, freedom, individuality, and trial in nature's primitive state. Certainly, the call to the south was related to the expansionist urge of manifest destiny.[1] Allie Fox's Central American paradise, like Squier's, does not really involve people, and especially not natives. Although Fox expresses a certain respect for the natives' freedom, his admiration does not extend to the culture of the Mosquito coast upon which he has intruded. Indeed, he continually calls the people savages, and it is apparent that he, like so many North Americans before him, considers the land under-used and empty.[2] Frederick Pike, in discussing the "ambivalent myths and stereotypes of civilization and nature [that] seem to lie at the heart of American attitudes toward Latin America," (xiii) notes that most North Americans assumed that the natives were incapable of progress "precisely because they could not get the upper hand over nature" (Pike 49). Allie Fox agrees: a savage, he says, is "someone who doesn't bother to look around and see that he can change the world" (Theroux, *Mosquito Coast* 157).

Often in U.S. literature on tropical America, this disparagement of the natives begins with arrival. The expected rapture of being in a tropical Eden yields to bewilderment, discomfort, disgust, and disappointment. Helen J. Sanborn, in *A Winter in Central America and Mexico* (1886), aptly captures the sense of vertigo or displacement that immediately strikes the touring North American:

> I wondered if I were in fairy-land; but then there were no fairies, for the inhabitants of this land dwelt in mud huts and were dark enough to be goblins. I felt like pinching myself to see if I were awake or dreaming, and said to myself, "Who am I?" "Where am I?" "Can this be part of the same earth on which I dwell?" (Sanborn 27)

Almost a century after Sanborn, Joan Didion felt a similar bewilderment when she arrived in El Salvador, which struck her as "a state in which no ground is solid, no depth of field reliable, no perception so definite that it might not dissolve into its reverse" (Didion, *Salvador* 3).

This bewilderment puts the travelers on their guard; something sinister—and certainly not very Edenic—seems to lurk in the land. Quite often they are frightened by the sudden excess of flora and fauna, or they are put out by the heat. But by far the greatest source of disappointment and dread are the natives of the country. Travelers like Sanborn wonder "with something of apprehension how we should fare when we came to penetrate this land and mingle with this uncivilized people" (Sanborn 27). One sight of the natives is enough to awaken a host of doubts. For one thing, the natives are black (in the eyes of North Americans) and black means primitive. Squier's narrator expresses typical shock upon seeing the natives: "There was a large assemblage on the beach, when we landed, but I was amazed to find that, with few exceptions, they were all unmitigated negros, or Sambos (i.e. mixed negro and Indian)" (Squier 58).

A typical convention of the literature is to single out from the "large assemblage" a native who stands for the whole race. Frequently, this individual is a customs agent, whom the arriving North Americans immediately hold in contempt. Squier describes "a very pompous black man," comically dressed, whose "final purpose seemed narrowed down to getting a dram, and pocketing a couple of dollars" (57). In early works, the tone is derisive. Later writers, however, drop the derision in favor of fear, using the occasion to establish an atmosphere of dread (e.g. Joan Didion's apprehension at having to "negotiate" customs in "a thicket of weapons" [Didion, *Salvador* 4]). In all cases, the travelers emphasize that a boundary has been crossed—the physical frontier, of course, but also a more nuanced border, as if the travelers had crossed into a bizarre Wonderland.

In sum, the arrival is a period for conflicting impressions from which travelers draw generalized conclusions about the "strangeness" around them. The ambivalence felt by Charlie Fox, narrator of *The Mosquito Coast*, best illustrates this tendency. From the ship, as he arrives, the Honduran coast looks "dazzling white," but up close he notices a "stinking air," and the town appears "yellow and jammed." "Everything was backward here," he concludes, and the shacks of the natives disgust him (Theroux, *Mosquito Coast* 101). Evening, however, softens his reaction; he hears a boy playing a flute, and the music casts "a soft spell on the beach, as purply-blue as the sky over the sea" (103). The town at night is "magic." He imagines "the whole place to be made out of green pillows, creepy-quiet and cool" (103). But with morning's harsher light, he changes his view once again. To Charlie, the town now appears "cracked and discolored and mobbed by people actually screaming above the braying car horns. There was no magic now, nor even anything familiar" (104). All his expectations become "a nightmare of summer ruin." Many Yankee travelers in Central America experience this same alternation of enchantment and disgust that Charlie feels.

The warning signs perceived upon arrival soon become indications of grave dangers; "an endemic apprehension of danger in the apparently benign" is the way Didion puts it in *Salvador*. Even tropical nature, which formerly held out Edenic promises to the traveler, is suddenly fraught with danger. It does not take long for North Americans to conclude that the tropics are inimical to whites. Soon after his arrival in Guatemala (1838), John Lloyd Stephens visited the grave of an American diplomat dead of yellow fever; Stephens himself was to die of a disease contracted in Panama. Squier's narrator, Samuel Bard, once so enthusiastic about his journey to Central America, quickly recognizes the perils: "Under the tropics, serious consequences often follow from these slight causes. I have known tetanus to result from a little wound, of the size of a pea . . ." (Squier 279). He warns against the "wickedness" of attempting to start colonies of whites on the "low, pestiferous shores, under the tropics" (58). And so it goes for nearly every traveler on record. Their accounts are not complete, it seems, without the experience of some horrible (and specifically tropical) illness. Richard Harding Davis's Captain Macklin becomes ill with malaria, as do several characters in O. Henry's *Cabbages and Kings* (1904), a collection of stories set in "Anchuria" (Honduras). One of these, a certain Halloran, "dried up to gristle and bone and shook with chills every third night."

Usually, the existence of these diseases—and their dangers for whites—is considered further evidence of the inferiority of the inhabitants of tropical lands. Mary Louise Pratt points out that "unexploited nature tends to be seen in this literature [travel books on Latin America] as troubling or ugly, its very primalness a sign of the failure of human enterprise" (Pratt 149). Diseases spread, the logic goes, because the people are physically unclean and morally not right with God. Danger is so rampant that even the more peaceful aspects of the tropics conceal hazards, especially for gringo minds and souls. The texts all issue an implicit warning: even when the tropics are apparently salubrious—with warm breezes, tranquil sunsets, and lazy afternoons—the North American had best beware. O. Henry, more than any other writer, broadcast this warning; his stories are filled with Anglos who have fallen under the spell of "this dreamy land, where time seemed so redundant." Tropical enchantment, no longer desired by Yankees once they experience its reality, turns out to be as inimical as the tropical diseases.

The big problem is that a Central American idyll means, inevitably, contact with Central American culture and all its supposed debauchery and amorality. The Yankee who is not careful will most likely succumb to turpitude, and the writers leave no doubt that this is a distinctly undesirable fate, one to be avoided at all costs. Squier encounters several lost and degenerate whites on his journeys. O. Henry uses allusions to Circe and the lotus eaters to call attention to the horrors that befall enchanted Yankees. Over and over, the laziness of the natives—which is perceived as the result of living in an environment where food is plentiful and can be had just by plucking it—is cited as a reason for avoiding Central America. In other words, the laziness is contagious. For example, the boat captain taking the Fox family to Honduras in *The Mosquito Coast* warns Charlie about the jungle that is to be their new home:

"Some people there have never seen a white man or know what a wheel is. Ask Reverend Spellgood. If they want to eat, they just climb a tree and pick a coconut. They can live for nothing. Everything they need is right there—free. Most of them don't wear any clothes. It's a free and easy life."

I said, "That's why we're going."

"But it's no place for you," the captain said. (83)

It is curious how often this alleged aspect of tropical life—the ease with which food can be obtained—is cited as a cause of native indolence. Considering the dreams of paradise which have lured the travelers to Central America, this sudden disapproval of the one Edenic attribute they find is inexplicable. Allie Fox, who has come to Honduras seeking freedom from restraints, goes so far as to ban bananas in his utopia because they encourage laziness.

But for the most part, North Americans find very little tranquility in Central America, especially where society and culture are concerned. A paradoxical dilemma emerges from which Central America cannot escape: when the place is pacific, it is dangerous, and when it is active, it is even more dangerous. More often than not, North Americans locate decadence in the violence, disorder, and corruption of Central America's "radically bad social order," to use the words of the famed filibuster William Walker.[3]

Most travelers from the north had nothing good to say about Central American societies. Pratt, in commenting on nineteenth-century travel writing, notes that "Spanish American society in general . . . is relentlessly indicted for backwardness, indolence, and above all, the 'failure' to exploit the resources surrounding it" (Pratt 151). In 1855, William Walker justified his invasion of Nicaragua by citing the need for "regenerating" the "worn-out" societies of the isthmus. A few decades later, it was popular novelist Richard Harding Davis's turn. A character in his romance *Captain Macklin* tells his fellow mercenaries what the place is like:

I know all of Central America, and it is a wonderful country [*sic*] . . . But it is cursed with the laziest of God's creatures, and the men who rule them are the most corrupt and the most vicious. They are the dogs in the manger among rulers. They will do nothing to help their own country; they will not permit others to help it. They are a menace and an insult to civilization, and it is time that they stepped down and out, and made way for their betters, or that they were kicked out. (Davis 199)

This character voices a frustration that soon entered official North American discourse, and has continued to guide U.S. policy at least until the 1989 invasion of Panama, which was supposed to rid Panama of the latest "dog in the manger," Manuel Noriega (the invasion's official code name, Operation Just Cause, reveals how little has changed in U.S. thinking). The U.S. Marines invaded Nicaragua as early as 1908 and controlled the country for the next four years, withdrawing (briefly) in 1912 after failing to establish a democracy. The U.S. blamed the failure on the Nicaraguans themselves. A 1913 article in *National Geographic* explained to the U.S. public that the "hopeless Nicaraguans" would never be fit for "good government." Like Davis's character, the article's author, William Showalter, did not blame outside intervention for contributing to the problems; they both considered Central America so hopeless that not even the U.S. Marines could save them.

Examples of this convention abound in U.S. discourse. A character in O. Henry's *Cabbages and Kings* makes a similar complaint of Honduras, where he is working as "private secretary to the president": "I get sick at times of this country. Everything's rotten. From the executive down to the coffee pickers, they're plotting to down each other and skin their friends" (Henry 593). Pratt comments that

Such a litany of criticism is anchored, of course, in the sheerest hypocrisy for it is [Latin] America's purported backwardness that legitimates the capitalist vanguard's interventions in the first place. Ideologically, the vanguard's task is to re-invent [Latin] America as backward and neglected, to encode its non-capitalist landscapes and societies as manifestly in need of the rationalized exploitation the Europeans bring. (Pratt 151–52)

The observations of Paul Theroux, who wrote of his travels by train through Central America, maintain a connection with those of nineteenth-century visitors, like Walker, to tropical America:

Central America was haywire; it was as if New England had gone completely to ruin, and places like Rhode Island and Connecticut were run by maniacal generals and thuggish policemen; as if they had evolved into motiveless tyrannies and become forcing-houses of nationalism. It was no wonder that, seeing them as degenerate states, tycoons like Vanderbilt and imperial-minded companies like the United Fruit Company took them over and tried to run them. (Theroux, *The Old Patagonian Express* 174)

These denigrations are engendered by the general North American feeling that society is not well-ordered in Central America. Theroux's crucial experience, for example, occurs at a soccer game, where the violent disorder of the crowd has infernal connotations for him.

This type of turmoil, with violence and terror inherent or given in the place, is also prevalent in the use that Paul Bowles makes of Central America as a setting. In Bowles's fiction, the dangers of the place are particularly acute for visiting North Americans, who are apt to be raped ("Under the Sky"), drugged and murdered (*Up Above the World*), brutalized ("The Echo"), or "disappeared," in the Spanish sense ("Tapiama"). Bowles's North Americans are generally unsympathetic characters who have wandered into the "primitive" world of Central America. They clearly do not belong there, and soon find themselves implicated in trouble. Western values do not provide comfort or guidance in this alien terrain; instead, they lead the characters deeper and deeper into danger.

For U.S. writers, violence always seems to lurk beneath Central America's surface. It threatens to erupt at any moment (these "eruptions" contributing in turn to the popularity of volcanos as natural metaphors for Central American society), and the North American feels particularly vulnerable. In early travel literature, confrontations with "bandidos" or showdowns with local mobs are common textual conventions. The people themselves are assumed to be inherently violent, and random encounters with locals usually present occasions for this violence to direct itself toward the vulnerable visitor. In a contemporary account, Joan Didion summarizes one such encounter by calling it "a pointless confrontation with aimless authority," yet another aspect of the "local vocation for terror" (Didion, *Salvador* 85).

Didion has a love-hate relationship with tropical places. Certainly her diction is more "tropicalized" than that of other North American writers. Her prose is full of the heat, light, liquidity, and dreamy listlessness that she associates with the tropics. Again and again Didion refers to "opaque equatorial light" or a "fluid atmosphere" or a "certain liquidity." In Didion's tropics, "surfaces dissolve," "nothing is fixed or hard," and things are "vaporous" or hold "a perilous attraction, like a mirage." One experiences "weightlessness"; one feels "listless" and "uneasy" as though "in a kind of waking dream." But she also, like so many other North American writers, associates the tropical ambience with turmoil: "few lessons get learned in tropical cities under attack from their own citizens. Lines only harden. Positions become more fixed, and privileges more fiercely defended" (*Miami* 45). In the end, Didion equates what is for her a destabilized tropical environment with a destabilized political and social situation, so that the peculiar combination of tropical terror and tropical unreality produce "a certain weightlessness, the heightened wariness of having left the developed world for a more fluid atmosphere, one in which the native distrust of extreme possibilities that tended to ground the temperate United States in an obeisance to democratic institutions seemed rooted, if at all, only shallowly" (Didion, *Miami* 23). The fact that Didion is writing about Miami here is significant, for her version of Miami sounds very much like her version of El Salvador. The subtext of her poetic descriptions is that the cancer of tropical violence and terror has spread northward to U.S. soil. Miami is the first tropicalized U.S. city, a portent of what may come if North Americans do not resist the tropical disease.

These, then, are the reasons given for resistance: Central America is deadly, diseased, dangerous, disorderly, dissolute, and decadent. If visiting North Americans are to remain sound of mind and body in such a place, they must protect themselves; they must resist the horrors of the land and its cultures. For this reason, in almost every text North Americans report an inclination, growing stronger with time, to reject the influence of both the tropics and Central American culture, and to insist on Yankee virtues in the face of tropical decadence. For those unable to resist, degradation and demise are inevitable.

This tendency is most apparent in O. Henry's short stories, where the "lotus-eater" theme recurs frequently. Several of O. Henry's Yankee characters have become wastrels on the "monkey coast," and it is clear that the malevolent influence of the tropics (along with a weakness for drink) causes the condition. Throughout *Cabbages and Kings*, O. Henry reiterates the dangers of tropical enchantment in what he calls "the land of the lotus." The characters who survive these dangers are those who resist and reject them. Thus, several of the characters who have spent the most time in O. Henry's fictional country of Anchuria—Billy Keough, Frank Goodwin, and Jim Clancy—are incessantly disparaging the place, as though their refusal to admit that anything good can be found there will somehow protect them from its insidiousness.[4]

A review of these derogatory comments on Anchuria reveals the extremity of the characters' prejudice. At various times, O. Henry's characters refer to the fictional Central American country as "a tropical mud puddle," "this grocery and fruit stand that they call a country," "the monkey coast," and the home of "missing links." This excessive disparagement allows the Yankees to protect themselves; asserting their superiority is considered the best way to mitigate the debilitating effects of life in the tropics: "Thus in all the scorched and exotic places of the earth, Caucasians meet when the day's work is done to preserve the fullness of the heritage by the aspersion of alien things" (Henry 616). It is telling that the narrator considers Anchurian things "alien," even though technically it is the Yankees who are alien.

The importance of this activity is revealed through several cautionary tales. One concerns the previously mentioned Halloran, a character who is trapped in Guatemala, unable to leave a railroad work crew because of a tropics-induced lethargy. "The fault's wid these tropics," Halloran says. "I've lost my grip. 'Tis the tropics that's done it" (622). A second example is Beelzebub Blythe, a drunkard for whom the tropics are an inferno: "Once in some Paradise Lost, he had foregathered with the angels of the earth. But fate had hurled him headlong down to the tropics, where flamed in his bosom a fire that was rarely quenched" (602).

O. Henry is not the only writer to note the danger of "the fetterless, idyllic round of enchanted days" in the hot countries. Squier offers some cautionary tales of his own, though in both cases the afflicted white man is not American but English. There was, perhaps, a political reason for describing lotus-eating British citizens. In the 1840s and 1850s, the U.S. was challenging British hegemony in the region; thus, comparing the faults of Englishmen (particularly their immorality in falling prey to tropical enchantment) with Yankee industry and diligence confirmed for Americans the righteousness of their manifest destiny over not only native inferiority but also old-world immorality. The cautionary tale, however, applied to all white men, no matter what their national origin: the dangers in the tropics, dangers inherent in both the hostility of the natural environment and in the indolence of native life, were deadly, and precaution was necessary.

This denigration of Central America in the works of North American writers has helped to deepen and harden the perceived distinctions between Yankee superiority and Central American inferiority. A political vision informs the subtext of their works, a vision that validated the difference between North and South, Yankee and Latin. North Americans, possessors of what they considered a stronger culture, have felt called upon and obligated to penetrate Central America and define it, interpret it, even capture it so that it might be saved from itself and redeemed. North American writers have re-produced Central America as a place of comic opera and decadence; anything serious in its political, social, or cultural life is discounted and dismissed. Central Americans have not been allowed political or ideological lives of their own. This reproduction was (and is) one way of justifying Yankee interference and domination: a trivial and comical people "require intervention by some civilized nation" (to use the words of Roosevelt's corollary to the Monroe Doctrine).

Nineteenth- and early-twentieth-century writers were certain of the efficacy of resistance, if only because they believed that Anglo-Saxon superiority ensured their ability to rise above the hindrances imposed by an inferior native culture. Writers in the later years of the twentieth century have sensed the same need for resistance on the part of visiting North Americans. In their works, however, the success of this resistance is by no means assured. Very often, in fact, characters fail precisely because of the inadequacy of the Anglo ideals upon which their resistance is based.

This failed resistance is exemplified in the stories of Paul Bowles and to a certain extent in Robert Stone's *A Flag for Sunrise*. But the single best example of a work that calls into question the efficacy of resistance is Paul Theroux's novel *The Mosquito Coast*. This is somewhat surprising, since among contemporary travel writers Theroux is the one most firmly in the tradition of O. Henry and Richard Harding Davis—the impervious and supercilious Yankee in Central America. As a traveler, Theroux resists tropicalization at every step. The disorder of the tropics and its inhabitants dismays him, and throughout his travel book *The Old Patagonian Express*—which devotes six chapters to Central America—he comments again and again on derelict buildings, trains, and people. His assumption is that Central Americans do not recognize their degeneracy, and at last he gets "sick of lecturing people on disorder." As a sign of his resistance, he makes a point of reading the lesser-known works of great U.S. authors. *Pudd'nhead Wilson* occupies much of his time on the train; he glances up from the book only to note more examples of Central American depradation.

The imperviousness and resistance to the tropics that distinguish Theroux's travel book are also important characteristics of Allie Fox, the protagonist of Theroux's novel. Fox is a pure Yankee. Although he has gone to Honduras in order to escape the constraints that North American society imposes upon the individual, Fox retains his Yankee energies and ideals. He sees himself as one of the last true North Americans, steadfastly committed to the libertarian values of the frontier. In American history, such a commitment led inevitably to the expansion of the frontier, to manifest destiny, and when the frontier vanished, to an imperialist expansion. *The Mosquito Coast* allegorizes that history and relocates it on the tropical frontier.

Because the North American continent can no longer offer him the freedom he needs, Fox heads south to a land he believes will be free from restraints. There, Fox's Yankee energies and ideals clash with a tropical environment and a tropical culture. Unwilling to remake himself in this new land, he resists the tropical environment and rejects the adaptations that native cultures have made to that environment. Moreover, he is certain that the best way to live in the jungle is by adapting it to his purposes. Thus, Fox, a self-proclaimed "Yankee with a knack for getting things accomplished," attempts to fix "haywire" Central America, confident that he possesses the capacity to do so.

At first things go well. Fox's self-built jungle village, Jeronimo, is "a masterpiece of order." "Control, that's the proof of civilization," Fox tells his family and the admiring natives. But maintaining that control—"the true test"—proves difficult. The tropics abrade the visitors until their world-conquering energy, represented by Fox's miraculous inventions (which stun the natives into worshipful subservience), is consumed by the chaotic jungle. This erosion is symbolized by the loss of Fox's proudest creation, the iceberg that he is towing upriver "to the hottest, darkest, nastiest corner of Honduras, where they pray for water and never see ice, and have never heard of cans, much less aerosol cans" (176). Fox fails in his attempt to deliver the ice, however.[5] Just as Fox's iceberg melts in the tropical heat before he can reach his destination, the energies of the Yankee begin to wear away. Resistance to the tropics fails. Manifest destiny grinds helplessly to a halt in the awesome jungle.

Frederick Pike argues that the North American frontier experience was supposed to follow a paradigmatic "dialectical process": "The civilized person arrives in America. He or she represents the thesis. Then the civilized person plunges into nature, embodying the antithesis. Ultimately, out of this process emerges the re-made human, the synthesis in which opposites fuse" (Pike 126–27). In U.S. mythology, this synthesis occurred again and again on the continental frontier. But when the frontier shifted to Latin America (as Pike demonstrates) and Anglos attempted to apply "the maximizing, extractive paradigm of capitalism" (Pratt 151), the synthesis somehow did not occur, and so the Yankees blamed the place and condemned it as evil. Allie Fox is but one example of a North American who does not experience the synthesis that is insisted upon in U.S. mythology.

Near his own end, Fox recognizes this failure but refuses to give in. His new appreciation of the Central Americans, however, stands in marked contrast to Theroux's own harsh judgments in the travel book:

He shook his head and said, "When I came here to the Mosquito Coast, I was appalled that these people had done so little to better themselves. They lived like hogs. I used to wince at their weedy crops and pathetic houses . . . That's what I used to think. Now after a year, it amazes me that they've got so much . . . I'm full of admiration for them." (291–92)

Still, Fox resists the kind of effective adaptation that has permitted the Zambus to survive in the tropics. Their type of survival seems too brutal to the North American. Ultimately, however, Fox is the one who does not survive. Resistance leads to his death.

Contemporary writers recognize the dangers of resistance. There is at least one contemporary writer, however, for whom these dangers, while real, provide the means to a deeper understanding of Central Americans. This is the poet Carolyn Forché, whose sequence of poems "In Salvador" (the first eight poems of *The Country Between Us*) is guided by the impulse to confront and cross cultural boundaries. Her poems take the persona and the reader through three stages of immersion. This process of immersion amounts to a deconstruction of the resistance motif.

The first stage of her immersion is the same experience of dislocation and de-familiarization that informs the works of so many U.S. writers. As with Joan Didion, it is a stifling terror that causes de-familiarization. This terror has a lasting effect on the persona, even when she has left El Salvador:

> . . . I was afraid more than
> I had been, even of motels so much so
> that for months every tire blow-out
> was final, every strange car near the house
> kept watch and I strained even to remember
> things impossible to forget.
> ("Return")

But Forché is led to a second stage in her immersion: the recognition that all North Americans, including herself, are implicated in this terror, since it is their government that manipulates the structures that create the terror. She has not recognized this earlier, having lived her life "in the heart/of the beast" without hearing it pounding ("The Island"). Forché learns more about the nature of the beast in El Salvador, especially through the person of the U.S. attaché there, a drunken man interested more in keeping fish than in keeping track of the situation in the country. The beast itself becomes embodied in the Salvadoran colonel, a product of U.S. training, who fills grocery sacks with human ears, the ears of his tortured victims. These things have happened in part, Forché realizes, because of our innocence, our lack of involvement, and our reluctance to question. North Americans are privileged and protected:

> There is a cyclone fence between
> ourselves and the slaughter behind it
> we hover in a calm protected world like
> netted fish, exactly like netted fish.
> ("Ourselves or Nothing")

Seeking to escape from this trap of Yankee making, the persona learns to overcome her culture-bound sensibilities and fears. She learns that resistance is inadequate and misdirected. Unlike travelers in other texts, she becomes a participant in Salvadoran life, learns its history, and hears its voices, such as that of the poet Claribel Alegría. Thus, Forché is led to a third stage of immersion, the impulse to witness, "to cry out until my voice is gone to its hollow of earth." For Forché, resistance has become engagement. This engagement is, in a sense, a direct attempt to address and to redress what we might call the "official resistance" manifested in the dominant form of discourse in North American life, the media. After her journey to El Salvador, the poet is aware that the prevalent U.S. image of the place is the one served up on television news: a violent and out-of-control El Salvador edited and adjusted to fit a two-dimensional sequence of images. This "official discourse" sanctions a sort of national resistance to those images. The impressions of El Salvador are conveyed in neatly controlled fifteen-second spots that adapt the images for the nightly news spectacle, alternating them with aspirin commercials, no less and no more important. The audience gets a dose, but only a small dose, and no harm is done. El Salvador is reduced to an object lesson soon lost among other images. The dominant discourse of the media thus inculcates resistance. Forché seeks to counter this discourse by exposing it and deconstructing it.

Several writers have alluded to Wonderland in their works on Central America. O. Henry in particular found correspondences between Central American reality and Lewis Carroll's fantasy. *Cabbages and Kings*, taking its title from the walrus and carpenter episode in *Through the Looking Glass*, develops what amounts to a running gag on the Wonderland theme. The implications of this set of allusions help illuminate the motif of resistance.

The idea, of course, is that Yankee travelers, like Alice, find themselves in an illogical place, where everything is backward, askew, or "haywire." And like Alice, the travelers—whether factual writers of travel accounts or fictional characters on a journey—resist the gravitational pull of the place's illogic. Alice demands reason and rationality (as she conceives them) and the Yankees demand order, efficiency, progress, and civilization. What both Alice and the Yankees forget is that *they* are the strange ones; it is their logic or ideals that are out of place, backward, or askew. By insisting that the natives of Wonderland and Central America have got it all wrong, by resisting the cultural geography of the place, by imposing their own maps, they are attempting to assert a superior, privileged world-view that simply does not obtain on the other side of the boundary. Ultimately, the Wonderland allusion betrays more than the writers intend; they share with Alice an inability to comprehend that things are different through the tropical looking glass and that this difference has its own distinct validity.

Notes

1. Many people in the United States in the nineteenth century were certain of a not-too-distant future in which the Anglo-Saxon race would control tropical America. As early as 1801, Thomas Jefferson envisioned a time "when our rapid multiplication will expand itself . . . and cover the whole northern, if not the southern continent, with a people speaking the same language, governed in similar forms, and by similar laws; nor can we contemplate with satisfaction either blot or mixture on that surface" (quoted in Horsman 92).

2. Reginald Horsman, in his excellent study *Race and Manifest Destiny*, demonstrates that North Americans were apt to consider the rest of the hemisphere empty and available for their own expansion.

3. Walker's book *The War in Nicaragua* is one of the central documents in the history of United States–Central American relations, a document as telling as the Monroe Doctrine or the Roosevelt Corollary. The book is significant for several reasons: (1) it is one of the first books written by a North American on Central America; (2) it is an exceptional exposition of the racial attitudes toward Latin America prevalent at that time; (3) it details a clash between North Americans and Central Americans that in many ways presages the numerous clashes that followed; and (4) it is a highly unusual travel book, perhaps unique, given that the traveler in this case ended up taking over the government of the country. For an extended analysis of Walker's prose, see my article "William Walker and the 'Discovery' of Central America."

4. My own experiences in the "gringo bars" of Central America have taught me that this type of talk still persists among the rather large expatriate community in the region. People who have spent years in Central America love to gather in these bars and decry the native culture. It is a curious contradiction.

5. An interesting parallel can be made with the opening chapter of García Márquez's *Cien años de soledad*, in which a band of gypsies succeeds in delivering the first chunk of ice ever to appear in remote Macondo. The gypsies succeed where Allie Fox, the North American "with a knack for getting things done," fails.

Works Cited

Bard, Samuel [Ephraim Squier]. *Waikna; Adventures on the Mosquito Shore.* New York: Hartford and Brothers, 1855.

Benz, Stephen. "William Walker and the 'Discovery' of Central America." *SECOLAS Annals* 24 (1993): 96–105.

Davis, Richard Harding. *Captain Macklin.* 1902. New York: Scribners, 1927.

Didion, Joan. *Miami.* New York: Simon and Schuster, 1987.

———. *Salvador.* New York: Simon and Schuster, 1983.

Forché, Carolyn. *The Country Between Us*. New York: Harper and Row, 1981.

Henry, O. *The Complete Works*. Vol. I. Garden City: Doubleday, 1953.

Horsman, Reginald. *Race and Manifest Destiny*. Cambridge: Harvard University Press, 1981.

Melville, Herman. *Typee*. 1848. Evanston: Northwestern University Press, 1968.

Pike, Frederick. *The United States and Latin America: Myths and Stereotypes of Civilization and Nature*. Austin: University of Texas Press, 1992.

Pratt, Mary Louise. *Imperial Eyes*. New York: Routledge, 1992.

Said, Edward. *Orientalism*. New York: Pantheon, 1978.

Sanborn, Helen J. *A Winter in Central America and Mexico*. Boston: Lee and Shepard, 1886.

Showalter, William Joseph. "The Countries of the Caribbean." *National Geographic* 24 (1913): 227–49.

Squier, Ephraim G. *See* Samuel Bard.

Stone, Robert. *A Flag for Sunrise*. New York: Knopf, 1981.

Theroux, Paul. *The Mosquito Coast*. Boston: Houghton Mifflin, 1982.

———. *The Old Patagonian Express*. Boston: Houghton Mifflin, 1979.

Torgovnick, Marianna. *Gone Primitive*. Chicago: University of Chicago Press, 1990.

Walker, William. *The War in Nicaragua*. Mobile, Ala.: Th. Goetzel, 1860.

Debra A. Castillo

The Tropics of the Imagination: "Quetzalcoatl and All That"

Late in *The Plumed Serpent* when Kate, tired of hot weather and hotter bodies, begins to muse about going back to cooler British climes for Christmas, she wonders if it is possible to have too much of the kinds of good things Mexico represents. When Ramón asks her if she has any particular good thing in mind, she responds, "Oh—Quetzalcoatl and all that" (Lawrence, *Plumed Serpent* 471). It is the uneasy tone of this response, both flippant and committed, that returns to me again and again as I read, a bit queasy myself, in the vast and growing bibliography of Anglo-America's fascination with Latin America: Katherine Anne Porter's stories, B. Traven's *Treasure of the Sierra Madre*, W. H. Hudson's *Green Mansions*, Graham Greene's *The Power and the Glory*, Malcolm Lowry's *Under the Volcano*, Paul Theroux's *Mosquito Coast*, Daniel Curley's *Mummy*, Harriet Doerr's *Stones for Ibarra*, Nicholas Shakespeare's *The Vision of Elena Silves*, or Lawrence Thornton's *Imagining Argentina*, where the dust-jacket artist imagines a Buenos Aires characterized by tropical foliage, long watery vistas, and colorful parrots. Kate's rejoinder to Ramón's question reminds me that in most of these books even the positioned critique of Eurocentrism occurs within the frame of a markedly Eurocentric paradigm. I want to explore this vexed dis-position towards/against Latin America in this paper in order to help me to come to terms with one of the facets of the underdiscussed underpinnings of Latin America's twentieth-century dependence on First World cultural artifacts, which from Latin America's side takes the form of a self-fulfilling exoticism, of seeing themselves as others see them, only more so.

Cultural circulation between Latin America and the First World offers a number of edifying exchanges. Before the "Boom" novel of the 1960s traveled outside Latin American borders to amaze and enchant us with a literary form often hailed as a Third World version of postmodernism with a magical-realist charge to it, there was a long tradition of Anglo-American and European authors who traveled to Latin America to seek exotic objects of knowledge or useful objects for trade. For example, Mexican critic José Joaquín Blanco explores the famous obsession with indigenous Mexico in writers like Artaud or Bataille, who, with a tourist's Spanish, rudimentary and second-hand anthropological concepts, no knowledge of Mexican history, and no understanding of indigenous languages, imagine and create a Mexico that fits their preconceived notions (Blanco 26). These notions then find their way into several of the many elaborations of postmodern theory where the staged exoticism of half-imagined indigenous practices resonated strongly with Western anti-canonical cultural projects. At the same time and in a parallel fashion, this transformed, fetishized, and transculturated version of indigenous America serves as the spur for what Mario Vargas Llosa calls the "sed de exotismo," thirst for the exotic, that has created an Anglo-European market for Latin American cultural artifacts. As George Yúdice notes in one of the most important and lucid elaborations of postmodern theory in the Latin American context, "not only did professionalized, superstar novelists like Fuentes or Vargas Llosa sideline 'vocational' writers . . . , they also sought to integrate with the growing consumer culture among elites . . . that made popular and indigenous cultures irrelevant unless they too integrated or 'transculturated' into consumer society" (Yúdice 11). It is no wonder that Latin America in general, and these novels in particular, are often acclaimed as postmodern *avant la lettre*, while concurrently metropolitan thinkers decry the lack of theory in Latin America.[1] Furthermore, there is something about the sidelining of indigenous cultures, while appropriating and even highlighting a certain aestheticized indigenism, that seems to me to mediate an important and underdiscussed thread of the modernism-postmodernism debate as it affects Latin America.

In the broadest possible terms, this debate involves questioning the processes involved in defining any particular cultural identity at all, and of tracing the conceptualizations of cultural identity with respect to their textual inscriptions. Any Western recognition of indigenous voices also and inevitably points toward the aesthetic and institutional models that frame this act of recognition within the context of a specifically Western institutional hierarchy. As Satya Mohanty reminds us, "Notwithstanding our contemporary slogans of otherness, and our fervent denunciations of Reason and the Subject, there is an unavoidable conception of rational action, inquiry, and dialogue inherent in this political-critical project" (Mohanty 26). If, on the one hand, metropolitan postmodernist critics and writers intuit a missing something or someone left out of traditional Western conceptual frameworks, on the other hand, the epistemological possibilities of native self-representation pose significant ethical and political challenges even to iconoclastic cultural projects. One typical postmodern reaction to the High Modernist canon has been to seek out these missing others to Western culture; the subsequent packaging of the exotic others has, however, tended to turn them into safely exotic artifacts for domestic consumption.

Accordingly, this study is a two-part project that will fit this strained relationship of texts and theories into an uneven dialogue between north and south. In the first part, I will explore two exemplary Anglo-American texts in this uneven cultural exchange, texts which enact variations on the theme of the cosmo-metropolitan's encounter with the irreducibly alien: *The Plumed Serpent*, D. H. Lawrence's classically obsessed modernist novel of an Englishwoman in a post-revolutionary Mexico convulsed by an Aztec revival, and *Keep the River on Your Right*, Tobias Schneebaum's impressionistic-ethnographic account of his stay with Amazonian cannibals. A second, complementary section will look at one of the representative texts in Latin America's "postmodern" exoticization of the alienated other within its borders: Mario Vargas Llosa's *El hablador* (*The Storyteller*). There is a grating consistency in all these texts. On the one hand, they all pose a commitment to indigenous America as a theoretical and artistic position by which the author achieves a significant insight into the workings of society and linguistic form. On the other hand, in each book this privileging of indigenous culture is jarringly matched with a tone ranging from dismissive to flippantly jocular: "Quetzal-coatl and all that."

Speaking from the Anglo-American side of the dialogue, Marianna Torgovnick's *Gone Primitive: Savage Intellects, Modern Lives* offers an exceptionally helpful account in focusing the terms of the discussion, although her principal examples are seldom drawn from the Latin American context, either represented or imagined. Torgovnick examines the multifarious ways by which certain societies in the Third World (those coded as "primitive") and their artifacts are not only consumed, but also constructed in the West, thus displacing the societies from the very matrix of meaning that, in Western eyes, should have positioned them as identities and licensed their voices in a shared dialogue. The primitive is that patina of the alien that allows Westerners to project their own dreams and fears and thereby to see themselves that much more clearly. It is much less a dialogue with another culture than a strained monologue about some detached and rejected essence of a Western self. Thus, she finds, "To study the primitive is . . . to enter an exotic world which is also a familiar world . . . The primitive does what we ask it to do. Voiceless, it lets us speak for it . . . The real secret of the primitive in this century has often been the same secret as always: the primitive can be—has been, will be (?)—whatever Euro-Americans want it to be. It tells us what we want it to tell us" (Torgovnick 8–9). It is this never-never land of projected fantasies that Torgovnick explores in her book: not the thing itself, but the history of giving voice to that thing; not the trope of the enigmatic native, but the story of Euro-American attempts to penetrate or to appropriate the enigma; not the drama of identity with its play of false analogies, but its potential, and therefore displaced, explosiveness. Here again, the indigenous peoples seem almost naturally to offer themselves up as ready-made postmodern artifacts, ripe for theorization. Furthermore, as James Clifford reminds us with reference to native objects that find their way into Western collections, these aesthetic artifacts return to us with a specific psychic charge: "At a more intimate level, rather than grasping objects only as cultural signs and artistic icons, . . . we can return to them . . . their lost status as fetishes—not specimens of a deviant or exotic 'fetishism' but *our own* fetishes" (Clifford 229).

In the Anglo-European works under discussion here, as in other similar novels from this tradition, violent death is the narrative crux—the metaphorical fetish—that serves as a convenient shorthand for the unleashing of primitive forces that can/will rewrite history, returning "civilized" men and women to their primitive origins, while at the same time underlining the absolute distinction between two theoretical stances, two historical moments, two cultures, two races, two gender orientations, so as to enact the thoroughly "civilized" drama of leaving the tropics, of stepping forward into the future and into the writing of the novel. Unlike the Latin American texts which, no matter how close their ties to the Anglo-American romances of the primitive, cannot resolve the strain of double voicing, cannot entirely lay the primitive to rest, the Anglo-American storyteller seems less problematically both to locate meaning in the primitive, and then to search out the conjectural uncodings of this constructed locus of signification. The effect in both Latin and Anglo-American texts is of a strained theatricality, but it hinges on a somewhat different misreading of the generalized/derived trope.

I

D. H. Lawrence's *The Plumed Serpent* stands out among the hundreds of novels and stories written by Anglo-Americans and set in Mexico for the particular forcefulness of Lawrence's obsession with, and equally forceful rejection of, that country and its people.[2] This fascinated attraction/repulsion is at the heart of his imaged rebirth of a cult of Quetzalcoatl. On the one hand, Lawrence found a challenge to his literary powers in the exoticism of the Mexican Indian, upon whom he intermittently projects a laudable lack of artificiality, a physical majesty, and a commendable fervor for uncontaminated religious rituals. In his depiction of this sensual and anti-rational other, Lawrence allows his own messianic ideas free rein. On the other hand, Lawrence is repelled by the actual Indians, who deviate from the script he has written for them with depressing frequency. The men creep along insect-like; "reptilian gloom" dominates their habitual outlook on life; they are idiotic and childlike in the intensity of their misguided fervor; despite their beautiful skins and "richness of the flesh" they stubbornly exist in "the complete absence of what we call 'spirit.'" They are, finally, a people very like the gods Lawrence insists they still worship: ugly, incomprehensible, violent, unreasoning, unlovable, ungraceful, unpoetic, charmless (Lawrence, *Mornings in Mexico* 35–36, 49, 53–55, 69).

Even worse, they terrify Lawrence with their obscurely menacing blankness: "And to this day, most of the Mexican Indian women seem to bring forth stone knives. Look at them, these sons of incomprehensible mothers, with their black eyes like flints, and their stiff little bodies as taut and keen as knives of obsidian. Take care they don't rip you up" (55). Lawrence's straightforwardly racist warning clearly addresses itself to a white, Anglo-European audience that can be expected to share his discomfort when facing an alien culture that refuses to be penetrated by the wise and poetic gaze of the British writer. Nevertheless, the positioning of that alien people also hints at something the white man reads as possessing a penetrating menace of its own. It is the stone knife that both compels and repulses Lawrence; he wants to appropriate the ritual of the stone knife on his own terms, freeing it from the dark people whose spiritless, brutish minds are incapable of manipulating its force. At the same time, he intuits that the Mexican Indians are, vaguely, in themselves the stone knives, and that they could turn on him. It puzzles and enrages him that the tool will not come quietly to his hand. After all, as Lawrence reasons, "That which is fit only to survive will survive only to supply food or contribute in some way to the existence of a higher form of life, which is able to do more than survive, which can really *vive*, live." In these terms, the Mexican Indian (reptile, insect, stone knife) is fit only for service:

> Life is more vivid in the Mexican who drives the wagon, than in the two horses in the wagon.
> Life is more vivid in me than in the Mexican who drives the wagon for me.
> We are speaking in terms of *existence*: that is, in terms of species, race, or type. (Lawrence, *Porcupine* 357)

There is no significant point to be gained in belaboring the obvious implications here. Lawrence found in Mexico the tabula rasa upon which to write the story of his own obsessions, and the alien other provides a more malleable form for this self-imagining than the resistant molds of his own countrymen. To the degree that Mexico confirms his fictional image, he loves it and its people; to the degree that it insists on deviating from his dream, on confirming a stubborn incomprehensibility, he rejects it utterly. Mexico exists precisely and specifically to nurture his infinitely more vivid species. Unsurprisingly,

Lawrence considered the tale of that fantasy, *The Plumed Serpent*, to be his best novel.

One of the curious twists in the reception of the novel is, as Ruffinelli points out and Torgovnick confirms, that "Mexico" serves both the author and his critics as a convenient symbol that does not require deconstruction. In Lawrence's account of Mexico, Torgovnick notes, "the primitive is put to the service of the West: its sensuality clarifies through contrast Western rationality . . . They have what the West has lost . . . The primitive lets Lawrence return to origins, rewrite Western history, and imagine a radically different kind of future" (Torgovnick 162, 169). The spiritual direction taken in the West is "pale" in both senses of the word, so Lawrence turns from Western Eucharist to black volcanic glass, from the prissy, bloodless Christianity to the sensual, bloody Aztec religion, resurrecting/creating an alternative past as his contribution to the discussion, between Westerners, of the West's ongoing dialogue with itself.

Ruffinelli would agree with this assessment, but he adds a Latin Americanist's perspective on this dialogue: "lo curioso es que la visión *mexicana* de Lawrence se juzga siempre a la luz de otros ojos *extranjeros*, es decir, a la sombra del desconocimiento del mismo país que Lawrence conoció y desconoció" [it is curious that Lawrence's *Mexican* vision is always judged by light of other *foreign* eyes, that is to say, in the shadow of an unfamiliarity with the same country that Lawrence knew and did not know] (Ruffinelli 93). What these shadowed foreign eyes see of Mexico, then, is the invented Mexico that Lawrence loves, and not the alien Mexico that Lawrence repudiates. Ruffinelli's own study intends to partially remedy that lack, and he concludes that, because of Lawrence's obsession with seeking a personalized version of utopia, that novelist underutilizes his opportunity to elaborate a theory of Mexico's own conscious return to its origins, in its effort to elaborate a coherent discourse of nationalism in the aftermath of the 1910–20 revolution. Yet, Lawrence's occasional insights are valuable, as the privileged position of the detached outsider often is valuable, in preserving certain sketches of landscapes, certain shades of perception about Mexican hermeticism and cruelty permeating the atmosphere in those years of recovery from the bloodiest war in Mexico's history (115).

It is the mix of insights and incoherence that has proved most disconcerting to the relatively few Mexican writers who have discussed this novel. What strikes me most, and concerns me the most, as a feminist Latin Americanist, is not only the enclosed and strictly delimited dialogue between Westerners that implicitly, if unwittingly, excludes Latin Americans from commenting on a work in which they are prominently positioned as subject/objects, but also the terms upon which Latin American thinkers insert themselves into that ongoing dialogue. Thus, for example, Octavio Paz praises Lawrence's depiction of landscape: "Lawrence's prose reflects the extremely subtle, nearly imperceptible changes of light, the feeling of panic when torrential rains begin to fall, the terror of darkness descending on the altiplano, the shimmering vibrations of the sky at twilight in harmony with the respiratory rhythms of the great forests and the pulsing heartbeat of women" (Paz *Alternating Current* 14). Strikingly, in this manner, Paz reiterates uncritically one of Lawrence's central metaphors, linking Mexican women to an anthropomorphized vision of landscape: "Mexican Indian women seem to bring forth stone knives" (Lawrence); "the sky at twilight [is] in harmony with the respiratory rhythms of the great forests and the pulsing heartbeat of women" (Paz). In both passages, the inanimate takes on life at the expense of the women, who are departicularized as the spirit of the mountain or the heartbeat of the land. In this respect, the Mexican woman falls a step below the male primitive/savage/native: not only does she exist outside rational discussion, but, as Torgovnick notes, "once she enters the narrative, she is made to embody the landscape, rendered throughout in the language of pathetic fallacy" (Torgovnick 155). She is reduced to a prop in the drama of identity.

Latin American(ist)s, it seems, enter the dialogue, if at all, only on Western terms, and only as confirmatory voices (if differently accented ones) in this conversation among men extending from Lawrence and Paz to more recent critics like Ruffinelli. It is a long conversation, echoed in the romantic Latin American novels contemporaneous with Lawrence, though unknown to him, of the early part of the twentieth century. In those Latin American nation-building novels, Doris Sommer finds, "the rhythms of male desire and female enthrallment . . . [raise] the ideal gender types to national proportions . . . by using different rhetorical moves: metonymic aggrandizement for the male; metaphoric substitution for the female" (Sommer 56). Men become fathers, rooted in the land; good women become the Land itself, birthing nationhood, whether in the form of good sons or obsidian knives. The praiseworthy or alienating quality determined as a consequence of this metaphoric substitution pales next to the fact of substitution itself, and significantly, all the metaphors of nation-forming derive from an examined overlay of Western models on non-Western landscapes and cultures.

Modern Mexicans look on their founding myths, including the myth Lawrence exploits, with a well-justified skepticism that derives partly from an uneasiness about the unresolved clash between European and indigenous thought systems. That clash is, in fact, central to Mexico's understanding of the Quetzalcoatl story. Quetzalcoatl, the winged serpent, the creator and comforter of humankind, the culture god signifying a spiritual regeneration, disappeared from the Valley of Mexico in 987. Prophecy foretold his return; Hernán Cortés's appearance precisely in a *ce acatl* year both fulfilled the prophecy and demonstrated the error in Aztec theological claims, thus blurring Mexico's origins in a case of mistaken identity—the white man is taken for the god. Quetzalcoatl has returned (to destroy Aztec civilization); Quetzalcoatl has not returned (the legitimacy of Aztec hegemony crumbles). It is, curiously, precisely this ancient and doubled myth of origins—the beneficent god Quetzalcoatl, founder of Tula and ancestor of the Aztecs, versus the destructive Spanish non-god, the false Quetzalcoatl, founder of New Spain and literal father of the first mestizo—that Lawrence adopts in his novel, suggesting a revitalized cult of Quetzalcoatl not so much as a religious rewriting of the Conquest, but as a legitimation of the spiritual purity of the noble savage. The unlikely partners for Ramón—the Quetzalcoatl figure as well as the lightly disguised figure of a Republican Roman—are a former revolutionary general, Cipriano Viedma, reincarnated through ritual as the war god, Huitzilopochtli, and Kate Leslie, the new white explorer, who is talked into both marrying Viedma and serving as his spiritual consort, the mother-virgin goddess that Lawrence, oddly, calls Malintzi.

Fortunately for the comfort of early-twentieth-century readers, canny (or post-menopausal) Kate Forrester Tylor Leslie (Viedma?) is spared the natural consequences of her marriage to the Mexican general. Though Kate has "gone native" to a suspect degree, miscegenation cannot occur, perhaps because white, European Kate is able to hold her own against the pressures exerted on her by charismatic Mexican men. Nevertheless, Lawrence's decision to make his protagonist a woman violates one of the more consistent traditions in this type of fiction—that of the white, male explorer—and deserves comment both in its own right and in relation to the results of this violation of narrative convention on the structure of the novel. I want to look at two passages that represent cruxes in this respect, the first between Kate and Cipriano, at the moment when he first tries to insist upon her conversion into a Mexican goddess. Why Cipriano (and Ramón) insist upon her participation in this ritual is not altogether clear. Apparently they choose her, in particular, because she is both an erotic object and an inherently superior being whose alienness and natural nobility contrast to the heavy physicality of the inscrutable and childlike Indians that surround them:

".. . You treat me as if I had no life of my own," she said. "But I have."

"A life of your own? Who gave it you? Where did you get it?"

"I don't know. But I have got it. And I must live it. I can't just be swallowed up."

"Why, Malintzi?" he said, giving her a name. "Why can't you?"

"Be just swallowed up?" she said. "Well, I just can't."

"I am the living Huitzilopochtli," he said. "And I am swallowed up. I thought, so you could be, Malintzi."

. . .

"Oh!" she cried to herself, stifling. "For heaven's sake let me get out of this, and back to simple human people. I loathe the very sound of Quetzalcoatl and Huitzilo-pochtli. I would die rather than be mixed up in it any more. Horrible really, both Ramón and Cipriano. And they want to put it over me, with their high-flown bunk, and their Malintzi. Malintzi! I am Kate Forrester, really. . . . I am sick of these men putting names over me." (406–7)

Kate's role, then, is to learn to become a savage, to "be swallowed up" in the resurrected ritual of the Aztec gods as her Mexican counterparts have been. Yet she is not swallowed up in the same way; the Mexican men allow their own "primitive heritage" to come alive once again in them; the foreign woman fights the parallel experience of a swallowing up in the alien culture as yet another unreasonable male demand for unconditional female submission to his wishes. In her own defense, Kate insists that she, like her creator D. H. Lawrence, "lives" in the peculiarly intense sense he gives to that word, and is thus due certain privileges on that basis alone. Becoming an Aztec goddess just isn't enough of a fringe benefit.

Malintzi, unlike Quetzalcoatl and Huitzilopochtli, was not an Aztec god-dess, though many of the attributes Lawrence gives her seem to derive from the qualities of a mother goddess like Coatlicue or Tonantzin, traditionally rooted to the land both as womb and grave. Malintzin (or Malinche, or Marina) was the name of Cortés's interpreter and mistress; she was also the mother of his mestizo son. Cortés called her "mi lengua" (my tongue), and her betrayal of her people, by tongue and body, is Mexico's enduring shame and most rep-resentative object lesson for the dangers of letting women out of the house and allowing them to speak. The invented syncretic maternal goddess Tonantzin–Virgin of Guadalupe has endured as Mexico's national symbol; Malintzin-Malinche, of course, has entered the common vocabulary as an insult meaning "traitor." Asking Kate to betray her people, in effect, by becoming the repre-sentative and spokeswoman for the revitalized Aztec religion neatly reverses and recapitulates Mexico's own origin myth, where Quetzalcoatl returned as a destructive white man with a traitorous indigenous woman as his spokes-woman and consort.

The second conversation occurs between Ramón and Kate sometime after the ceremony in which she accepts her role as the virginal goddess Malintzi, as Cipriano's counterpart and "the soft lodestone to magnetise his blade of steel" (424). In this conversation, Ramón clarifies the price of Kate's ritual deification:

"It is wonderful, really," said Kate, as they rowed over the water, "how—how splen-did one can feel in this country! As if one were still genuinely of the nobility."

"Aren't you?" he said.

"Yes, I am. But everywhere else it is denied. One here feels the full force of one's nobility. The natives still worship it."

"At moments," said Ramón. "Later they will murder you and violate you, for having worshipped you."

"Is it inevitable?" she said flippantly.

"I think so," he replied. (478)

Nobility is Kate's birthright; she believes she is intrinsically superior because her blood is "another, finer fluid" than that of the commoners and the Mexican peasants who taunt her with their "strange, reptilian insistence" that *Blood is one blood*" (456). It is because these commoners, despite their resistance, respect the superiority of her more refined spirit, her finer blood, that they have chosen her, a foreigner, to become the incarnated Malintzi. Furthermore, at the very point in which her natural nobility is acknowledged and inserted into a "Latin American" meaning system—the triad Quetzalcoatl/Huitzilopochtli/Malintzi—her foreignness dissolves and her legitimacy not only as the silent mother/virgin goddess, but also as the voice of/for Mexico is established. She provides the connection to European high culture that the educated mestizos, Ramón and Cipriano, are unable to make alone. At the same time, Ramón reminds her, the common people's animal resentment will eventually bring her down. To the degree that her difference from them cannot be internalized (her orientation is modern/spiritual to their primitive/corporeal), she becomes the obvious sacrificial victim, both the unwanted element that must be cast out as well as the representative of the best that can be achieved through miscegenation. In Lawrence's novel, however, this delicately avoided topic of the potential vitality of a miscegenated race and culture, in equal parts desired and undesirable, resists its own spiritualized/brutalized conception in ritual and in narration.

Kate's ambivalence to the Mexican Indians is concocted of inherited prejudices combined with the author's own particular obsessions. Thus, for Torgovnick, Lawrence retells "in personalized terms the two major stories about primitive peoples he inherited from the nineteenth century: primitive peoples as dangerous and irrational . . . ; primitive peoples as the idealized noble savage . . ." To these inherited stereotypes Lawrence adds his own gendering twist: the first, or "feminine," story represents "the primitive as degeneration, as a cautionary tale for the modern West; the second, 'masculine' version, is the primitive as regeneration, as the last best hope for the modern West" (Torgovnick 159). What is interesting to me, however, is the degree to which these inherited prejudices intersect with Mexico's own, creating a partial overlap, but one with an entirely distinct political edge. The mystique of the superior quality of white people's blood sounds familiar in miscegenated Mexico as the trope of an inherited (from the Spanish) passion for "purity of the blood" that undergirds the classist and racist prejudices of Mexicans to this day. At the same time, alongside the obsession with pure blood, the myth of the glorious

Aztec past helped the colonial creoles endow their struggle for an independent identity from Spain with a moral or spiritual authority. Thus, Paz writes, Sigüenza y Góngora proposed to the viceroy the idea of using Aztec, rather than Roman, emperors as the theme of a triumphal arch celebrating good government. Furthermore, Paz finds, "noteworthy, too, is the frequency with which, in all texts of this period, there appears the adjective 'imperial' applied indifferently to the Aztec state and Mexico City" (Paz, "Flight of Quetzalcoatl" xvii). Even more interestingly, the same general division that Lawrence, with his nineteenth-century prejudices, discerns between the degenerate and the regenerative forms of the primitive obtains in seventeenth-century Mexico as well, where the exaltation of the disappeared Aztec past—a mythic invention parallel to the equally mythologized Roman empire in stature and spiritual status—is paired to an absolute denigration of and disgust for the living Indian. Early-twentieth-century Mexico, despite its official exaltation of "the cosmic race" (Vasconcelos) unmistakably downgraded the indigenous component of that mixture of blood as shiftless peons while pointing ritually to Benito Juárez, the Indian president, as a sign of a national lack of racial prejudice. Patriotism, consequently, in the post-revolutionary period familiar to Lawrence, as in the period preceding independence, involves a resurrection of an invented past, along with a rejection of the living present.

Finally, Lawrence's image of the revived religion of Quetzalcoatl seems to have less to do with coincidental parallels to Mexican myth, nation-forming or not, and a good deal that aligns it closely with the work of his contemporary Georges Bataille, who imagines a sinisterly subversive Aztec America, one that offers a devastating critique of the rational obsessions of the civilized world. In his reading/celebration of the Aztec civilization, Bataille emphasizes the value of openly affirmed human sacrifice, and he explicitly underscores the fiercely intense sensuality of the sacrifice in his masculinist fantasies. The Inca civilization, says Bataille, is dull, but the Aztecs, "the liveliest, the most seductive" of the American natives, had "air and violence, . . . poetry and humor" (Bataille, "Extinct America" 4–5). In another article Bataille clarifies that he wants "to become part of the history of sacrifice, not of science," and while he "had nothing more serious to say of the reasons for our joy than the Mexican has of his own satisfaction," he hints that "only when death is at stake does life seem to reach the extreme incandescence of light" (Bataille, "Sacrifice" 68). Like Lawrence, Bataille seems to feel that the joy reaches a special incandescence when the element of miscegenation is factored into the sacrifice:

An Englishwoman, transfigured by a halo of blond hair, abandons her splendid body to the lubricity and the imagination (driven to the point of ecstasy by the stunning odor of decay) of a number of nude men.

Her humid lips open to kisses like a sweet swamp, like a noiseless flowing river, and her eyes, drowned in pleasure, are as immensely lost as her mouth. Above the entwined human beasts who embrace and handle her, she raises her marvelous head, so heavy with dazzlement, and her eyes open on a scene of madness. (Bataille, *Visions of Excess* 85)

Bataille's vision, like that of innumerable pulp novels, juxtaposes the Barbie-like image of the blonde Western beauty against the pornographic gaze filtered through "primitive," over-sexed, and racially othered men. It is precisely the contrast between the iconic beauty of the woman and the iconic bestiality of the men that proves so stimulating; madness and death are the natural concomitant results, intensifying the erotic charge for the implicit white male voyeur. In Lawrence too, the revival of the old gods requires blood sacrifice, though the assurance that the men executed as part of the Huitzilopochtli ritual, mere brutish Indians after all, are criminals deserving of death placates Kate's more queasy conscience.

As in Lawrence's novel, Tobias Schneebaum's narrative of his eight months in the Amazon with the Akarama people tells of the writer's encounter with a primitive people that represent at the same time the virile noble savage and the degenerate cannibal. In telling this story, Schneebaum too focuses on a fetishized act of ritual violence. Furthermore, Schneebaum structures his tale as that of an educated Westerner who, like Kate in *The Plumed Serpent*, is both detached from the Latin American culture observed, and ritually and spiritually part of that culture. Like the British writer, he blurs his own subjectivity into that of the native, thus lending the account an insider's authority. Schneebaum, with the ostentatious rejection of the ethnographer's reasoned and distanced account of his field work in favor of a more subjective account of his experiences, treads close to the novelist's territory. He is at the same time a Western person who marks his ethnographer's training in the text. Implicitly, then, he is apparently taking a step closer to the native than the imagined fetish object of a Lawrence or a Bataille. If as in Lawrence, the Latin American initially seems mysterious, unfathomable, and intensely male, nevertheless, the Anglo-European, by virtue of adoption into this alien culture, soon learns everything there is to know, even to the point of becoming, as Schneebaum does, the spokesperson for "my people" and privileged explicator of "our way of life" (Schneebaum 130, 177). These people, as we know from reading the prologues to the book, are a cultural variant lost to humanity. They have no speech, no future.

Schneebaum is deeply aware of the audience in whose terms "our way of life" needs both explication and defense. After opening the story of his travels *in medias res* with a chapter that begins, "Manolo came into the clearing below me . . ." (3), Schneebaum starts his second chapter, with a mental clearing in this rapidly sketched narrative jungle, through direct address to the reader:

"Now that I've begun this diary, these letters, whatever they are, it is difficult to know how to go on . . . And I think of all those who will read this. My friends, that is. You, that is" (16). The readers become friends, people with similar intellectual and aesthetic interests and ideological goals, and these multiple friends (literate and unlettered) condense into those of his friends who can read and who both sympathize with and influence the form of this telling: the shadowy shapes of "C" and "M," the anthropologist and the artist, and perhaps, the less shadowy shape of the Spanish wanderer, Manolo, whose tortured homosexuality causes him to exile himself in the jungle, in the furthest outpost of Catholicism. These friends are further condensed into the figure of the letter's recipient, the intimate ur-Friend, "You, that is." That is to say, me. I, the letter's recipient, am participating in a long, and long-distance, conversation with my friend who, writing from the immediacy of the moment, from the day-by-day experience, needs my insight, my detachment, in order to evaluate the adventure as a whole. "There will be no pretense of objectivity here," Schneebaum warns (16). He is feeling his way along, depending on instincts, and he continues, inviting my participation, "I must tell my own story in this same way; perhaps you will connect it all together and analyze my motives and methods" (20). Not only am I urged to listen to the story, but to perform the eminently postmodern occidental critical act of forging connections among scattered fragments and theorizing about methodological issues based on sparse evidence.

One effect of the method is immediately clear. Schneebaum quickly establishes a relation of immediacy and intimacy between himself and the reader that suggests his powers of intuition and empathy, hinting at the strikingly unique qualities of his sensibility (and of his sexuality) that allow him not only to make contact with the Akarama and avoid being eaten in the initial meeting, but also to become one with that people in what is, after all, a relatively short stay. Furthermore, the letter-writing strategy, with its intimate, informal tone, and its half-bewildered account of developing events, permits Schneebaum a latitude in narrative construction decried in the more formalized accounts of ethnography or anthropology. In some sense, Schneebaum's intense self-awareness can lead us to the conclusion that his little book sets the precedent for (post)modern cultural anthropology and serves as a primer for the exploration of the relation of modern ethnographical studies to indigenismo. We readers (I, that is) tend to forget quickly how multiply hedged and shaped this letter/diary actually is.

Schneebaum's visit with the Akarama took place in 1955, when he went to Peru on a Fulbright fellowship. And, he notes in a preface to the original 1969 edition of *Keep the River on Your Right*, "although I kept notes at the time, it has taken me all these years to come to the actual writing of the pages that follow"—a very delayed letter, indeed, and one reciprocally conditioned by the late 1960s and Rachel Carson rather than the mid-fifties. Time enough for contemplation, one would think. Time for analysis to have taken place at some level. But again, analysis is left to me, that is my job as reader, my job because I can *read*; Schneebaum places himself, the writer, fictitiously on the "primitive" side of the divide, ranged alongside those who neither read nor find any reason for analyzing actions.

Schneebaum is also aware that the readers of the second edition of the narrative are different from the first edition's readers twenty years earlier. Readers in 1988 are more consciously concerned about the problem of deforestation in the Third World, have been appalled by the Union Carbide disaster in India, and remain deeply incensed by Western insensitivity to other cultures. As the author tells us in his new preface to the 1988 edition, he discovered a few years after the book originally came out that the entire Akarama people had been wiped out by trans-Amazon highway constructors, who used incendiary bombs to kill them. It is not so much, or not only, that the 1960s were "a simpler time, a more beautiful time," but that memory makes it so; thus not only nostalgia, but also outrage condition the old-new story of the Akarama people. Curiously, however, Schneebaum's own outrage is more for himself than his Akarama friends: "I had searched out that particular encounter without realizing the fulfillment that would thereby come to me . . . An entire culture disappeared, and with it went a whole section of my life" (Schneebaum preface). What we readers—what I—tend to forget is that *Keep the River on Your Right* is, precisely, a narrative of a period in our friend Tobias Schneebaum's life. As is more obviously the case in Lawrence's novel, the Akarama in Schneebaum's narrative serve as the correlative of the other within; they focus and rechannel and empower his repressed sex/sensuality. His trip to the deepest, most unexplored regions of the Peruvian Amazon is a homecoming and a self-encounter.

Thus, one of the most striking things for me, as I read Schneebaum's narrative, is the network of allusion he deploys to define himself *and* his reader in terms of a shared cultural heritage. On his first night in the Mission, his mind overflows with possibilities that derive from a well-established background in Tarzan comics and afternoon television serials: "Of course, nothing happened; there were no snakes, no tigers, no headhunters, no tarantulas. Yet my mind overflowed with all these possibilities" (9): his mind, and, by osmosis, mine as well. The image that prevails is not that of an uneventful evening, but rather of a jungle full of potential adventure and rife with dangerous encounters with exotic men and beasts. Schneebaum's decision to journey, like Kurtz and Marlowe, into the heart of darkness, to go, *Star Trek*–like, where no one has gone before, ratifies this first impression. Perhaps because his command of Spanish is shaky, and he speaks the other languages of the region not at all, Schneebaum, like Lawrence, is freer to dream, to invent the "rightness" and love he feels bursting out around him in all directions. "It is becoming the realization of a dream, my being here," he says, "it's as if I were back in *Bomba the Jungle Boy*, my favorite reading in my early teens" (19). Events are profounder, richer, sillier, by relation to the pop-culture context.

Our shared cultural context includes not only Tarzan and Bomba, however. He also expects me to share his interest in T. S. Eliot, to navigate in the ideological waters familiar to *The Nation*'s readers, to sense this friend's connection to Hesse's *Steppenwolf* (he borrows Manolo's Spanish translation to read by candlelight while native men and women are conducting orgies on the beach under the crescent moon), to recognize his allusions to Proust: "the shock of cold water was my madeleine" (41). The first moments of his encounter with the Akarama function as another madeleine, a shock of forememory of an event yet to take place. From the beginning, he feels that he can understand these people without the slightest familiarity with their language, that an empathic bond allows them to communicate with each other (76, 78–79). I, his reader, am evidently meant to share that bond as well. But in 1988, and even perhaps in 1969, we might well suspect that Schneebaum, like the crazy old priest in the frontier mission "most of the time . . . makes himself misunderstood" (26), that the experience of mutual comprehension might be considerably less mutual than he imagines, that in constituting himself the speaker for the people, he is, again like Lawrence, actually speaking only for a construction of his own desire.

He sees the Akarama in terms of certain basic categories—human, and eaters of other humans—and as he hopes they are—"the first men who had ever walked upon the earth." This implicit confusion of what he is, or how he sees himself, with what he hopes and what he sees of the Akarama conditions all of his (mis)understandings of his adoptive people, his longing for their pristine innocence, for their knowledge, as well as his recognition that he is forever expelled from the Eden of their lives:

In writing, I think. That is, in writing here, it has become necessary to put thoughts together to go down on these pages . . . And coming upon my people, now my lovers, my friends, I shed my past as I did my clothes, even knowing inside me that I could never be a Michii or Yoreitone, that a shirt, though gone now in shreds, though it no longer is an object for which I have any desire or need, remains forever something that I know has somewhere a use, and I can never strip myself of the knowledge of how to open a button, how to put my arms in sleeves, how to put the tails inside a pair of pants. To become Michii, I must not only rid myself of the need to write, but also of the very knowledge that writing exists . . .

Time after time they ran their hands over my chest and belly and penis. They touched with gentle fingers my nose, my eyes, my ears, my hair, and they prodded into my navel with their noses. They repeated one word over and over, Habe, habe, and it has taken me all this time to understand its meaning: "ignorant one." (69–71)

Schneebaum knows that he is ignorant because he writes, that in order to understand the Akarama and to be like them he has to forget his knowledge of Eliot and Proust and Bomba the Jungle Boy. Yet, at the same time, he realizes that he thinks in writing, and that he will continue to write during his time with the Akarama, using whatever makeshift ink and paper he can devise. The end result of all of his thinking, and all of his writing, has a single, simple conclusion. He now understands the most basic fact of all; he sees the Akarama as brothers, lovers, friends, *his* people, while they see him as a mascot, a pet, an "ignorant one." He continually puzzles over why these eaters of their fellow human beings have not eaten him; it does not occur to him (or at least does not occur to him in the pages of this narrative) that they might see him as inedible.

As is the case with Lawrence's novel, there is a violent blood ritual at the heart of *Keep the River on Your Right* that seals the spiritual relationship between the white Euro-American and the native Latin American. In *The Plumed Serpent*, Kate witnesses executions and accepts her elevation to a goddess; in *Keep the River on Your Right*, Schneebaum takes part in a graphically described male fertility ritual of hunting, killing, and eating men from another Amazonian group, followed by ritual homosexuality. The entire process, Schneebaum hints, is at the same time a deeply religious ceremony, a celebration of life, a declaration of identity, an assertion of the hunting male's dominance over his prey, and a nutritional necessity. This is *The Heart of Darkness* from Kurtz's side of the divide between barbarity and civilization, a *Heart of Darkness* where the values are, Bataille-like, inverted: "I was hypnotized by movement always up and down, kaleidoscopic lights that flickered through my iris, a chant that soon became a roar that drained out thoughts that came my way . . . I took a piece of meat that Michii held out and ate and swallowed and ate some more, and entered the circle again to dance" (106). At the same time, Schneebaum feels a wondering guilt at having gone so far native that he eats human flesh, that he loses both writing and thoughts in the chant "Mayaariihá," "roaring jaguar."

The roar of the jaguar sounds throughout the rest of the narrative, paired to its minor key partner, an obsessively repeated, *written* sentence: "I am a cannibal." In sharing the Akarama males' ritual meat, he declares himself irrevocably one of them; in reflecting upon his participation in their communion, he knows that he is equally irrevocably set apart. No matter how deeply he goes, or thinks he goes, into their practices, he is not one of them. He suffers a crisis of identity; they do not. Their laughing attitude towards death, their frankly ritual homosexuality are intensely unlike his own lacerated needs, at least insofar as we, his friends, can filter them through the writings of and conversations with his alter ego, the other writer in this narrative, the Spanish homosexual Manolo, whose only reader is the one man who understands him, his friend, Tobias Schneebaum. For all his love of Bomba and other exotica, and despite his conversion experience with the Akarama, for Schneebaum the drama of meaning is played out in a field that has nothing to do with Michii, Yore-itone, or his other Akarama companions. Schneebaum, inevitably, processes these experiences in terms that have to do with letter writing for a Western-educated audience, albeit a sympathetic one, and not for his Amazonian friends. "I am a cannibal," he writes, "but I am no savage" (181). For the Akarama people, neither of the two clauses has any linguistic or existential referent, and the distinction Schneebaum makes between "cannibal" and "savage" is utterly meaningless, as would be the distinction Western society makes between people according to sexual preference. "Here I am," they say simply, "a roaring jaguar." Tobias Schneebaum, for all his adventures, is still, or perhaps more intensely, Bomba, the jungle boy, a little lost, oppressed by lingering twinges of superiority.

But what of the Akarama? Just as the reader of the 1960s is different from the reader of the 1980s, so too I posit that the Akarama, as given to us by To-bias Schneebaum, need to be read differently. The Akarama of both decades are deeply misunderstood people. Previously taken to be bloodthirsty, primi-tive savages, Schneebaum shows us that they are really happy, loving, commu-nity-oriented people. While the community he describes seems strangely de-void of women, there are any number of good reasons for Schneebaum's inability to mingle with the female groupings as easily as he does with the men. Yet because even the Akarama men whom Schneebaum personalizes by reference to a name and a couple of personality traits seem so sketchily drawn, the reader is ultimately left to her own devices. Thus, the Akarama of the 1960s are genial inversions of their hippie counterparts up north. They groove on peace and togetherness, love and understanding, and are real back-to-nature folks. If they seem a bit simple, they are endearing in their simplicity. The reader of 1988, unlike the reader of the 1960s, knows the Akarama have been brutally extinguished, and our sympathy for them is conditioned by this fore-knowledge. Theirs is now a tragic story of the cruelty and violence of the white man, whose inexplicable conviction of his rightness and superiority colors this moral tale. Darinimbiak's death seems a foreshadowing; the curing of Pendiari and Awaipe's ills, an ironic commentary on the greater tragedy to come. Schneebaum ends his narrative with the reflection: "I go where my legs will take me and if I look ahead, it seems like time gone by, for I see myself no mat-ter where I go, forever here" (184). His memory—here and now in 1969, or here and now in 1988, or here in the now of this critical study—is all that re-mains of an entire people, but it is a people processed and reprocessed as the site of self-construction, of critical analysis. "Here I am," says the Akarama, only a memory now, the roaring jaguar stilled in the jaguar-skin throw rug, the "here" unaccountably shifting locale.

There are several points that need to be made briefly, and by way of conclusion, about the body of texts represented by these works. (1) For reasons that still require exploration, ritual violence, or what I've been calling a Western fetishization of violence—as opposed to banal or inexplicable violence—plays an essential role in these narrations about the exotic, "other" America, and ritual is linked to an explicit, temporally conscious positioning. In these works, time is manipulated as a value structure, either to contrast a timeless, primitive existence (Akarama, Mexican Indians) with a time-bound one (Schneebaum's New York; Kate's London),[3] or to suggest a variation on what Bataille calls the "empty toxicity" at the doubled end of history when modes of consciousness and production and modes of excess, sacrifice, and art will join (see Stoekl 107–8). One compelling feature of this paradigm is the linking of sexuality and violence with the "primitive" culture, suggesting that the familiar postmodern trope of the end of history also predicts a return to this imagined primitive past. I do not believe that the underlying connection with utopic and/or pastoral discursive traditions is insignificant. (2) Issues of domination also need to be explored. Both Lawrence and Schneebaum, in their different ways, manipulate an ingrown sense of superiority as a tool for opening up and understanding an alien culture. In his article "The National Longing for Form," Timothy Brennan hints at the imbrication of such a desire for mastery with self-indulgence, and with destruction, as well as with the colonialist's unconscious linkage of "to enlighten" with "to control." Brennan focuses on the motives that have, in a large sense, been at the basis of imperialism. "The 'novel of empire' in its classic modernist versions . . . has been blind to the impact of a world system largely directed by Anglo-American interests, however much it involved itself passionately, unevenly, and contradictorily in some of the human realities of world domination" (Brennan 48). Likewise, Torgovnick reminds us that the sense of the literary recuperation of the primitive upon which such works as Lawrence's and Schneebaum's depend is neither coherent nor particularly well-founded, and that closer scrutiny uncovers nationalistic biases, ethnocentric prejudices, and sexist values that are now impossible to defend (Torgovnick 3). At the same time, the strong connection between nation and narration needs to be uncoupled and explored, especially, as is the case in these texts, when the underlying notions about narrative construction seem at odds with the concept of nation under discussion. This problem seems particularly acute when exploring the origins (Lawrence) or boundaries (Schneebaum) or gender inflections of stories/myths/rituals about narration/nation.

These trends are disturbing ones, and implicitly undercut much of the overt theoretical and political discursive positionings of postmodern thought. Other scholars, similarly aware of this problem, have turned to the Third World for more authentic, or at least more culturally sensitive, renderings of this postmodern indigenist paradigm that I have been discussing through my comments on the novel by D. H. Lawrence and the personalized ethnography of Tobias Schneebaum. As Michael Fischer notes, "bifocality, or reciprocity of perspectives, has become increasingly important in a world of growing interdependence between societies: members of cultures described are increasingly critical readers of ethnography. No longer can rhetorical figures of the 'primitive' or the 'exotic' be used with impunity; audiences have become multiple" (Fischer 199). Postmodern readers can no longer safely or simply appropriate indigenous cultural objects as our own fetishes—they remain stubbornly connected to their native source. In response to such epistemological complications, we in the Anglo-European academy have a tendency to supplement or displace the felt incompleteness and recognized Western bias in earlier versions of postmodern indigenism by turning to renowned Latin American writers and thinkers who have also taken up such concerns. It will be my contention in the second half of this paper that texts like Mario Vargas Llosa's *El hablador* (*The Storyteller*), which seemingly presents a response to Kate's Malintzi and Schneebaum's Bomba the Jungle Boy, in actuality distance themselves very little, if at all, from the strong, if discredited, paradigm represented by such works as those of Schneebaum and Lawrence.

II

Torgovnick ends *Gone Primitive* with the reminder that her book is itself biased in particular ways, and offers only one study among many possible studies of the phenomenon: "The present study has traced, in essence, a male-centered, canonical line in of Western primitivism—without question the major line . . . But I can imagine alternative lines of primitivism that would, necessarily, be based on an entirely different selection of texts. Some of those texts would be produced by women; many (whether by men or women) would probe alternative versions of knowledge and social order, including many marginalized in the West" (Torgovnick 248). Mario Vargas Llosa is deeply suspicious of the "sed de exotismo," thirst for the exotic, relieved in these works of the canonical sort, and finds particularly invidious the exploitation of ingenuous "proletarian" Third World writers by well-fed European leftists to confirm their own preconceptions about Latin America and their own frustrated romanticism about their own countries. The simple fictions about Latin America, says Vargas Llosa, are what they demand and what they get; such fictions feed both their Bomba-the-Jungle-Boy exoticism and their ideological programs. On the occasion of a speech by a working-class Peruvian brought to address a group of Danish intellectuals, he writes with distaste of the Danes' enthusiastic reception of an exceptionally one-sided and biased account of life in Peru:

La razón principal es, sin duda, ese fenómeno de *transferencia* tan frecuente en los intelectuales europeos que dicen interesarse en América Latina. En realidad, se interesan en una América Latina ficticia, en la que han proyectado esos apetitos ideológicos que la realidad de sus propios países no puede materializar, esas convicciones que la vida que viven desmiente diariamente. La compensación de su frustración es ese otro mundo, al que se vuelven a mirar a fin de que les muestre siempre lo que quieren ver . . . [The function of the third-world writer] consistía en resarcirlos vicariamente de la desgracia que es para ellos—los pobres—vivir y escribir en un país culto y democrático donde los sindicalistas prefieren ver la televisión, en sus casas propias, en vez de editar las novelas de los escritores revolucionarios que les elevarían la conciencia. (Vargas Llosa, *Contra* 343–44)

[The main reason is, doubtlessly, that very common phenomenon of *transference* in European intellectuals who say they are interested in Latin America. What they are really interested in is a fictitious Latin America, onto which they have projected those ideological appetites that the reality of their own countries cannot materialize, those convictions that the life they live contradicts on a daily basis. The compensation for their frustration is that other world, the one they go back to again and again so long as it shows them exactly what they want to see . . . [The function of the third-world writer] consists in vicariously indemnifying their disgrace, which for those poor intellectuals consists of living and writing in a civilized and democratic country where union organizers would rather watch television, in their own homes, rather than publish the novels by those revolutionary writers who would raise their consciousnesses.]

Vargas Llosa, then, decries oversimplification of complex Latin American realities in order to exploit specific Latin American difficulties for first-world aesthetic enjoyment, and finds particularly reprehensible the political erotics of a continuing exoticism that insistently rewrites Latin America in terms of Western intellectual desires. From his point of view, amply supported by many thoughtful critics, his own difficult, highly fragmented, self-reflexive, eminently postmodern novels make their claim on Anglo-European attention through reference to a nuanced multi-cultural Peru reaffirmed in its multifarious vitality rather than displayed as an uncomplicated and easily marketable folklore. To counter first-world intellectuals, or writers like Lawrence and Schneebaum, who find western tools of analysis adequate for the study of any culture, in *El hablador* Vargas Llosa proposes a model in which the production of knowledge is a joint undertaking. A western-trained narrator and a Machiguenga storyteller speak alternatively in the text, implicitly to each other and to us, who find their complementarity and the grounds for dialogue in the textual interstices. The immediate attractiveness of such a work is that, unlike those works studied by Torgovnick, in *El hablador* Vargas Llosa, ostensibly at least, does not pretend to speak for or from the margins of his own (in Western terms) marginalized society. Instead, his point-of-view character speaks from the very center of that society—Lima, Peru, and Florence, Italy—while giving the Amazonian storyteller (almost) equal space to speak in his own voice.

Nevertheless, the question I want to ask this text is, first of all, to what degree does Vargas Llosa's affirmation of the political and artistic complexity of such work as his lay claim to Western attention through a deployment of stylistic techniques that are both white-male canonical and "universal" rather than local in orientation, and secondly, how much of the authority of Vargas Llosa's novel derives from the reader's sense that in it, unlike in traditional ethnographical accounts, the novelist speaks for the margin because in this book he licenses his own, differently constituted, margin to speak for itself?

In *El hablador* the problem almost too easily breaks down into a question of narrative orientation. There are two narrators, both Peruvian: one speaks from Florence, having chosen the route of westernization (though he agonizes about writing the story of the Machiguenga Indians), the other from the unexplored (by westerners) rain forest of the Amazon. In depicting a reality that is at least double, Vargas Llosa would seem to respond to those European intellectuals he describes who want Latin America to retain a straightforward, fairy-tale simplicity. Yet, at the same time, his bid for relevance comes uncomfortably close to duplicating their analogous anxiety. Those European intellectuals he critiques want Latin America to provide a standard of relevance for their ideological programs, to provide them with the forum that their own people, too involved in television to bother, deny them. But when he turns to his own society, Vargas Llosa describes the Latin American writer as a person similarly, although for different reasons, without a place: "En una sociedad en que la literatura no cumple función alguna porque la mayoría de sus miembros no saben o no están en condiciones de leer y la minoría que sabe y puede leer no lo hace nunca, el escritor resulta un ser anómalo, sin ubicación precisa, . . . una especie de loco benigno" [In a society in which literature has no real function whatsoever because the majority of the members of that society do not know how to read, or are not able to do so, and the minority that knows how to read and can read never does so, the writer turns out to be an anomalous being, without any precise position . . . a type of benign madman] (Vargas Llosa, *Contra* 93). Western intellectuals look to Latin America for the practical validation of their theories; Latin American intellectuals, hints Vargas Llosa, look to Europe for their reading public. Vargas Llosa, then, is concerned with the writer as exile and exemplary citizen, and with the strained linguistic/literary modes of coding a text for two different and incompatible audiences, the more-or-less indifferent educated elite of his own country, and the relatively uninformed reader abroad. I need not go into the implications of this practice. Several years ago Fernández Retamar pointed out the orientalizing tendency in his contemporaries' targeting of the reading publics in Europe and North America, and he has eloquently explored the issues involved in inscribing a Latin American identity for (or against) a supposedly "universal" audience. His *Calibán* confronts the issue of cultural and linguistic alienation not only in relation to the Spanish-speaking Latin American's relation to indigenous and other minority peoples, but also in terms of a vexed consciousness of the overriding effects of cultural imperialism.

There is a second issue beyond the ironies involved in a fall into exoticism when the frenzy to escape such orientalizing tendencies is at its height, however. Not only are Europe and Latin America caught in a mutually validating narrative bind involving the very heart of postmodern critical and theoretical practices, but both the Europeans he critiques and Vargas Llosa himself use the exotic as the validating trope of authenticity. Like the ingenuous proletarian writer who repeats to the Danish audience all the stereotypes about an exotic Latin American city that they most desire to see fulfilled, so too Vargas Llosa, the Latin American city dweller, looks to the exotic margins of Peru for the image of an authentic narrative voice. If the Western intellectual or the metropolitan storyteller is a barely tolerated benign madman, the same is not true in the Amazon. The Machiguenga storytellers, the narrator tells Mascarita, "son una prueba palpable de que contar historias puede ser algo más que una mera diversión . . . Algo primordial, algo de lo que depende la existencia misma de un pueblo" [They're a tangible proof that storytelling can be something more than mere entertainment . . . Something primordial, something that the very existence of a people may depend on] (Vargas Llosa, *Hablador* 92/*Storyteller* 94). The Machiguenga storyteller is at the center of his culture in a way the Latin American novelist or Western intellectual can never hope to be, but his very existence there, on the margins, describes the conditions by which they can imagine a way out of the multifarious postmodern fictional impasses and achieve cultural empowerment. Fiction in the Amazon is not just the amusing lie that supplements reality,[4] it is the reality that constitutes a community, validating the old ties between a nation (however defined) and narration in a particularly strong sense. Academic fascination with such a model of dynamic, empowered ethnicity is entirely to be expected, since this model allows for a reimagining of the interplay between speaker and society that we, in our twilight admissions in conference corridors, uncomfortably suspect to be highly attenuated in postmodern theorizing and literary practice.

Furthermore, while the fully empowered Machiguenga oral storyteller is new, the novel that runs simultaneously along two well-defined tracks has become a well-established feature of Vargas Llosa's recent work; *La tía Julia y el escribidor* and *Elogio de la madrastra* both use a similar technique of setting up two narrative voices, and Carlos Alonso suggests in an article on *tía Julia* that the divided novel "can be read as an example of that more general current within postmodernism which seeks to explode the chasm between high and low cultures by using popular forms and discourses to produce objects that ostensibly belong to high literary culture" (47). Clearly, if we agree with Alonso, we conclude that Vargas Llosa is concerned with setting two discrete narrative modes side by side so as to abstract the essential components of storytelling. What is so interesting about Vargas Llosa's recent efforts, however, is that he "explodes the chasm" in the chasm itself, in the double and double-voiced text, unlike as in, say, *Historia de Mayta* where he exploits/explodes the detective formula from within for high-art ends. Vargas Llosa's doubled text reminds me again of Barthes's formulation that "Culture . . . recurs as an edge," an edge defined in the aestherotic seam between pleasure and violence, between modernity and the primitive: the destroyer mourning/reveling in the loss of what he has destroyed.

Vargas Llosa's double narrative, then, is caught in a bind that is at least triple. (1) The Machiguenga storyteller represents the best hope for a revitalized, constructive narrative tradition at the center of culture rather than at the destructive seam, but the westernized novelist who tries to write a story about the Machiguenga oral storyteller is unable to find a voice that is either "authentic" (102/104) or even "credible" (152/158). (2) Ethnography, the alternative traditional method of explicating the primitive to the modern, is suspect on both cultural and ideological grounds. Concern about non–Latin American investigators' motivations for field study in the Amazon is widespread, and not only in fictional accounts.[5] As one of Vargas Llosa's characters says, not entirely tongue in cheek: "la Etnología es una seudociencia inventada por los gringos para destruir las Humanidades" [ethnology is a pseudo-science invented by gringos to destroy the Humanities] (34/32), and the Instituto Lingüístico de Verano or the Dominican priests who staff a mission at Urubamba, both organizations acknowledged in Vargas Llosa's endnote, implicitly have their own nefarious reasons for wanting to study Amazonian Indians and their languages (e.g., veiled hints that such organizations have been the object "de virulentas controversias," "of virulent controversy" [69/71]). (3) To go native—in Schneebaum's terms, to blur the distinction cannibal/savage—would seem to find a way out of the contradiction by replacing the western-oriented, canonical author with an indigenous figure. Nevertheless, the indigenous storyteller by definition does not enter into any dialogue about authorship, living or dead, and remains completely outside the burning conflict in postmodern aesthetic modes. Without the intervention of the modern, westernized author-figure, there is no book. Without a reader who accepts narrative fragmentation, there is no community bound together (rather than cut on the edge) of the story.

What Vargas Llosa attempts, then, is a both/and operation: he includes both the native informant (the Machiguenga storyteller) and the analytic framework (the westernized intellectual). The storyteller blurs all temporal modes into a continuous present line: "'Estamos vivos,' decían. Y ellos seguían andando" ["We're alive," they said. And they went on walking] (44/43). Like Schneebaum and the Akarama, they live in the "here," with no time or inclination for western-style analysis. The intellectual, in contrast, emphasizes the retrospective mode of meditative reflection upon a history now "visto con la perspectiva del tiempo" [with hindsight] (21/19), where the tell-tale marker "ya" indicates the direction contemplation must take: "¿Sentía ya esa fascinación de embrujado por los hombres del bosque y la Naturaleza sin hollar, por las culturas primitivas, minúsculas, desperdigadas . . . ? ¿Ardía ya en él ese fuego solidario brotado oscuramente de lo más hondo de su personalidad . . . ? Sí, ya había comenzado todo eso" [Did he already feel that spellbound fascination for the peoples of the jungle and for unsullied nature, for minute primitive cultures . . . Was that ardent fell feeling, spring from the darkest depths of his personality, already burning within him . . . Yes, all that had already begun] (15/12–13). The narrator's "ya" ("already") betrays his methodology, his repeated "already" marking the repetitious and necessary scene of analysis of an event not yet, and already defined. This narrator, our westernized guide to the Amazon, is aware of the role of the reader, aware of his own role, aware as well of the institutional status of a certain kind of privileged intellectual activity that creates its own, albeit rejected, community, one defined by a shared matrix involving Kafka and Proust, Corín Tellado and popular television programs, local news and literary gossip. This familiar narrative territory, alternating with the impossibly exotic realm of the Machiguenga storyteller, inevitably suggests its own blurring of edges, it own narrative recharting. For the storyteller's odd mish-mash of news and gossip retold and mixed with myth and traditional tales, all spiced with ritual expressions begins to sound suspiciously similar to the westernized writer's combination of travelogue and gossip about friends, flavored with references to reading, spiced with literary allusions. Reduced to its essential components, the wandering storyteller begins to look like the jet-setting novelist, just as the novelist adduced the *hablador*'s kinship with the European troubadour, the Brazilian *caboclo*, the Irish *seanchaí* (see 158–59/164–65). The Machiguenga serves, ominously, as a defamiliarization device in the continuing story of the Western intellectual's long monologue about himself, never fully escaping into (or from) the social matrix that declares the Western writer a benign madman and the Machiguenga storyteller a defining element of community. Slyly, the story about the Machiguenga storyteller does get written; our mistake would be to take it as a Machiguenga story rather than a talented westerner's variation on his own autobiographical tale.

Vargas Llosa's triple bind is understandable, perhaps inescapable. And the nature of that problematic suggests not so much the enlightened multi-cultural Latin American as someone far more similar to the Danish intellectuals Vargas Llosa belittles before finally rejecting. Like them, Vargas Llosa chooses a specific and stereotypical representative of an exotic culture so as to reaffirm predrawn conclusions, not in this case about the revolution of the proletariat, but rather about the role of the committed writer in (post)modern society. What is of concern to me, however, is the particular framework of literary allusion chosen to surround the Machiguenga elements. In this novel, the overt text of the westernized narrator's admiration for the social status of the Machiguenga storyteller is paired with a repressed subtext hinting at the impotence of the Machiguenga people, who need a converted westerner to come in and revive their dying civilization, and also implying the physical and spiritual monstrosity that is the most they can hope to achieve for themselves in the best of cases.

The narrator's first image of the Amazonian tribes is accompanied by a grimace of distaste. What else, he asks, can a modern, cosmopolitan Peruvian feel for those subhuman beings that sit around naked in the jungle, gabbling incomprehensibly and eating lice? "Esos hipibos, huambisas, aguarunas, yaguas, shapras, campas, mashcos representan en la sociedad peruana . . . un horror pintoresco, una excepcionalidad que los otros compadecían o escarnecían, pero sin concederle el respeto y la dignidad que sólo merecían quienes se ajustaban en su físico, costumbres y creencias a la 'normalidad'" [In the Peruvian social order those Shipibos, Huambisas, Aguarunas, Yaguas, Shapras, Campas, Mashcos represented something that he could understand better than anyone else: a picturesque horror, an aberration that other people ridiculed or pitied without granting it the respect and dignity deserved only by those whose physical appearance, customs, and beliefs were "normal"] (29–30/28). The narrator's original "picturesque horror" ostensibly changes as the novel progresses, and he too begins to appreciate and yearn for the unquestioned respect in which the Machiguengas hold their storytellers. Nevertheless, underlying this superficial change persists the image of an unredeemable, incurable monstrosity.

The first monstrosity lies in the Indians' "perfectionism," their lack of human compassion: new mothers will bury alive or drown babies born with physical handicaps or deformities of any sort (27/25). Yet, despite this horror of deformity, despite their tendency to let themselves die if afflicted by even the most minor illness, the Amazonians seem to support more than their share of human grotesques. The spiritual monstrosity that the narrator "knows" about finds its parallel in the physical deformation all around him when he reaches the Amazon. He describes his impression of Urakusa, an Aguaruna town; first, the "espectáculo acostumbrado" [familiar spectacle]: "tetas colgantes, niños de vientres hinchados por los parásitos, pieles rayados de negro" [dangling tits, the children with parasite-swollen bodies and skins striped red or black], and then something new, "un espectáculo que nunca olvidé: el de un hombre recientemente torturado" [a spectacle I have never forgotten: that of a man recently tortured] (the torturers were whites and mestizos who objected to the Aguaruna leader's foresight in trying to improve living conditions for his people) (72–73/74). The implication is that the unassimilated Indians are monstrous; the semi-assimilated ones are victims of horrible and subhuman treatment; the fully assimilated (e.g. city-dwelling) Indians are merely pathetic. As the narrator rhetorically asks himself later, "¿de 'salvajes' libres y soberanos habían empezado a convertirse en 'zombies' . . . ?" [Or were they, rather, from the free and sovereign "savages" they had been, beginning to turn into "zombies"?] (157/163). The poles of his transformative equation are not insignificant; they suggest no roles for the Indian in westernized imagination other than minor parts in either "Tarzan" or "The Night of the Living Dead." By contrast, the linguists and anthropologists who immerse themselves in this world are "personajes faulknerianos de una sola idea, testarudez intrépida y alarmante heroísmo" [a character out of Faulkner—single-mindedly, fearlessly stubborn, and frightening heroic] (178/184).

On one of the narrator's subsequent trips to the Amazon, he travels with the Schneils to visit a Machiguenga town, in itself an anomaly for this people whose most basic, traditional belief is that the world continues to exist because they never stop walking. Characteristically, the narrator's first impression is of deformity: "uno de los niños tenía la cara destruida por esa especie de lepra que es la uta" [the face of one of the children was eaten away by a form of leprosy known as uta] (162/168)—but the monster is not shunned by his peers; instead, he interacts freely with the other children. The narrator wants to emphasize both the physical horror and the unquestioning acceptance of monstrosity; in order to maintain the argument, however, he has to make a baroque and rather unconvincing distinction between the Indians' monstrous pursuit of perfectionism that leads to infanticide of children with birth defects, and their natural lack of discrimination against those unfortunate individuals whose handicaps or deformities occur after birth, the only way he can maintain the strong linkage between monster and savage.

The narrator reinforces this connection through the figure of Saúl Zuratas, or Mascarita, who is inextricably linked to Kafka's man-monster Gregor Samsa on the one hand and the Machiguenga on the other. This young man, deformed by an immense mole covering one side of his face, is monstrous in various senses of the word. The drunk in the bar summarizes society's uninhibited reaction to his appearance:

—¡Puta, qué monstruo! ¿De qué zoológico te escapaste, oye? . . .

El borracho alargó las manos hacia él, haciendo contra con los dedos, como los niños cuando les mentan la madre.

—Tú no entras, monstruo. . . . Con esa cara, no debías salir a la calle, asustas a la gente. (16)

"Son of a bitch! What a monster! What zoo did you escape from? . . ."

The drunk stretched out his hands, making hex signs with his fingers, the way children do when they're called bad names.

"You're not coming in here, monster. . . . With a face like that, you should keep off the streets. You scare people." (13–14)

Mascarita's enormous mole is a variant on the prominent nose stereotypically thought to be the physical sign of a Jewish heritage, and, indeed, Mascarita's father is a Jew, but as the child of a mixed marriage, a monstrous birth, he is rejected by both his parents' peoples on those grounds. Mascarita is also monstrous in his humor, in his rejection of western models of knowledge, in his passionate commitment to the peoples of the Amazon. He is obsessed with Kafka, and especially "The Metamorphosis," "que había releído innumerables veces y poco menos que memorizado" [which he had read countless times and virtually knew by heart] (19/17), and has a pet parrot he calls Gregorio Samsa. It is, in fact, Kafka's tale of the man-insect that serves as the most persistent literary touchstone for the entire novel. The Machiguengas and Gregor Samsa are Mascarita's twin obsessions, and through this obsessive linking they become identified. Mascarita is a Gregor Samsa; in the Machiguenga world "a los monstruitos, a los gregorio samsas, los despeñaban" [little monsters, Gregor Samsas, were hurled from the top of a mountain] (27/25). At the same time, the Machiguengas are the Gregorio Samsas of Peru; only among them can another Gregorio Samsa hope to feel at home. Soon, through an incomprehensible metamorphosis, or conversion experience, Mascarita becomes a Machiguenga; more, he is the Machiguenga storyteller quoted in this book. The Machiguenga, it seems, have no native storyteller left, for although *habladores* are spoken of in the plural, the only one we hear of, meet, or see depicted is this adopted member of the tribe, the monster, the misfit, who can only find acceptance among these picturesque and primitive people.

If Mascarita's conversion had been complete, the novel would fit more neatly into the tradition of tales of the primitive in which romantic and monstrous interpretations jostle for priority. Monstrously, Mascarita's conversion, like his physical metamorphosis, is halted halfway. Once he is fully accepted as a *hablador*, that is, as one of the people upon whom the very existence of the Machiguenga depends, he employs that power to redefine the nature of the community, at first subtly, later more blatantly. From the first, there is a mystery surrounding this albino graft onto the tribe. The Machiguengas, a friendly and open people, "no tienen reservas sobre nada. Pero sobre los habladores, sí" [They don't keep anything to themselves. Except anything having to do with the habladores] (169/175); the cosmopolitan narrator surmises that these people were not, and had no need, to protect the institution of the storyteller; quite the contrary, since the storyteller was at the root of their sense of community. Instead, "lo protegían a él. A pedido de él mismo, sin duda" [They were protecting him. No doubt because he asked them to] (179/185), and the specific taboo spread to the abstract level.

Mascarita also changes the nature of the Machiguenga belief system in other, even more fundamental ways. One of the horrors of assimilation, says the narrator, is the process by which an independent people is converted into a herd of victims, losing the primordial, untouchable depths (167/172) by learning to sing the national anthem in Machiguenga and to tell Bible stories in broken Spanish. Mascarita changes the fundamental nature of his adopted people in just such basic ways. The Machiguenga never travels alone; they are a wandering but gregarious people. Mascarita refuses any companion except his parrot. The Machiguenga do not use names: "su nombre era siempre provisional, relativo y transeúnte: el que llega o el que se va, el esposo de la que acaba de morir o el que baja de la canoa, el que nació o el que disparó la flecha" [Their names were always temporary, related to a passing phenomenon and subject to change: the one who arrives, or the one who leaves, the husband of the woman who just died, or the one who is climbing out of his canoe, the one just born, or the one who shot the arrow] (81/83). Mascarita does not dissolve name into function in such a fashion; instead, he insists on retaining his nickname, and on hearing it repeated back to him, preserving his unique identity, attaching the Spanish word "Mascarita" to the abstract Machiguenga word for "one who speaks": "lo llamo con una palabra que inventé para él. Un ruido de loros pues. A ver, imítenlo. Despertémoslo, llamémoslo. El lo aprendió y lo repite muy bien: Mas-ca-ri-ta, Mas-ca-ri-ta, Mas-ca-ri-ta . . ." [I call him by a name I invented for him. A parrot noise. Let's hear you imitate it. Let's wake him up; let's call him. He's learned it and repeats it very well: Mas-ca-ri-ta, Mas-ca-ri-ta, Mas-ca-ri-ta . . .] (224/234).

Finally, as the narrator hints, Mascarita's transformation has less to do with his adoption of the Machiguenga belief system than with his Jewish prejudice towards another community that, like his own, is both marginalized and wandering (233/243). Certainly, the long, boring hours he spent in synagogue and the other long hours he spent in a Christian society have their effect on the stories he tells his adopted people. Like the Bible instructors, but more insidiously, Mascarita inserts the stories of those other peoples into the compendium of news and legend. He tells the story of "Tasurinchi-jehová" and the Machiguenga-Jews who were cast out by the Viracocha-Christians and set to wander the earth. I do not want to suggest that what is at issue is the question of retaining some sort of illusory purity of the untouched primitive as an alternative social matrix. What is at issue in this novel is a problem of competing narrative modes—westernized and Amazonian—in which the eccentric, monstrous form of narration is subsumed, almost imperceptibly, into a parody of the same old Judeo-Christian tale. It is perhaps because Mascarita retains his westernized sense of self and heritage and identity that the narrative "I" can so easily recreate the long-desired story of the Machiguenga *hablador*, and do so, moreover, in a form that exactly reproduces the seemingly less authentic (because more overtly western-biased) accounts of ethnographers like Tobias Schneebaum and Kenneth Good (the latter does, in fact, also include the intermittent voice of the native informant in the brief italicized paragraphs provided by his partially westernized Yanomama wife, Yarima). We could, in fact, argue that Vargas Llosa's account, compared to the accounts of the European thinkers he criticizes, is all the more disturbing because in it the Machiguenga voice seems less mediated, seems more like a transcription of the native speaking out or speaking back in his own voice, on his own terms, from the margins of the margin.

Like Schneebaum's narrative or Lawrence's novel, then, Vargas Llosa's *El hablador* describes the experience of giving oneself over to another way of seeing. This is, in itself, an honorable endeavor. What ultimately disappoints, however, is that in the Latin American novel, as in the British and the American's works, the apparent duality of vision is coupled to no interplay. We see what Kate or Tobias or Mascarita sees, and we have an intuition about what the Mexican or the Akarama or the Machiguenga does *not* see, but at all times we are still looking through the mediated vision of Western eyes. Politically, this narrative technique conforms perfectly to Vargas Llosa's pro-acculturation stance with respect to indigenous peoples in the Americas.[6] Because Vargas Llosa's novel only *apparently* privileges (or gives equal time to) the autoethnography of the Machiguenga, there is no bifocal or multiply conceived discursive encounter in the narrative, no countervision to throw the westernized conclusions into relief or put them in perspective. While in each case we are told, endlessly, about a contradiction between a western individual and a non-western collective subject, in each case the collective transposes itself into narrative as a mediated transcription of a single individual's idiosyncratic vision. As William Rowe says in a recent article, "Those parts of the text that present the voice of Zuratas as a Machiguenga 'storyteller' read like a bad *indigenista* novel . . . These passages . . . have virtually no intellectual content" (Rowe 60–61).

In her reading of J. M. Coetzee's *Foe*, Gayatri Spivak suggests that "there can be no politics founded on a continuous overdetermined multiplicity of agencies" (Spivak 166), and she continues: "perhaps that is the novel's message: the impossible politics of overdetermination (mothering, authoring, giving voice to the native 'in' the text; a white male South African writer engaging in such inscriptions 'outside' the text) should not be regularized into a blithe continuity, where the European redoes the primitive's project in herself" (174). Coetzee's novel, Spivak reminds us, does not hold together in a continuous narrative space. Tellingly, for all their surface fragmentation, all three of the books examined in this paper do hold together as the exotic "there" reveals itself as another face/mask of the western "here." All of them suggest that they are limit texts—this is as far as we can go into the jungle—when in fact they mark only the first threshold we must cross.

"We" the readers may resist co-optation into the cultural community of the text's value system on various grounds. As Torgovnick writes, "the language of 'us and them' . . . is powerfully, almost infinitely seductive. Today we seem to have a choice of which 'us' is 'us': the humanist 'us' . . . or the imperialist 'us'." And, Torgovnick adds, even if we are able to choose among the multiple and fragmentary versions of "us," "we still need to ask what is excluded from the 'us'" (Torgovnick 145). Clearly, all three of these works show, both the humanist "us" and the imperialist "us" share a common Anglo-European cultural frame and both, in Mary Louise Pratt's succinct formulation, "continue to locate the whole planet with respect to a European-based historical narrative" (Pratt 8). Neither Tobias Schneebaum's subjective ethnography nor Vargas Llosa's ostensibly de-centered and multiply voiced novel shift this undertheorized cultural bias. Alternative knowledge systems, including those of women-centered and non-western-determined texts, are still all too often among those excluded from the expansive, universalizing "us." The politics of postmodern indigenism continue to betray the fact that in our western textual universe "Quetzalcoatl and all that" still have limited consequences for our revisionary intellectual projects, and until we begin to address the implications of this bias our postmodern theorization of indigenous disruptions as textual resistances will remain seriously flawed.

Notes

1. There is a vast and growing bibliography on postmodernity in Latin American fiction and culture. Among the clearest and most succinct discussions available in English are Yúdice, Beverley, García Canclini, and Benítez Rojo.
2. See Dewey Wayne Gunn, who identifies more than 450 novels, plays, and narrative poems on Mexico between 1805 and 1973 by British and U.S. writers.
3. It ought to be noted that these structures respond to narrative conventions rather than objective reality. Schneebaum finds a charming simplicity in the Amazonian measurement of time and space in terms of walking distance: the Akaramas are "four sleepings" from the Mission, for example (Schneebaum 50), and he doesn't understand if the cycles of ritual cannibalism respond to anything other than whim. In *The Plumed Serpent*, Quetzalcoatl's seasonal character is, as Clark notes, "more Mediterranean than Mexican" (Clark 114), and Lawrence's references to the "uncounted, unregistered, unreckoning days" of pre-Columbian times fits oddly with the time-bound Aztecs and their meticulous attention to a calendar more exact than that of their western conquerors (see Clark 108).
4. I am refering to Vargas Llosa's formulation in *Kathie y el hipopótamo* that "la ficción no reproduce la vida: la contradice, cercenándole aquello que en la vida real nos sobra y añadiéndole lo que en la vida real nos falta" [fiction does not reproduce life. It contradicts life, paring away all that in real life is excessive and adding that which real life lacks] (Vargas Llosa 11).

5. See Kenneth Good for a U.S. take on this issue.
6. Vargas Llosa writes, for example, that "if forced to choose between the preservation of Indian cultures and their complete assimilation, with great sadness I would choose modernization of the Indian population because there are priorities" (*Writer's* 36).

Works Cited

Alonso, Carlos J. "*La tía Julia y el escribidor*: The Writing Subject's Fantasy of Empowerment." *PMLA* 106 (1991): 46–59.

Barthes, Roland. *The Pleasure of the Text*. Translated by Richard Miller. New York: Hill and Wang, 1975.

Bataille, Georges. "Extinct America." *October* 36 (1986): 3–9.

———. "Sacrifice." *October* 36 (1986): 61–74.

———. *Visions of Excess: Selected Writings, 1927–39*. Translated by Allan Stoekl. Minneapolis: University of Minnesota Press, 1985.

Benítez Rojo, Antonio. *The Repeating Island: The Caribbean and the Postmodern Perspective*. Translated by James E Maraniss. Durham: Duke University Press, 1992.

Beverley, John. "Postmodernism in Latin America." *Siglo XX/Twentieth Century* 9 (1991–92): 9–29.

Blanco, José Joaquín. *La paja en el ojo: ensayos de crítica*. Puebla: Editorial U. Autónoma de Puebla, 1980.

Brennan, Timothy. "The National Longing for Form." In *Nation and Narration*, edited by Homi K. Bhabha. New York: Routledge, 1990.

Carpentier, Alejo. *Tientos y diferencias*. Buenos Aires: Calicanto, 1967.

Clark, L. D. *Dark Night of the Body: D. H. Lawrence's The Plumed Serpent*. Austin: University of Texas Press, 1964.

Clifford, James. *The Predicament of Culture, Twentieth-Century Ethnography, Literature, and Art*. Cambridge: Harvard University Press, 1988.

Fernández Retamar, Roberto. *Calibán: Apuntes sobre la cultura en nuestra América*. Mexico: Editorial Diógenes, 1971. Translated by Edward Baker as *Caliban and Other Essays*. Minneapolis: University of Minnesota Press, 1989.

Fischer, Michael M. J. "Ethnicity and the Post-Modern Arts of Memory." In *Writing Culture: The Poetics and Politics of Ethnography*, edited by James Clifford and George E. Marcus, 194–233. Berkeley: University of California Press, 1986.

García Canclini, Néstor. *Hybrid Cultures*. Translated by Christopher L. Chiappari and Silvia L. López. Minneapolis: University of Minnesota Press, 1995.

Good, Kenneth, with David Chanoff. *Into the Heart: One Man's Pursuit of Love and Knowledge Among the Yanomama*. New York: Simon and Schuster, 1991.

Gunn, Dewey Wayne. *American and British Writers in Mexico, 1556–1973*. Austin: University of Texas Press, 1974.

Lawrence, D. H. *Mornings in Mexico*. 1927. Salt Lake City: Gibbs M. Smith, 1982.

————. *The Plumed Serpent (Quetzalcoatl).* 1926. New York: Vintage, 1959.

————. *Reflections of the Death of a Porcupine and Other Essays.* Cambridge: Cambridge University Press, 1988.

Mohanty, S. P. "Us and Them: On the Philosophical Bases of Political Criticism." *Yale Journal of Criticism* 2,2 (1989): 1–31.

Pacheco, José Emilio. "El México de los novelistas ingleses." *Revista de la Universidad de México* 18,12 (1964).

Paz, Octavio. *Alternating Current.* Translated by Helen Lane. New York: Viking, 1973.

————. "The Flight of Quetzalcóatl and the Quest for Legitimacy." Foreword to Jacques Lafaye, *Quetzalcóatl and Guadalupe: The Formation of Mexican National Consciousness 1531–1813.* Translated by Benjamin Keen. Chicago: University of Chicago Press, 1976.

Pratt, Mary Louise. Contribution to symposium on Edward Said's *Culture and Imperialism. Social Text* 40 (Fall 1994): 2–10.

Rowe, William. "Liberalism and Authority: The Case of Mario Vargas Llosa." In *On Edge: The Crisis of Contemporary Latin American Culture,* edited by George Yúdice, Jean Franco, and Juan Flores, 45–64. Minneapolis: University of Minnesota Press, 1992.

Ruffinelli, Jorge. *El otro México: México en la obra de B. Traven, D. H. Lawrence y Malcolm Lowry.* Mexico: Nueva imagen, 1978.

Schneebaum, Tobias. *Keep the River on Your Right.* 1969; 2nd ed. London: GMP Publishers, 1988.

Sommer, Doris. "Not Just any Narrative: How Romance Can Love Us to Death." In *The Historical Novel in Latin America,* edited by Daniel Balderston, 47–73. New Orleans: Ediciones Hispamérica, 1986.

Spivak, Gayatri. "Theory in the Margin: Coetzee's *Foe* Reading Defoe's *Crusoe/Roxana.*" In *Consequences of Theory,* edited by Jonathan Arac and Barbara Johnson, 154–80. Baltimore: Johns Hopkins University Press, 1991.

Stoekl, Allan. *Politics, Writing, Mutilation: The Cases of Bataille, Blanchot, Roussel, Leiris, and Ponge.* Minneapolis: University of Minnesota Press, 1985.

Torgovnick, Marianna, *Gone Primitive: Savage Intellects, Modern Lives.* Chicago: University of Chicago Press, 1990.

Vargas Llosa, Mario. *Contra viento y marea (1962–1982).* Buenos Aires: Sudamericana, 1983.

————. *Kathie y el hipopótamo.* Barcelona: Seix Barral, 1983.

————. *El hablador.* Barcelona: Seix Barral, 1987. Translated by Helen Lane as *The Storyteller.* New York: Farrar Straus Giroux, 1989.

————. *A Writer's Reality.* Syracuse: Syracuse University Press, 1991.

Yúdice, George. "Postmodernity and Transnational Capitalism in Latin America." In *On Edge: The Crisis of Contemporary Latin American Culture,* edited by George Yúdice, Jean Franco, and Juan Flores, 1–28. Minneapolis: University of Minnesota Press, 1992.

II

In the Heat of the Night:
Sexuality (South) of the Border

Susana Chávez-Silverman

Tropicolada:
Inside the U.S. Latino/a
Gender B(l)ender

In this essay, I explore racialized and gendered representations of Latina subjectivity—variously encoded as tropical, exotic, hyper-eroticized sexuality, or elided, or textualized as a site of productive and complex *mestiza* hybridity—in four contemporary American writers, both well-known and emerging. Although image analysis has been largely superceded, if not irrevocably discredited, in most theoretical camps, and although I certainly do not wish to undertake the naive, nationalist substitution of "positive images" or even to suggest that we can have "unmediated access to . . . the real [Latina/o] community" (West 28), nevertheless, because of the prevalence of (indeed the alarming increase in, nationally and particularly in my home state, California) anti-Latino biases within the dominant culture, I believe, as does Chon Noriega, in the critical vindication, the "recuperation" of image analysis as *one* among many current alternatives, "as a vital cultural reclamation project that researches . . . and evaluates our [aesthetic] representation" (Introduction xii). I position my work—rather than Manichaean image analysis seeking the comforting binaries and reversals of black and white (perhaps brown and white), good and bad—as part of a project described by Homi K. Bhabha: "The point of intervention should shift from the identification of images as positive or negative, to an understanding of the processes of subjectification made possible through stereotypical discourse" (Bhabha 71). One of the results of these "processes of subjectification" is that Latinos/as are rendered, if not literally "invisible" to ourselves and to the dominant culture, as Noriega would have it, visible *only* as stereotypes.

Kate Braverman's Latina Tropical

> No need to hear your voice when I can talk about you better than
> you can speak about yourself. —bell hooks 343

This first section of my essay comprises a reading of Kate Braverman's second novel, *Palm Latitudes* (1988) and a consideration of the author's literary project as it impacts on the contemporary representation of Latinas. Henry Louis Gates, Jr., has cautioned against the "burden of representation" "ethnic" authors are made to carry if they are held accountable for writing in an "authentic" African American [or Latino, Asian, lesbian, etc.] voice (Gates, "'Ethnic and Minority' Studies" 294). He writes equally strongly, however, about the dangers of essentialism which lurk if we attempt to forbid outsiders from representing our culture on the basis of their outsider status:

It is not just a matter of the outsider boning up while the genuine article just writes what he or she knows . . . the distasteful truth will out: like it or not, all writers are "cultural impersonators" . . . our histories, individual and collective, do affect what we wish to write and *what we are able to write*. But that relation is never one of fixed determinism. No human culture is inaccessible to someone who *makes the effort* to understand, to learn, to inhabit another world. (Gates, "Authenticity" 29, 30; emphasis added)

It is not my intention, in discussing *Palm Latitudes*, to condemn Kate Braverman for choosing to write about a culture other than her own; I seek, rather, to problematize this choice and how it has played out in the resultant novel and its critical reception. The *Kirkus Review* finds Braverman's "effort to fix invisible lives in our hearts and memories" ultimately a "failed [effort]," "perhaps because . . . Braverman has not quite fixed [these lives] in her own." What "effort" does the author make, in Gates's words, to "inhabit another world"?

I will borrow from Gayatri C. Spivak the notion of "worlding," which she has described as the consideration of the Third World as "distant cultures, exploited but with rich, intact . . . heritages waiting to be recovered, interpreted, and curricularized in English translation" (Spivak 262). The "worlding"—a version of *hegemonic tropicalizing* (which Frances R. Aparicio and I have described in our introduction to this volume)—in *Palm Latitudes* deals not with the Third World as distant culture but rather with what we could call the domestic Third World, or "third woman," the Latina here at home—my home— in Los Angeles.

It is irresistibly tempting to set aside, momentarily, the requisite post-structuralist separation between author and text, because in interviews and reviews of the novel, author, authorial intent, and text often seamlessly converge. In an interview about her novel, Braverman has stated: "I'm working with the Tropical Princess of Danger motif . . . I do see Los Angeles as a ruined tropical kingdom, and I love it that way. I love the sense of corruption and vitality. And I do believe that geography is destiny" (Jenkins 1). In her introduction to the interview, Joyce Jenkins quotes *Los Angeles Times* book reviewer Carolyn See: "[Braverman is] a burglar, stealing the steaming, still-beating heart of Los Angeles and slicing it open" (1). The Aztec-inflected imagery is quite apt, since *Palm Latitudes* does indeed enact a kind of fierce burglary, if we locate that "still-beating heart" within the novel's three Latina protagonists' breasts.

These women live in Los Angeles, in an area which is immediately recognizable as the predominantly Latino Echo Park. Yet in Braverman's hands the barrio is transformed into an alienating, chillingly defamiliarized, lunar landscape. *Her* Los Angeles is nocturnal nightmare or sun-scorched disaster zone: "The central city will stand without pretense, deserted as if by a collective perception of contagion" (Braverman, *Palm Latitudes* 10). However, the novel opens onto a political (if overdetermined and fetishized) reality, with a sinister caveat about the dangers of life for undocumented, poor Latino immigrants:

In this City of the Angels, you can trust nothing . . . there is La Migra, la policía . . . en Nuestra Señora la Reina de los Angeles, it is best to be silent, invisible. You who are brown in this white realm, be as your stained courtyard walls, hidden, camouflaged . . . vanish into the indigenous . . . you who have no visa, no passport, no identification." (9)

But you *will* have a voice here, the novel seems to promise. Your story will be told. Whose story? The setting immediately loses its incipient claim on political realism and specificity, transforming into a generic pre-apocalypse nightmare nightlife: "The pattern of this city is familiar, the scent and rhythm and texture . . . it is repeated everywhere. Sunsets through half-drawn drapes, sending a coral flush across alleys of bougainvillea and dust and dogs. The earth shivers as if with fever" (9).

The reader is introduced to the flamboyant Francisca Ramos as she leans—perfect "Tropical Princess" image—against a palm tree. For six pages she is merely "La Puta de la Luna," apparently Other to the stereotypical Latino identity paradigm established in the novel's opening paragraph: undocumented workers, brown, silent, invisible. "La Puta de la Luna," writes Braverman, "is a flagrant exception" (9). In the pages that follow, Francisca Ramos is described as a predatory feline who "paces and hunts," who "prefers to experience the night as it actually is, raw, hungry, and lawless" (10). Her indifference and disgust toward men respect no hierarchies of color or class; in fact: "the Spanish-speaking men are no better . . . they still smell of dirt roads, muddy, rain-ruined plazas in insignificant villages . . . later, these Mexicanos will smell of jails, and bus stations and tequila . . . they will marry women and beat them, father children and desert them. It is a pattern they will repeat past exhaustion . . . she is of another species entirely" (11–12).

"La Puta de la Luna" is portrayed as an independent woman, with a rich, quasi-mystical inner life, wholly unavailable to her johns or to "more serious" men who would love to offer her more. In oddly impersonal, yet gaudy and sensuous prose, Braverman's third-person narration alternates between Francisca's remembrances of her colorful past and her empty, dangerous present. A village girl who becomes a servant to a series of *patrones*, she ends up serving the fabulously wealthy Colombian Ramón Cárdenas and his (predictably) icy gringa wife.

Francisca's exceptional status, marked with regard to other "Mexicanos" in the novel's opening pages, shows up much earlier, chronologically, when the *curandera* of the village of her birth remarks, "You are an oddity here, an orchid among weeds" (43).[1] This prefigures her difference—distance—from the Mexicanos in her new home, Los Angeles, and begins to suggest her proximity to and co-optation by the dominant culture. Francisca's apartment, for example, "belongs to her alone"; she owns "many sets of matched pure cotton floral-print sheets" (51). She has weekly manicures and haircuts at Bullock's Wilshire; she does not shop downtown—"El Centro is for refugees" (51), and while she is pampered at Bullock's "a Mexicana scrubs her floors, cleans her windows, mops and polishes and dusts" (55). Francisca's thoughts about writing (tagging, or graffiti), reported in the third person, are significant: "the walls of a liquor store have been spray-painted with the emblems of local madmen and incarcerated heroes. This script is primitive . . . the expression asserts itself, even in a degraded form. The impulse cannot be erased. She stares at the graffiti, noting that the signatures are perfectly arched like the arc of a matador's cape" (52). This ethnocentric, ludicrously mixed-metaphor, pan-Hispanic discourse (madmen, primitives, and matadores!) attributed to a Central American prostitute begs any explication.

The cause of Francisca's psychic pain and self-hating alienation is prostitution, which has hardened her heart against men and yet affords her the luxury of economic privilege, which distances her from other Latinos and "refugees." In representing an "exceptional" Latina character—this term, and variations upon it, are repeated throughout this section and indeed, throughout the entire novel—Braverman only ends up reifying various elements endemic to the stereotype of the Latina. Francisca Ramos's story concludes with the following epiphany, which draws geography into Braverman's move toward historical and cultural non-specificity and tropicalization, which we have seen in this first section:

The air was steaming, greasy, stained, chaotic, mad. She realized then that the region had been delirious for a millennium . . . there were no longer any sacraments, not in the jungle or the city . . . no, not in blood or marriage, words or rites or images or magic . . . she recognized then . . . that the world had fallen apart. [. . .]

"Las latitudes de las palmas," she says.

Yes, of course, she realizes, it stretches from Mexico City and El Salvador, through Havana and Miami, across the Islands of the Caribbean, from Caracas to Los Angeles. It is that particular air of slow rotting, that special scented steaming poison masquerading as emeralds, spice, clouds. (89–90)

Interestingly, the point of view of the observing eye/I echoes nearly verbatim any one of Braverman's worldly yet prodigiously eloquent heroines. "It seemed the air had . . . been transmuted and flowed like a poison," entones twenty-seven-year-old Rose in *Lithium for Medea,* "reaching up for the pale drained useless sky" (Braverman, *Lithium for Medea* 118). Ten years later, Jessica Moore, the fortyish protagonist of the story "Points of Decision" in *Squandering the Blue*, claims that "all other cities and ports have been a disappointment . . . always the reality was a clutter, a sense of debris and degradation, exiled history, smog, amputated gods, and misery in the streets, in the alleys and the terraces." For Jessica Moore, "the Hawaiian Islands are the exception . . . the islands defy . . . linear assumptions. There is nothing simple about them" (146–47). Ironically Hawaii—tropical setting sine qua non—escapes Braverman's tropicalizing, nihilistic gaze. The closing words of the first section of *Palm Latitudes*, quoted above, conflate all tropical locales—even those with the geo-political differences of Havana and Miami, or the cultural differences of Caracas and Los Angeles—into one degraded dystopia.

In contrast with her third-person treatment of Francisca Ramos's story, Braverman chooses to present Gloria Hernández in the first person, constructing the illusion that it is this Chicana's own voice we are hearing. The narrative of Gloria's story is more intimate, engaging, and ultimately more horrifying than Francisca's. Married as a teenager in Mexico, she crosses the border illegally with her husband Miguel, eventually ending up in a little house on Flores Street in Echo Park, across from the so-called *bruja*, Marta Ortega. Gloria represents herself as others see her, a nondescript housewife and mother: "My family and neighbors on Flores street . . . pronounced me rubble, a dead moon, useless . . . I was undemanding as adobe, as yucca . . . I had the patience of agave . . . my world was Flores Street, my white cottage with its glistening orange-tiled roof" (93–94). This woman is represented by the iconically Latin symbols of Southwestern vegetation, which are deployed to signify her silence, ignorance, and passivity. Yet, like Francisca Ramos, she has an extraordinary inner life and an incongruously erudite, poetic voice: "I did not learn English, read newspapers, or form opinions . . . No one recognized the elegance of my resistance, my intricate immunity . . . I am speaking of the subliminal tremors which make all nations, customs and artifacts of women and men temporary . . .

I always possessed this awareness . . . I kept my unique abilities shrouded and locked" (93).

Her extraordinary psychic and prophetic "awareness" notwithstanding, Gloria is presented as totally dependent on Miguel, who is her link to the outside (Anglo) world. She is pathetically insecure; gradually this insecurity causes her to become convinced that her husband is infatuated with Barbara Branden, the alabaster-white, politically correct social worker who has moved in next door, who speaks excellent Spanish and reads revolutionary Latin American poetry with Miguel and his two sons. Portents of disaster abound. Gloria is alienated from her husband and children as they embrace Anglo ways, symbolized by their passion for sports and their fixation on Barbara Branden. The Santa Ana zephyrs blow, Marta Ortega's prize-winning orchids shrivel and die in the unnatural heat. Finally, in the conclusion of part II, Gloria's language echoes the description of pre-apocalypse Los Angeles with which the novel opened:

It might have been noon, a pitch-black noon on a planet of only singed darkness and virgin water. The moon was inordinately flagrant, elegant, and purposeful . . . I felt her heat, her rhythm, how sultry she was . . . I knelt in the dirt, startled by an unmistakable connection to the earth . . . and I realized that certain forms of ecstasy . . . often mistaken for insanity are not expressions of madness but revelation. (184–85)

On this fevered night, rendered in overheated prose, Gloria Hernández plunges a knife in Barbara Branden's chest and kills her. The narrative we have just read—her (his)story—is what she has dictated, in a mental hospital, to her social worker.

In the final section of the novel, narrated, like the first section, in the third person, signs point irrevocably to a cataclysm. "It was a season of indisputable omens," muses Marta Ortega, "even before Gloria Hernández went insane" (193). Unhappily married and twice divorced, mother of two exotic, neurotic, trendy Westside daughters named Angelina and Orquídea, grandmother of too many pot-smoking, advice-seeking grandchildren to count, Marta Ortega's life history and discourse bear more than a passing resemblance to the middle-class Anglo mothers in *Lithium for Medea* and *Wonders of the West.* However, she is meant to be the most quintessentially Latina figure of all, the barrio sage or bruja. Ancient yet ageless, like the matriarch Ursula in *Cien años de soledad,* all-seeing and all-knowing Marta has watched the slow racial integration of Echo Park, befriended the gay Anglo couple who have moved in next door, knows exactly where La Puta de la Luna's favorite corner is. Her strange prescience is inexplicably devoid of agency: the only thing she predicts with certainty is her own death. At the novel's climax she walks slowly along Sunset Boulevard, toward Echo Park, where she will lie down and await her death:

"Marta Ortega lies wrapped in a common Mexican blanket beneath a palm that is one of dozens ringing an insignificant circular lake in the center of a city park which is a vortex, an opening into a realm of texture and fragrance where no passport is required" (382).

We are back in the passportless, tropicalized geography Braverman inhabits. In this world, there is no possibility of redemption or regeneration, no way out at all, in fact; more significantly, there is no way for these Latinas to constitute anything *other* than three faces of an archetypal, Latina Eve, never mind their Echo Park address. Although Braverman's tropical masquerade has convinced most of her critics of its transcendence, mythic value, and "authentic" Latin flavor, in these times of Proposition 187 and the so-called "California Civil Rights Initiative," traveling passportless, at least for Latinos, is dangerous. As she wafts her Latina heroines through the verdant regions which level out Madrid, Caracas, or Los Angeles, cholo writing, the arc of a matador's cape, or the blue robe of La Virgen de Guadalupe, Kate Braverman has not really gone anywhere, has not even left the master's house.

Her unmediatedly tropicalizing gaze in *Palm Latitudes,* which seamlessly overlaps with dominant Anglo stereotypes of the Latina, suggests Braverman's unfamiliarity—surprising in a Los Angeles–based writer—with recent "autoethnographic" texts and local performances by writers and artists such as Gloria Anzaldúa, Cherríe Moraga, Alicia Gaspar de Alba, John Leguizamo, Guillermo Gómez-Peña, Coco Fusco, and Culture Clash, to name just a few, who have for the past several years been working out hybrid, polyvocal, *retropicalizing* versions of Latino identity.[2]

My critique of Kate Braverman centers on her insistence that "nationalities, languages, rituals and gods are irrelevant" (Braverman, *Palm Latitudes* 55), and on the unacknowledged privilege this assertion implies. Indeed, my reading of Los Angeles would substitute Mary Louise Pratt's "contact zone" for Braverman's "palm latitudes," for, as recent events in our city have surely shown us, Los Angeles *is* a contact zone: a "social space where cultures meet, clash, and grapple with each other, often in contexts of highly asymmetrical relations of power" (Pratt 34).

Guillermo Gómez-Peña's Gender Trouble

Unlike Braverman, Guillermo Gómez-Peña, a self-described "nomadic Mexican artist/writer in the process of Chicanization" (Gómez-Peña, *New World Border* 1), is keenly aware of the politics of location. Although he too eschews passports ("no one needs a passport to enter my performance continent" [7]), he directs his audiences to "swallow their fears and to question any ethnocentric assumptions they might have about otherness, Mexico, Mexicans, other languages" (7). Gómez-Peña has repeatedly critiqued essentialism and nationalism in Chicano identity politics—most notably in his collections *Warrior for Gringostroika* (1993) and *The New World Border* (1996)—and is lately elaborating the postmodern notion of "the hybrid": "a cultural, political, aesthetic, and sexual hybrid. My version of the hybrid is crossracial, polylinguistic, and multicontextual" (Gómez-Peña, *New World Border* 11–12). Nevertheless, in contradictory fashion, he also lays claim to a Chicano identity, albeit embattled: "many essentialist Chicanos still have a hard time considering me a Chicano" (21).

Gómez-Peña's MacArthur-winning performance pieces probe the thorny issues of self and other, unsettle national, linguistic, and cultural borders, attempting to transcend the binaries implicit in canonical conceptualizations of the border. In his most recent critical writing, Gómez-Peña addresses a panoply of politically sensitive, vexed issues: "Men of color are active protagonists in the history of sexism, and Anglo-American women share the blame in the history of racism . . . U.S.-born Latinos and Latin Americans cannot fully understand one another" (14). Nevertheless, his most recent performance pieces still demonstrate a disturbing inattention to gender issues, for all his theoretical sophistication and "hybridity."[3] For example, page 2 of the program for "The New World (B)order" reads: "This performance is part of 'The Year of the White Bear,' a larger interdisciplinary project created by Gómez-Peña in collaboration with Coco Fusco." However, the credits give Gómez-Peña top billing as sole writer and director, billing Fusco as performer only.[4]

The piece deals with a political/cultural upheaval called *gringostroika*, which moves people of color—especially Latinos—from margin to center. Into this reconfigured border geography, Gómez-Peña (as El Aztec High-Tech) and Fusco (as Pop Semiotician and Miss Discovery 1992) arrive on the scene to describe and mediate. The bulk of the performative description of five hundred years of Columbian hell and its postmodern reversal is left to Gómez-Peña. In a disappointing echo of his own indictment of Anglos perceiving and representing Latinos exclusively as images and symbols (Gómez-Peña, *Warrior* 40), the "Pop Semiotician" never seems to make it onto the stage. Instead, she is displaced by Miss Discovery 1992, as Fusco contorts her silent body across the stage, looking like an unfortunate cross between Beauty Queen and robot, dressed in a grass skirt (shades of "The Couple in the Cage") and skimpy leopard-print bra top.[5] The few words uttered by Fusco were often a sort of overdubbing, their semantic content all but erased by Gómez-Peña's voice.

It is important to note that "The Couple in the Cage," a video chronicle of Gómez-Peña's and Fusco's mock traveling performance titled "Two Amerindians Visit . . . ," in which they pretend to be members of an indigenous tribe from the Gulf of Mexico displayed in a cage (and arguably the most compelling segment of the entire White Bear/New World (B)order project), was produced by Fusco and Paula Heredia. "The Couple in the Cage" clearly articulates and undermines the borders between "civilization and barbarism," between the primitive and the civilized, viewer and viewed, subject and object.

Clearly in her guise as "Pop Semiotician," in an interview with the *Los Angeles Times*, Fusco eloquently mediates and defers the borders in her own life and work, decisively reversing the expected gender binaries. She characterizes herself as "more analytical" and Gómez-Peña as "more intuitive and playful." In addition, when asked about press coverage of their collaborative efforts, she points out the sexism that frequently results in her exclusion from press photos. However, as I have pointed out above, the performance piece itself reifies the very body/brain border Fusco's interview unsettles. Finally, after some insightful observations about how the flip side of oppressing people is to fetishize them, Fusco almost does precisely that to her then-companion: "By focusing on [Gómez-Peña] and developing him as a sort of celebrity, the press distances itself from the content of our work." In literally according Gómez-Peña the last word in *her* interview, Fusco unwittingly replicates the press's rock-star treatment of him.

Perhaps this silencing of Fusco follows logically upon the way in which the complex sociopolitical problematics of the border are often distilled, in Gómez-Peña's work, to the intensely private angst of one individual's quest for identity. Even unwittingly, this is reflected in a 1991 interview with Jason Weiss. In describing the characters of an earlier play, "1992," it seems patently clear to me that Gómez-Peña is (also) talking about himself:

Most of the characters I work with are hybrids, half traditional and half contemporary, half Mexican and half Chicano. They include El Aztec High-Tech, El Caballero Tigre, El Mariachi Liberachi, and El Warrior for Gringostroika. They are mythical characters. Each articulates within himself a series of cultural contradictions which are at the core of the U.S. Latino experience . . . In a sense, I am rediscovering America through my own immigrant experience. I turn the continent upside down . . . to become the speaking subject. (Weiss 11)

All the disclaimers about increased sensitivity to gender issues, hybridity, and bridge-building do not hold up in the face of this highly individualistic, doggedly male-centered, and Odyssean (or, dare I say, neo-Columbian) discourse. Even in 1996, the representation of Latina subjectivity in Gómez-Peña's work remains a persistent blind spot.

Moving away now from these versions of *hegemonic tropicalizing* I have been examining within the dominant Anglo and the Latino cultures, I would like to turn now toward two writers whose works embody, for me, very different and exciting instances of Latina cultural competence.[6]

Sandra Cisneros's (Loose) Women

Sandra Cisneros (like Gómez-Peña a MacArthur winner), whose early books were published by Chicano presses, has more recently "crossed over" to Random House and Knopf, with whom she published her latest books, *Woman Hollering Creek* (1991) and *Loose Woman* (1994). I would like to consider, first, the story "Eyes of Zapata" from *Woman Hollering Creek*, and then move briefly to her most recent poetry. In the hauntingly beautiful "Eyes of Zapata," Cisneros creates a different version of the Mexican Revolution, a re-visioning of Emiliano Zapata through the eyes of Inés Alfaro, one of his mistresses.

In an arresting opening, the very first paragraph of this story by a woman author about Revolutionary hero Zapata focuses the reader's gaze, in dizzying extreme close-up through the lens of Inés's eye, on Zapata's male member: "I put my nose to your eyelashes. The skin on the eyelids as soft as the skin of the penis, the collarbone with its fluted wings, the purple knot of the nipple, the dark, blue-black color of your sex, the thin legs and long thin feet. For a moment I don't want to think of your past nor your future. For now you are here, you are mine" (Cisneros, *Woman Hollering Creek* 85). Within this singularly bold, close-up angling of the lens which is protagonist Inés's eye (and whose precise angle the reader's gaze replicates), rather than merely "remembering" as repetition, like traditional masculinist historical narratives of the Mexican Revolution, Cisneros anchors a fiction crafted, rather, to "remind" the reader of what has been silenced, what has not shown up in the master narrative, on the big screen of history: the woman's I.

Just as Zapata lies supine and disarmed in slumber under the erotically charged, microscopically penetrating gaze of Inés, so too the reader is held fast under the sensuous, too-close-for-comfort spell of her words, which draw us, along with the narrator, down on top of the hero's sleeping, phallically elongated yet helpless body. We too are here, we are hers. Inés takes inventory of Zapata's *indumentaria* for the reader, his hero's trappings: "your black trousers with the silver buttons . . . your embroidered sombrero with its horsehair tassel . . . the handsome black boots, your tooled gun belt and silver spurs." But she immediately replaces the overdetermined image of the warrior, displaces it with a question, which inverts with lovingly mocking disrespect the common Revolutionary form of address "mi general": "are you my general? Or only that boy I met at the county fair in San Lázaro?" (85)

Cisneros's deconstructive portrait—exposing, subtly, layers of never-seen vulnerability—begins by eroticizing the hero, laying him bare under her female gaze. Next she reduces him to an adolescent. He will be repeatedly imaged thus throughout the story, often haughty, or on horseback, but he will be a boy, and Inés will be his match. *"Small, but bigger than you, Miliano,"* in the words of Zapata's friend Francisco Franco (108). The traditional image of Zapata is initially revised in "Eyes of Zapata" by his passive eroticization and youth. Cisneros further undermines history's collusion with patriarchy by presenting Zapata as a feminized object of beauty, for example: "Hands too pretty for a man" (85) or "Your voice, Miliano, thin and light as a woman's, almost delicate" (106). However, Cisneros's revision is not merely a binary reversal; each feminizing description, such as those above, contains its own opposite. After remarking on his pretty hands Inés notes that Zapata's fingers smell sweet from his Havana cigars, restoring (the comfort of) masculinity to the image, which had foregrounded the feminine, leaving the reader with a curious sense of ambiguity. Commenting on Zapata's beautiful voice, Inés adds: "And yet I know what that voice of yours is capable of" (106).

Perhaps even more compelling, in terms of a specifically feminist revisioning of history, is the image of Inés herself. Invisible in historical accounts of Zapata's *hazañas*, it is Inés, much more than Emiliano, who takes center stage in Cisneros's story. Following her description of Zapata's pretty hands, Inés remembers how he used to call *her* hands *"exquisitas."* She deconstructs the semantics of this trite compliment, "as if they were something to eat. It still makes me laugh remembering that." Then, back in the feminine mode, she laments how fast her hands have aged, "The skin as coarse as the wattle of a hen." But she reverses this complaint, attributing their premature aging to "the hard man's work I do clearing the field with the hoe and the machete." Furthermore, she is "not afraid of hard work or of being alone in the hills" (86). Inés's self-presentation, from the second page on, is that of a woman in love, yes, but her love object is variously feminized and infantilized (she frequently croons lullaby-like to him while he sleeps), only faintly sketched in his role of military leader, whereas she represents herself as capable, even more capable than a man, than "her general." For example, Inés often seems to have an infantry soldier's expertise: "I know every cave and crevice, every back road and ravine . . . I scout the hillsides, the mountains" (87–88). Emiliano, on the other hand, is "tired, sick and lonely with this war" (87), craving comfort from Inés.

Finally, there is Inés's magical power to transform herself into a *tecolote*, a power she inherits matrilineally from her mother (reputed to be a "perra," and a "bruja," as is she) and passes on to her daughter, Malena. Inés first takes flight after performing a ritual with one of Zapata's handkerchiefs; she is heartsick that he has taken other lovers and even married another woman. She flies initially out of jealousy and grief, and then to keep watch over Zapata. But her final flight—the last section of the story—is not just the individualistic flight of a woman betrayed; it is, rather, a soaringly panoramic *pronóstico,* a revisionist fast-forward at once lyrical and stoic in which the woman's idiosyncratic and intimate version replaces the broad-brush-stroke historical "facts" we think we know.

In the last three pages of "Eyes of Zapata," Inés envisions Zapata's death, but rather than a blaze of glory his death is represented as a simple betrayal, one among many others. The ultimate banality of his death is suggested by the detail spent in the narration of Inés's mother's horrific murder, betrayed by her lover, a stake driven through her sex by the village men, the ultimate misogyny of the scene—"a man's sombrero tipped on her head, a cigar in her mouth, as if to say, this is what we do to women who try to act like men"—agonizingly underscored by its eerily muted beauty: "The star of her sex open to the sky. Clouds moving soundlessly, and the sky changing colors" (111). With Inés's final flight Cisneros, in the words of Frances Bartkowski, "recall[s] and invent[s] a potential past to suggest a utopian future" (Bartkowski 38).

Here I do not mean utopian in the sense of future perfect, nor am I trying to suggest that the story is unproblematic. Rigid gender roles are probed and the absoluteness of the master narrative is shaken loose, however, the overdetermined sign of the *bruja*, who beats out the competition and still gets her man in the end, remains well within the confines of the heterosexual Chicano imperative. Nevertheless, I do see a feminist impulse in Cisneros's deliberate privileging of fictive ambiguity over historical facticity, and it is in the creation of a literary space where the Latina's agency can be so forcefully yet so lyrically articulated that I find Cisneros's major—stunning—achievement in "Eyes of Zapata."

Unfortunately, I find that this feminist vision is not sustained in Sandra Cisneros's latest book, *Loose Woman*; for that matter, there are only a few poems in *My Wicked Wicked Ways* (1987) that I would characterize as feminist to any degree.[7] Mostly, what I read in both volumes is what I would call a *self-tropicalizing* bad girl: images, often beautifully crafted, of *la otra*, the sometimes defiantly, sometimes bitterly unmarried woman. Not the self-abnegating Latina matriarch, true, but merely an embrace of the other side of the puta/virgen binary (Anzaldúa 84) always already allowed to Latinas by the dominant culture. One example, I think, will suffice to illustrate my point.

In "Loose Woman," the final poem in the eponymous collection, Cisneros uses gendered and sexualized imagery along a cross-cultural axis. The speaker attempts to re-script her subjectivity as powerful by agreeing with an unnamed plural observer's representation of her:

> They say I'm a beast.
> And feast on it. When all along
> I thought that's what a woman was.
>
> They say I'm a bitch.
> Or witch.
> I've claimed
> the same and never winced.

> They say I'm a *macha*, hell-on-wheels,
> *viva-la-vulva*, fire and brimstone,
> man-hating, devastating,
> boogey-woman lesbian.
> Not necessarily,
> but I like the compliment.
>   (Cisneros, *Loose Woman* 112)

The third stanza above demonstrates the speaker's obsession with the image of the lesbian as brash, dominant, and anti-male, which overlaps neatly with the dominant culture's script for the butch dyke. The speaker hastily retreats from the semantic possibility of her lesbianism ("not necessarily"), although she executes a neat little flirty half-turn ("but I like the compliment").

In the final stanza, the speaker claims the loose/wicked persona attributed to her by "the[m]" throughout the poem:

> I'm Bitch. Beast. Macha.
> *¡Wáchale!*
> Ping! Ping! Ping!
> I break things.
>
>   (115)

But what has she, in fact, really broken? In attempting to enact a reversal from within—to uncritically embody in her poetry available stereotypes (perra, slut, lesbian, not to mention specifically *tropical* images such as mangoes, golden earrings, incense, etc.)—is to fail to recognize that wickedness/ looseness is always already allowed to Latinas.

Alicia Gaspar de Alba's *Fronterótica*

In "Beggar on the Córdoba Bridge" (1989), up-and-coming Chicana poet/critic Alicia Gaspar de Alba's first volume of poetry, the author crafts a luminous series of tightly knit poems which together textualize what I have called a *borderotics/fronterótica*—a specifically mestiza lesbian journey of desire—which avoids the self-tropicalizing pitfalls present in Cisneros's poetry, instead reaching out to transform—re-tropicalize—traditional Chicano/a and lesbian images and symbols.[8]

In "Domingo Means Scrubbing," the child-speaker's subjectivity is conjoined in a plurality—"our"—absorbed in and given over to sensuous pleasures. The poem opens onto liturgical and familial Latino rituals, "scrubbing our knees for Church," "Domingo means one of our tíos/passing out quarters/ for the man with the basket." Both of these spaces, however, yield to the more powerful forces of sensation and pleasure: "me putting mine [my quarter] under/my tongue like the host." Sensation centers first around innocent delights—menudo and raisin tamales—and then moves subtly into the realm of the forbidden, sneaking same-sex *besos* with a female cousin "under the willow tree." Predominant images of orality underscore a tight structural cohesiveness, from the lozenge-like quarter lodged under the tongue, through food, drink, and kisses.

The final stanza effects a return to closure and a disavowal of the forbidden, transgressive sexual border crossing represented earlier. These sanctions come from within the speaker's Chicano culture, "La Llorona/knows what you kids are doing!" and from within the family, represented by the mother's voice, which reinscribes the strict gender-specific appropriateness of domestic activity: "Amá coming out of the house/to drag the girls inside/pa' lavar los dishes" (Gaspar de Alba 6). If the speaker was able to step outside—metaphorically and literally—for a stolen girl-kiss, "Amá" leaves the circumscribed and culturally overdetermined confines of the casa only to "drag" the speaker and her (female) cousins back inside, recuperating the child-speaker for more traditional Chicano and culture norms. "Amá" and what she represents—Chicano culture's stake in patriarchy—has the last word, at least for now.

In "Making Tortillas," Gaspar de Alba plays with the polysemy of the notion of "tortillera," in standard Spanish, literally a "maker of tortillas," but in Chicano as well as Peninsular Spanish slang, a term for lesbian. Slyly and sensually retropicalizing the negativity with which the term is imbued within the Chicano patriarchy, Gaspar de Alba takes the lesbian out of the ghetto, so to speak, by resemanticizing "tortillera," by taking the "tortilla-maker" decisively out of the kitchen:

> My body remembers
> what it means to love slowly,
> what it means to start
> from scratch . . .
>
> Tortilleras, we are called,
> grinders of maíz, makers, bakers,
> slow lovers of women.
> The secret is starting from scratch.
>
> (44–45)

With this elegant, sexy poem, Gaspar de Alba also loosens—thankfully, for me—the stereotypical, almost obligatory association of the Latina with the kitchen and cooking.[9]

In "La frontera," the eponymous opening poem of the collection (which I actually read as the culmination of a circular journey of discovery), "la frontera" is a site/sight which alludes to and does not elide problematics of nationality, ethnicity, and violence called to mind by more traditional Chicano renderings of the border:

> La frontera lies
> wide open, sleeping beauty.
> Her waist bends like the river
> bank around a flagpole.
> Her scent tangles in the arms
> of the mesquite. Her legs
> sink in the mud
> of two countries, both
> sides leaking sangre
> y sueños.
>   I come here
> mystified by the sleek Río Grande
> and its ripples and the moonlit curves
> of tumbleweeds, the silent lloronas,
> the children they lose.
> In that body of dreams,
> the Mexicans swim for years,
> their fine skins too tight to breathe.
> Yo también me he acostado con ella,
> crossed that cold bed, wading
> toward a hunched coyote.

(5)

Even as it subtly engages border "issues," the poem moves surefootedly beyond binary constructions and expectations as it names la frontera as a female, open zone. Motifs of struggle and conflict are suggested rather than made concrete by images less real than elliptical. The text foregrounds synaesthetic images of horizontality, sensuousness, fluidity. The line "yo también me he acostado con ella," uttered in Spanish—to dramatic and intimate effect in this English-dominant poem—does not preclude the more standard geopolitical reading of the border, yet surely the line's erotic charge—particularly read in the context of other images in this poem and within the larger framework of the collection as a whole—is the predominant sign, even, I would argue, the organizing principle of "La frontera" and of the collection as a whole.

Woman or river? Erotic reverie or anguished geopolitical lament? In Gaspar de Alba's postmodern *borderotics*, it is both/and, not either/or, as we can see in the deliberately ambiguous final image of the "coyote": timeless emblem of Southwestern renegade, or outlaw mercenary border crosser. In Gaspar de

Alba's "Beggar on the Córdoba Bridge," the figure of the Chicana lesbian and, in a broader sense, the textualization of *fronterótica*, is deployed to foreground the deep ambivalence, the sense of differentiation and hybridity, in the borderlands.

Notes

1. An example of Braverman's ignorance (or refusal) of geo-historical detail is the fact that Francisca is fleeing a war-torn country which, given the story's temporal frame and some of the novel's hints—"the guerrilleros had bombed the power plant," "other men crossed the border or journeyed into the mountains to join the forces of the insurrection" (19), for example—is probably Nicaragua or El Salvador, but, incongruously, "when the fighting reached the streets of the capital, [Francisca's first] patrón and his wife and daughter fled to Guadalajara" (23), and this is not presented as an international flight.

   In addition, the village curandera repeatedly invokes "La Virgen de Guadalupe," a quintessentially Mexican (and Chicano)—not Central American— saint.

2. I use the term "autoethnographic" in the sense described by Mary Louise Pratt in "Arts of the Contact Zone": "autoethnographic texts are representations that the so-defined others construct *in response to* or in dialogue with those [ethnographic] texts . . . they involve a selective collaboration with and appropriation of idioms of the metropolis . . . [they] are often addressed to both metropolitan audiences and the speaker's own community" (35).

3. Interestingly, although Gómez-Peña offers a mollifying tip of his *sombrero* to persistent critiques of his sexism in *The New World Border*—"my women friends have consistently pointed out the hypocrisy of my hiding behind ethnicity to avoid gender issues" (14)—he continues to do precisely that. He effectively writes woman out of his script by not publishing the version of the performance piece "The New World Border" on which he originally collaborated with Coco Fusco, his former companion.

4. The program to which I refer is from September 1993, when I attended the performance at Highways Performance Space in Santa Monica, California.

5. Indeed, despite his recently published protestations to the contrary, Gómez-Peña's gender politics—the representation of women, Latina or Anglo, in his work— seems not to have changed at all. In a review of "Califas," performed by Gómez-Peña and his then-partner Emily Hicks in 1987, Carl Heyward remarks on Hicks's "mute" persona, "at once whore and madonna" (*High Performance* 97).

6. I am indebted to the first anonymous reader for the University Press of New England, for invigorating the revision of this essay by suggesting that I emphasize in my analysis an examination of Latino/a "cultural competence."

7. It is well to remember that *My Wicked Wicked Ways* is a much earlier work,

published in 1987. Interestingly, however, although there is no real feminist tone to the volume—in fact, the title seems to suggest an uncritical *self-tropicalizing* tendency—much later, in "Redefining Legacies: Power in Transition," her keynote speech at the Women's Caucus for the Arts 1995 National Conference in San Antonio, Texas, Cisneros makes explicit what she meant by "wicked": not something "defined by a man, or . . . a white woman." No, wicked, at the time, when the poet was in her twenties, was something as simple yet so terrifying for a Latina, as leaving her father's house to live alone and to write.

8. For a more extended study of Gaspar de Alba's poetry as well as my theorization of *fronterótica*, see my "Chicanas in Love: Sandra Cisneros Talking Back and Alicia Gaspar de Alba 'Giving Back the Wor(l)d,'" forthcoming in *Chasqui: revista de literatura latinoamericana*.

9. For playful yet brilliant structural riffs on this association, see the "Recetario" and "Preface," especially, in Debra A. Castillo's *Talking Back: Toward a Latin American Feminist Literary Criticism* (Cornell, 1992); see also the section "Salpicando la Salsa, the Writer as Cook" of Chapter 6 in Tey Diana Rebolledo's *Women Singing in the Snow: A Cultural Analysis of Chicana Literature* (Arizona, 1995).

Works Cited

Anzaldúa, Gloria. *Borderlands/La Frontera*. San Francisco: Spinsters/Aunt Lute, 1987.

Bartkowski, Frances. *Feminist Utopias*. Lincoln and London: University of Nebraska Press, 1989.

Bhabha, Homi. "The Other Question: Difference, Discrimination and the Discourse of Colonialism." In *Out There*, edited by Russell Ferguson et al., 71–87.

Braverman, Kate. *Palm Latitudes*. New York: Penguin Books, 1988.

———. *Lithium for Medea*. New York: Penguin Books, 1989.

———. *Squandering the Blue*. New York: Random House, 1989, 1990.

Cisneros, Sandra. *Woman Hollering Creek*. New York: Vintage/Random House, 1991.

———. *Loose Woman*. New York: Knopf, 1994.

Ferguson, Russell, Martha Gever, Trinh T. Minh-ha, and Cornel West, eds. *Out There: Marginalization and Contemporary Cultures*. Cambridge, Mass.: MIT Press, 1990.

Gaspar de Alba, Alicia, et al. "Beggar on the Córdoba Bridge." In *Three Times a Woman: Chicana Poetry*. Tempe, Ariz.: Bilingual Press, 1989.

Gates, Henry Louis, Jr., "'Authenticity,' or the Lesson of Little Tree." *New York Times Book Review*, Nov. 24, 1991: 26–30.

———. "'Ethnic and Minority' Studies." In *Introduction to Scholarship in Modern Languages and Literatures*, edited by Joseph Gibaldi, 288–302. New York: MLA, 1992.

Gómez-Peña, Guillermo. *Warrior for Gringostroika*. Saint Paul, Minnesota: Graywolf Press, 1993.

———. *The New World Border: Prophecies, Poems and Loqueras for the End of the Century*. San Francisco: City Lights, 1996.

Heyward, Carl. Review of "Califas." *High Performance* 41–42 (Spring–Summer 1988): 97.

hooks, bell. "marginality as site of resistance." In *Out There,* edited by Russell Ferguson et al., 341–43.

Jenkins, Joyce. "The One Intoxication: An Interview with Kate Braverman." *Poetry Flash* (Dec. 1990): 1, 11, 19–20.

Kirkus Reviews. Review of *Palm Latitudes.* 471–72.

McKenna, Kristine. "An Artist Is Uncaged." *Los Angeles Times*, September 14, 1993.

Noriega, Chon, ed. *Chicanos and Film: Representation and Resistance.* Minneapolis: University of Minnesota Press, 1992.

Pratt, Mary Louise. "Arts of the Contact Zone." *Profession* 91: 33–40.

Spivak, Gayatri C. "Three Women's Texts and a Critique of Imperialism." "'Race,' Writing, and Difference." *Critical Inquiry* 12:1 (1985): 262–80.

Weiss, Jason. "An Interview with Guillermo Gómez-Peña." *Review: Latin American Literature and Arts* 45 (July–December 1991): 8–13.

West, Cornel. "The New Cultural Politics of Difference." In *Out There,* edited by Russell Ferguson et al., 19–36.

David Román

Tropical Fruit

The literature of resistance, according to renowned Uruguayan writer Eduardo Galeano, holds the potential to "radically alter the course of our history" (Galeano 125). Galeano's stirring manifesto to "rescue the word" assumes the tactic of identity politics for the indigenous people of the Americas—that is, "our history"—in order to challenge the naturalizing processes of hegemonic oppressions resulting from both colonial domination and postcolonial nationalist tyranny. In his "In Defense of the Word: Leaving Buenos Aires, June 1976," Galeano joins a longstanding tradition of Latin American and Caribbean critics who have for decades insistently demonstrated the symbiotic relationship between literature and ideology: how one tradition of politicized writing of the Americas has intervened in dominant narratives to initiate revisionist histories; histories which begin to account for the experiences of those who, for various and specific reasons, have suffered oppression.[1] And yet with the increasing production of these revisionist histories comes the task of locating the limits and ramifications of such counter-hegemonic practices. In order to avoid replacing the historical documentation of colonization and tyranny with a universalizing and monolithic record of the oppressed, it becomes necessary for cultural historians to problematize and interrogate these emerging revisionist histories. Literary, cultural, and historical theorists must continue to call into question the differences between history and fiction, truth and myth set forth by revisionist writers. Moreover, such all-embracing and potentially totalizing categories as "revisionist history" and "resistance literature" need to be persistently contextualized. In short, we must continue to challenge ourselves to identify cross-cultural practices of revision and resistance without obscuring, as Santiago Colás reminds us, "the historical, geographical, and ideological *heterogeneity* that political resistance can take" (Colás 93).

   In order to unravel some of these concerns, I will isolate one tendency apparent in contemporary resistance literature of the Americas. I focus on the depiction of Latin/o gay men by three prominent and widely read novelists of the Americas who set—as an immediate goal—the precise task that Galeano demands of writers living in an age of revolutions. I point out not simply the limits of such an identity-based politics but also the ramifications of what I will be identifying as "bilateral tropicalizations." I will focus on three nearly contemporaneous novels—the Chilean writer Isabel Allende's political romance of 1984, *De amor y de sombra* (translated in 1987 as *Of Love and Shadows*), Jamaican writer Michelle Cliff's 1987 postcolonial feminist utopia, *No Telephone to Heaven*, and *Afterlife*, a 1990 novel about three AIDS widowers in West Hollywood, written by Paul Monette, a white gay man living with AIDS in the United States. By examining three different constructions of the Latin/o gay man, or what I'm calling half-jokingly the "tropical fruit," I hope to demonstrate how such tropicalizations are not necessarily confined to North American writers, but instead involve, and are produced by, a complex intertextual and bilateral ideology around the sexuality of Latin/o gay men that runs equally south and north.

All three of these novelists introduce Latin/o gay characters who, to varying degrees, participate in the revolutionary cause that each writer documents. None of these three writers is a Latin/o gay male. Each one, however, identifies as an "insider"—that is, as a supporter of, or a participant in, a revolutionary counter-hegemony—who sees writing as a revolutionary act that disrupts dominant and officially sanctioned constructions of history, national ideology, and the cultural mythologies that result from both. I foreground the representation of the Latin/o gay man in order to demonstrate how one system of counter-hegemonic practice ends up duplicating an equally troubling system of exclusion, both narrative and material. In each of these novels, the Latino gay man undergoes an inscription that positions him either as an exotic and highly volatile contagion that, while serving the revolutionary cause, must be contained in order for the new system to gain a sense of authorized legitimacy; or as the wise yet monstrous sphinx who, while enigmatic, serves as the embodiment of the unknown other. In either case, these characters become the locus from where the novelist invokes a radical politics of difference that by the end results in the character's self-erasure or death.

I would like to address some preliminary concerns regarding the scope of this essay before proceeding to my three case studies of the tropical fruit.

1. I am fully aware that various Latin American and Latino authors identify themselves as "gay" and have long written about issues of homosexuality and its relation to politics and revolution. The works of the Argentine writer Manuel Puig, Cuban writer Reynaldo Arenas, and the writer John Rechy from the United States are but three of the most prolific and successful writers who address these issues. And while I recognize that these writers themselves are complicit in the larger construction and circulation of representations of

Latin/o gay men in the Americas, I'm interested instead—and only for the moment—in interrogating the constructions of Latino gay men by non-gay Latinos who write resistance literature, especially in texts which have gained wide circulation and consumption in the literate circles of the Americas.

2. I employ the term resistance literature in the manner explained by Barbara Harlow to discuss political literature written in conjunction with a resistance movement. Harlow suggests that resistance literature sets out to accomplish a revolutionary transformation of existing social structures and, moreover, that the texts themselves must be seen as "immediate interventions into the historical record, attempting to produce and impart new historical facts and analyses" (Harlow 116). While my essay may seem to privilege literature as the primary form that resistance can take, I am aware of the crucial interplay between literary practice and social praxis.

3. Let me also briefly address the implications of naming and taxonomizing same-sex sexual activity in relation to Latin/o men. That is, the descriptive term "Latino gay men" itself is often a misnomer; to identify as "gay" already connotes a certain bourgeois privilege that many Latin/os either do not share or refuse outright. The Chicano gay sociologist Tomás Almaguer, for example, writes that "the Mexican/Latin-American sexual system confers meaning to homosexual practices according to sexual aim (and not sexual object choice)—that is, the act one wants to perform with another person (of either biological sex)" (Almaguer 77). Almaguer joins various other sex theorists in proclaiming the need to understand the configuration of gender/sex/power that is "articulated along the active/passive axis and organized through the scripted sexual role one plays" (77). Despite my general agreement with these ideas, I want to foreground "gayness" in order to challenge the often misdirected and homophobic assumption that results from this type of logic: the denial of the reality of homosexuality as a possible identity based on the "sexual aim" epistemology. Perhaps, I would argue, a homosexual identity based on sexual object-choice is so taboo in Latin American cultures that the only tolerated manifestation of male same-sex desire is precisely through the "sexual aim" system. Regardless of the source of the anti-gay sex and gender systems in place in Latin/o cultures, homosexual identities are at least imagined in the three novels I discuss, and these characterizations involve a type of tropicalization. I want to avoid complying with the paradigmatic binarism that posits gay identity, on the one hand, as a denial of an imagined "authentic" Latino ethnicity and Latino identity, on the other hand, as an indicator of internalized homophobia.

4. I use "tropicalization" in this essay in the spirit of this anthology's reference to how dominant cultures inscribe the "Other" in relation to their own reigning ideologies around race and ethnicity, and, as I will argue, male (homo)sexuality. Thus, what emerges in these narratives is the "tropical fruit,"

the Latin/o man who because of his sexuality is configured at once as both exotic other *and* sexual outlaw. It is often this very intersection of ethnicity and sexuality that needs to be named and contained within political narratives of resistance. Thus, the positive-valenced transgressiveness of the "sexual outlaw"—who holds the possibility of being the ultimate transgressor/resister of oppressive systems—is absorbed into the primary function of the narratives, one where the tropical fruit's radical potential is appropriated to serve the issues of the main characters. I hope to demonstrate the ramifications of such textual practices on the larger canvas of social narratives that circulate in dominant cultures invested in a politics of what Adrienne Rich so usefully identifies as compulsory heterosexuality.

I. Tropical Fruit: Mario

In Isabel Allende's romance *Of Love and Shadows*, Mario, the successful beautician who serves as personal confidant to Irene, the novel's heroine, has, unbeknownst to her, formed a pact of solidarity to engage in subversive activities against the militaristic dictatorial regime in an unnamed country with Irene's love interest, Francisco. The novel—high in melodrama and written in the popular style of romance fiction[2]—charts the political awakening of Irene alongside a heterosexual love plot that has its central lovers (Irene and Francisco) investigate and then suffer the tyranny of the militaristic dictatorship. Irene and Francisco discover a hideous crime—the political killing and cover-up of a group of peasant workers thought to be organizing against the government. This event is based in fact. In 1978, the remains of fifteen peasants buried alive in 1973 were discovered in the Lonquén mines.[3] Mario is a minor character in the novel, introduced in a few brief pages in the beginning of the novel, only to return for a short cameo at the end. Here is how Allende introduces the character:

Mario had no tolerance for bad taste, and years ago had conquered any tendency toward promiscuity. He had come from a miner's family of eleven children. He has been born and raised in a gray town where the dust from the mines coated everything with an impalpable and deadly patina of themselves . . . He had delicate hands and a spirit inclined toward fantasy, a quality his father had tried to beat out of him. Drastic measures had not, however, cured his effeminate mannerisms or altered his inclinations. As a child, if the family turned their backs for an instant, he slipped away to entertain himself in solitary pastimes that provoked pitiless ridicule: he gathered stones from the river and polished them for the pleasures of seeing colors shine; he scouted the dismal landscape looking for dry leaves to arrange in artistic compositions; he was moved to tears by a sunset, wanting to capture it forever in a line of poetry or in a painting he could imagine but felt incapable of realizing. Only his mother accepted his peculiarities, seeing them not as signs of perversion but as evidence of a soul that was different. (Allende 85)

Allende spends the next few pages describing Mario's coming-out process, resulting in part from his father's efforts for him to have sex with a female prostitute who warns the son to "go away, far away boy, where no one knows you, because if you stay around here they'll end up killing you" (86). Allende continues, "In all his life he had never received better advice. He dried his tears and promised to never spill them again over a manliness that in his heart he did not desire. 'If you don't fall in love, you will go far,' the woman told him as she said goodbye" (86). Mario arrives at the capital city and quickly ascends into the highest echelons of the fashion scene, but not before he undergoes plastic surgery, maintains an artificial tan, and slaves over various diets and exercise regimes in order to hold "a slender, trim physique" (88). He becomes such a sensation that the wives of the most influential politicians and military leaders not only sport his hairdos at the most elite gatherings but, more importantly, choose him as their confidant.

On the one hand, Allende describes Mario in the homo-ignorant rhetoric of difference which can only imagine homosexuality within the clichéd stereotypes typical of most depiction in Latin American literature.[4] Allende, while seemingly sympathetic, inadvertently ends up duplicating a discourse that positions Mario as exotic, effeminate, and hyper-sexualized (although discreet). Yet, on the other hand, it is only Mario who—because of this massive social trivialization of his existence—is able to serve effectively the heterosexual lovers in their escape from death and facilitate their inevitable romantic reunion.[5] When Irene and Francisco are forced into exile because of their journalistic exposé of the horrific practices of the military dictatorship, Mario—who "had acquired experience in such matters [escape and disguise] during the course of his clandestine activities" (259)—conjures up a disguise for their successful escape. His dedication to the cause is only usurped by his devotion to the heterosexual lovers:

> "You're risking your life for us," said Francisco.
> "I'll fix some coffee—we all need it," Mario replied as he left the room. (259)

In *Of Love and Shadows*, the Latino "gay" man—trivialized by dominant culture and yet associated with the politics of revolution—serves as both the revolutionary catalyst and as an instrument propelling the reinscription of heterosexual love. He is both sign and symbol of difference, marked by the heterosexual characters both in and out of the revolutionary cause as the location where dominant identities (heterosexual and/or militaristic) are validated and enforced. By the end of the novel, the heterosexual lovers make it across the border to safety. Implicit in this ending is the notion that heterosexual union is indeed safety, a convention of romance fiction. As Janice

Radway has explained: "[E]ven as the narrative conveys its overt message that all women are different and their destinies fundamentally open, the romance also reveals that such differences are illusory and short-lived because they are submerged or sacrificed inevitably to the demands of that necessary and always identical romantic ending" (208).

Most critics of *Of Love and Shadows* read the happy ending in the novel as the triumph of love over shadows, neglecting to unpack the merged ideologies of patriarchy and heterosexuality in the novel's conclusion. Ambrose Gordon, for example, celebrates the ending as an indication that "[l]overs can meet and love deep in the shadow, can in time escape and live together in hope for return; moreover, they can bring about that day" (Gordon 535). Only Gabriela Mora challenges such an idealization of heterosexual union in her feminist reading of the novel. For Mora, Irene's political potential is seriously undermined by the ending which suggests that Irene's motivation to uncover the crime at the mines was only a device for her to win Francisco, and for Allende, it is a plot device that has less to do with the literature of resistance and much more to do with the conventions of romance.[6] I am not suggesting, nor do I think that Mora is suggesting, that romance fiction cannot serve to challenge hegemonic ideologies. Radway has already demonstrated how such practices offer one possible—albeit limited—occasion for social change. Rather, and here is where I see Mora's critique of the novel most useful, for Latin-American writers, critics, and readers to idealize the reinscription of heterosexual love without interrogating its politics imposes serious limitations on the liberatory possibilities for resistance literature in the Americas. And yet, if the form of the romance reinscribes the heroine within the confines of patriarchy, as Mora argues, the fate of the tropical fruit is much less determined.

Allende provides no closure for Mario, no discussion of Mario's future. Having served his function to provide heterosexual stability, he remains (presumably) alone and unloved. Mario is left with his wigs, make-up, and pot of coffee to answer to the very same authorities that propelled the heterosexuals' exile. But it is precisely at this juncture of assumed pathos and radical politics that Mario was first introduced, his identity always configured by a dominant culture which inevitably—as Allende unwittingly demonstrates—misreads him. Such misreadings provide Mario the possibility of manipulation; an agency which, while by its very complicity in hegemonic homophobia it plays into stereotypes, does alter the social networks which produce them. Mario's success, however, can never be evaluated since it escapes the scope of Allende's novel. In short, Allende does not concern herself with the full possibilities of Mario's political contributions to the movement of resistance, only in his actions to secure the union its heterosexual triumph.

II. Tropical Fruit: Harry/Harriet

Michelle Cliff's 1987 novel *No Telephone To Heaven* offers yet another, although very different, example of the tropical fruit. Unlike Allende's popular romance, which invests in traditional narrative methods, Cliff's experimental narrative challenges dominant rhetorics of difference on various levels at once.[7] Cliff writes of the colonization of Jamaica and the subversive strategies of usurpation proposed by a new generation of radicals involved in antiimperialist guerrilla warfare. Like Allende's Irene, the central character of Cliff's novel, Clare Savage, embarks on a journey of political awakening. Throughout her journey, she identifies more and more with her homeland, a landscape that through the novel is understood as female. Harry/Harriet, the transgendered character who serves as her political mentor and initiator, while not "gay" per se, can be identified as the novel's "tropical fruit."[8] S/he serves as the medium through which Clare reunites with the land of her mother and grandmother. Harry/Harriet's exoticism as rendered by the text becomes the center of a radical politics out to unsettle dominant cultural myths of gender, race, and nation. And while Mario's main service is to the heterosexual love plot in Allende's novel, Harry/Harriet, by the end of the *No Telephone to Heaven,* becomes *the* means for Clare Savage to reunite with her ancestors.

Unlike *Of Love and Shadows*, which never explores Mario's contribution to the resistance movement beyond helping the heterosexual lovers escape, *No Telephone to Heaven* places Harry/Harriet at the forefront of the novel's issues. Moreover, throughout the novel Cliff offers an in-depth treatment of the character. Harry/Harriet continuously punctuates the novel with a radical politics that provides the reader a rare opportunity to engage the interrelated connections between colonization, gender, and sexuality. The initial enigma of the character's sexuality and identity—while disruptive of set binary categories of male/female and hetero/homo—is nonetheless by the end of the novel gendered. No longer Harry and now Harriet, his symbolic castration marks the transition from patriarchal oppression to matriarchal deification that Cliff sets up as the oppositional strategy through the novel. While such a feminist utopian (re)vision of indigenous culture provides a brilliant and convincing response to colonization, it calls into question positions of difference within such an imagined world. In *No Telephone to Heaven*, Harry/Harriet is understood to represent the highest form of political consciousness, the mentor to the novel's central protagonist. Despite such an exalted position, Cliff shuts down the fluidity of the he/she identity by having Harry/Harriet transform into Harriet. Cliff first describes Harry/Harriet in contrast to the protagonist Clare Savage and within the context of the underlying homophobic ideology of Jamaican society:

While Clare had been dragging her ass through parts unknown, as Harriet put it, her friend had been studying the healing practices. At the university and with old women in the country, women who knew the properties of roots and leaves and how to apply spells effectively. How to temper dengue fever, to slow TB, to stop gangrene in its tracks. Some of the old women saw their knowledge used at the cancer treatment centers for rich Americans, springing up here and there. One old woman, one who kenned Harriet's history, called her Mawu-Lisa, moon and sun, female-male deity of some of their ancestors.

None of her people downtown let on if they knew a male organ swung gently under her bleached and starched skirt. Or that white powder on her brown face hid a five o'clock shadow. Had they suspected what would they have been reduced to? For her people, but a very few, did not suffer freaks gladly—unless the freaks became characters, entertainment. Mad, unclean diversions.

Had they known about Harriet, they would have indulged in elaborate name-calling, possibly stoning, in the end harrying her to the harbor—perhaps.

And still she was able to love them. How was that? (Cliff, *No Telephone to Heaven* 171)

This passage offers the context for Harry/Harriet's transformation to Harriet. Harry/Harriet, like Mario in Allende's novel, must fashion an identity that fits into the reigning ideology of the counter-hegemonic resistance movement and also one that bows to the intolerance of "the people downtown." If, in *Of Love and Shadows*, Mario aspires to and mimics the class privilege of Irene and Francisco, in *No Telephone to Heaven*, Harry must become Harriet to find solidarity in the woman-centered and feminist-based ideology of Cliff's indigenous Jamaica. Both Mario and Harry/Harriet, moreover, face the always possible emergence of homophobic violence. In Cliff's novel, Harry/Harriet's transformation to Harriet suggests not only the ways in which the sex-gender systems of Cliff's Jamaica are locked within a binary system of identification which insists upon clarifying the blurred positions of those neither accommodated by traditional gender roles nor by conventional sexual identifications, but also the potential ramifications for those outside such epistemologies. The novel is not interested in explicating or concentrating on the specific challenges faced by the transgendered. In other words, Harry/Harriet cannot remain Harry/Harriet even within the radical political agendas set forth in the novel. Harry/Harriet must become Harriet in order to participate in both the anti-imperialist resistance movement and Cliff's own attempts at a revisionist history of Jamaica.

Cliff describes the horrific annihilation of the guerrilla activists at the end of the novel as the completion of a cycle. The guerrilla activists who attempt to subvert the neo-colonial enterprise of a North American film crew on the island are literally burned into the landscape of Jamaica. When discussing her novel, Cliff explains how this ending relates specifically to Clare: "In her death she has achieved complete identification with her homeland. Soon enough she will be indistinguishable from the ground. Her bones will turn to potash as did her ancestors' bones" (Cliff, in *Critical Fictions* 69). But what about Harry/Harriet? In order to share in the anti-androcentric impulse of such a conclusion, Harry/Harriet must symbolically fabricate an identity that, while modeled on a form of separatist feminism, can never truly be available to someone who originally self-identifies as a transgendered Jamaican. Fiona Barnes, in her insightful reading of the novel, explains how Cliff "constructs *No Telephone to Heaven* as a heteroglossic Caribbean narrative in order to counter the hegemonic and monolithic scripts of various Western experts (historians, economists, literary critics/theorists, and politicians)" and also to "expose the newest and subtlest form of neo-colonialism in the Caribbean: cultural cannibalism" (Barnes 23). While such an agenda already involves an impressive intervention in western culture's dominant mythifications of the Caribbean, Cliff—like Allende—relies on the tropical fruit as the basis for her imagined political reconstruction, and in doing so perpetuates the mythification of the tropical fruit as exotic other. Harry/Harriet, and not Clare, is presented as the abhorrent mark of difference. And despite Clare's affinity, indeed her deep affection, for Harry/Harriet—"Harry, you make me want to love you" (130), Clare confides to him after he tells her of his brutal rape as a boy by a British officer—Cliff suggests, even in this scene where the effects of imperialism are played out on the body of the tropical fruit, the limits of Harry/Harriet's inclusion as such within the feminist utopian image of the ending. Moreover it needs to be noted that *No Telephone to Heaven,* while radically different—narratologically, politically, geographically, and ideologically—from *Of Love and Shadows*, still shares with Allende's novel the focus on a heroine as the single protagonist. While an argument could be made that the freedom fighters of Cliff's novel constitute a collective protagonist that unsettles some of the individualization of most *bildungsroman* narratives and even novels of political awakening, by the end of the novel and despite the complete eradication of all of the guerrilla revolutionaries, the reader is left with the privileged perspective of Clare and the symbolism of her death.

III. Tropical Fruit: Dell

If in both Allende's and Cliff's novels, the tropical fruit is the locus of a transaction between either men and women (*Of Love and Shadows*) or between women (*No Telephone to Heaven*) that serves a radical politics of counter-hegemony, in AIDS activist and best-selling writer Paul Monette's novel *Afterlife* (1990), the Latino gay man demonstrates yet a third variation of the topos. In effect, he embodies the fate of all exotics at the hands of U.S. dominant culture, where differences among the people of the Americas are conflated in the larger construction of the "alien." *Afterlife* tells the story of three AIDS widowers who, having met in the most dire of circumstances, continue their friendship past the long, round-the-clock hospital vigils of the first encounters. The three surviving gay men—Steven, Sonny, and Dell—each represent three very different ways of reacting to AIDS: grief, denial, and anger. Monette begins the novel a year after their initial meeting and depicts how each widower copes with the loss of his partner and with his own HIV-positive status. Stephen, the novel's central character, "who ballooned in a year from 160–185" (Monette 1), hosts their Saturday gatherings; Sonny, on the other hand, lives at his West Hollywood gym, flexing muscle and attitude with a vengeance that can only be countered by a heavy dose of California New Age mysticism; and Dell, the novel's most enigmatic character, rages against an anti-gay television evangelist when he's not on the 900-number phone-sex lines. Each man undergoes a powerful journey that results in a complete restructuring of his life. Together they teach each other about the challenges and possibilities of living in the afterlife—"this extra piece of time after a lover dies" (7).

The main narrative strategy of *Afterlife*, as in Allende's novel, is the convention of romance. Monette's most political message is that gay men living with HIV can indeed continue to have both love and sex in a variety of relationship configurations. While Monette spends considerable time in his fiction providing a fully realized depiction of all three AIDS widowers, the narrative is essentially generated by the marriage plot. In this case, however, the union involves two white gay men who are both HIV positive. While the conventions of both romance and the marriage plot novel are imbedded in deeply conservative ideologies, the placement of gay men at the center of the courtship radically alters the limits of the form.[9] *Afterlife* reads like Jane Austen in West Hollywood: courtship, social critique, irony, and, of course, AIDS. Add to this love story a dash of the best revolutionary resistance narratives and you have the first gay novel written about AIDS that fuses personal love interests with political activism. While Allende unproblematically invests in the fictions of heterosexual romance and thereby perpetuates the gridlock of heterosexuality as the normative sexuality within counter-hegemonic movements, Monette defamiliarizes romance fiction by altering not its thematics or plot conventions but rather its protagonists. Steven and his new lover Mark play out the conventions of romance within the ideology of safe sex. These new negotiations and practices necessary for survival are never dogmatically set up as the new normative sexuality for gay men, or a mere performance of heterosexual marriage models. Instead, their courtship and reunion signal one possible alternative for gay men living in the midst of AIDS. Not all the AIDS widowers in *Afterlife* are looking for love; some prefer justice instead.

Dell, a Mexican immigrant and one of the three AIDS widowers, finds meaning and purpose in terrorist activities that call attention to the horrors of AIDS and the insidious discriminations that affect people with AIDS, especially, but not exclusively, gay men. Dell stands out as the exotic other in the landscape of West Hollywood's urban white gay male culture. His public terrorist tactics of confrontation—claiming to have spilled HIV-contaminated blood in the public reservoir, threatening to abduct and inject HIV into members of the County Board of Supervisors who were withholding funds for HIV testing sites, destroying the files of a fanatic television evangelist who blames gay men for AIDS, for example—are fueled by anger and pain and unmatched by any of the other gay men who deal with AIDS in the novel. Dell, in fact, becomes the location of all fantasies of revolution, usurpation, and violence. By the end of the novel he dies on an assassination mission—a successful one, no less—that results in his self-sacrifice to the cause. He embodies the U.S. myth of foreign other, a "terrorist" willing to risk all for the revolution. While the other (white) characters find romance, spirituality, and community, Dell is presented as a social other/outsider. Although he is tolerated by white gay men sympathetic to his anger and loss, he is annihilated by a dominant culture which can only view him as *the* threat to its own welfare. Dell Espinoza is never judged by any of the other gay characters as the ethnic stereotype that the novel's dominant institutions—in particular the media—construct. While the media insists on producing a composite of the "terrorist": "hispanic male, mid-thirties, probably gay" (50), the other widowers and the kinship networks they establish for themselves allow for Dell's multiple identifications. Nor do the other Latino characters share Dell's ideas of activism. Linda, Dell's lesbian sister, calls Steven once she hears of Dell's assassination of Mother Evangeline, the television evangelist:

> "What's he done?" she cried in anguish. "How could he do this?"
> "Honey, I'm sorry," Steven said brokenly, feeling the rush of protectiveness. "There was no way to know. He had a pain we couldn't touch." This sounded, even as he said it, as mindless as the TV expert.
> "But he *killed* somebody. Why?"
> Steven bit his tongue, because he realized the killing didn't bother him. That part at least seemed to have some social value. As to why, it was perfectly clear why. Mother Evangeline was a pig. (277)

Of the three novelists I have discussed, Monette comes closest to recognizing the fate of the tropical fruit. From one perspective, this view falls into the domain of tragedy; in dominant cultures there exists no place for the Latin/o gay man that does not already socialize him as alien. And yet, because of his multiple positions in relation to oppositional discourses, the Latin/o gay man posits the radical possibility of dismantling hegemonic practice simply by asserting his self-identity.

If the trope of the tropical fruit—as I have described it—is understood within the counter-hegemonic literature of the Americas to signify Latino and Caribbean gay men, in the hegemonic narratives of U.S. politics such distinctions are either lost or rendered obsolete. Perpetuations of the "tropical fruit" are evident in the hegemonic fictions of the U.S. government and its policies on AIDS and people of color of the Americas and begin to demonstrate the effects of this conflation of race, sexuality, and national identity. One only needs to recall how often the concept of tropical fruit has emerged in U.S. responses to AIDS. Rhetorics of quarantine and contagion continue to surface in discussions of AIDS, and the realities of people with HIV and/or AIDS in U.S. prisons comes very close to actualizing these reactionary and racist agendas. Viewed at once as dispensable trivialities and yet simultaneously as the site of (heterosexual) contagion, gay men of color in particular will find little comfort in these narratives of the Americas refusing them any self-identification. But gay men of color should not be the only people alarmed by the production of tropicalizing discourses. The trope of the "tropical fruit" extends into the imaginings of dominant culture to mean all people of African descent as well as Latin and Caribbean: remember, for example, the racist claim (blame) for Haiti as source/origin of AIDS, a process still in circulation with the widespread discrimination of Haitian refugees.[10]

In 1992, under the Bush administration, 233 HIV-positive Haitian asylum seekers and about sixty family members were detained in the first mass-isolation facility for HIV-positive people organized by the U.S. government. The refugees at the camp in Guantánamo Bay Naval Base in Cuba had to await the decision of President-elect Clinton, who promised throughout his campaign to change U.S. immigration and HIV policies.[11] Despite the recommendations from various Health officials, the Justice Department under the Bush administration stopped processing the claims for political asylum because of two legal disputes. At issue was whether HIV-positive people should be permitted to enter the U.S. and whether the Haitian refugees had a right to enter the U.S. to have their claims heard. On June 8, 1993, a federal judge ordered the release of all Haitians held at Guantánamo and the immediate closing of the camp.[12] Although the sexuality of the Haitians held at Guantánamo Bay wasn't a point of discussion in the media, the conflation of race, sexuality, and contagion highlights precisely what I am describing as the phenomenon of the tropical fruit. Upholders of the policy that restricts people with HIV from entering the United States argued that the Haitians would expose people in the U.S. to AIDS and burden the U.S. health-care system. In the process of defending this policy, supporters of the ban demonstrated the effects of a tangled logic produced and maintained by xenophobic, racist, and homophobic tendencies, the very tendencies that construct what I have called the tropical fruit. The tropical fruit always appears in the fictions of hegemony as the exotic and enigmatic other. He is the location of a given culture's fears and anxieties, the boundary of a culture's own imagined borders.

Even in the counter-hegemonic narratives of the 1980s and 1990s, writers committed to social change invoke the character of the tropical fruit as a means to comment on the revolution at hand. Yet the tropical fruit—himself resistant to any ideology of containment within compulsory heterosexuality and/or homophobic discourse—remains outside the center, problematically positioned as Other despite the social restructurings these novels imagine. On the one hand, such a marginalized position allows for the perpetuation of this mode of tropicalization regardless of any North/South or colonial/postcolonial imagined border of difference. Yet on the other hand, it is from this marginalized location that the tropical fruit begins to intervene in the dominant binary systems of identification that characterize all of the Americas. As I have argued, the Latino and Caribbean gay man emerges as tropical always, but he remains throughout these narratives politicized; a reminder of the inevitable social, cultural, and discursive necessity to continue a radical politics that recognizes the need to restructure social institutions and policies in order to accommodate and affirm the various differences between and among us.

The dilemma of the Haitian refugees held for nearly twenty months at Guantánamo Bay remains a case in point, for the Haitians "detained, segregated, and held incommunicado behind barbed wire and under armed guard" (Coughlin, "Age of AIDS") remind us that the fictional and discursive tropes perpetuated in literature—even in resistance and revisionist historical literature—almost assuredly materialize in the lived realities of people of color in the Americas regardless of sexual orientation or identity. The perpetuation of such tropicalizing discourses, while an indication of the limits of the politics of tolerance, finally demonstrates that Galeano's call to "rescue the word" is deeply connected with the need to rescue life as well. Resistance literature and revisionist narratives of the Americas can begin to actualize these claims by avoiding the pitfalls of nationalist, racist, and homophobic rhetoric. The salient obviations often operative in counter-hegemonic practices—in this case, the discursive production throughout the Americas of the Latino gay man as the tropical fruit—boomerang back to these borders from a different angle. As the Haitian refugee camp makes clear, there remains the seemingly unalterable equation in North American discourse that imagines all cultures outside its borders within the topology of the tropical fruit. Thus the need to deconstruct the mythification of such a phenomenon in the literature of so-called resistance becomes all the more urgent and all the more worthwhile.

In other words, counter-hegemonic practices within the Americas need to be more imaginative in formulating the coalitions available for cultural and political resistance. Despite the specificity and heterogeneity of resistance movements in the Americas, in U.S. government policies—those regarding

AIDS and HIV in particular—all people of color of the Americas are conflated as alien others; sexuality remains, then, undifferentiated in this system where racial and national categorizations rule. In order to challenge the oppression and exploitation within such a system, the resistance literatures of the Americas need to counter the tropicalizing tendencies within their own narratives. The bilateral traffic in tropicalization perpetuates the configuration of alien and other, but unlike other locations within representation where such a proliferation destabilizes the systems producing such a paradigm,[13] tropicalization, at least in our current historical reality, seems to always involve a certain degree of appropriation, if not reinscription, by the omnipresent discourses of both colonization and imperialism, and compulsory heterosexuality and homophobia.[14]

Notes

This essay was first presented at the November 1992 American Studies Association in Costa Mesa, California, and then revised in the summer of 1993 for publication. My discussion of AIDS is therefore informed by (and limited to) the specific historical events up through this time. I would like to thank the editors of this anthology, Susana Chávez-Silverman and Frances Aparicio, for inviting me to participate in the initial ASA session and in this volume, Kate Shanley and Lauren Berlant for offering me helpful suggestions for thinking through some of these ideas, and Yvonne Yarbro-Bejarano for her generous support and critical insights.

1. See, for example, Roberto Fernández Retamar's seminal study *Caliban and Other Essays* for the historical processes of resistance. For a reading of Retamar, see José David Saldívar's insightful critique in *The Dialectics of Our America*, especially Part 1.
2. On the characteristics of romance fiction as well as its reception among North American women readers, see Janice Radway's *Reading the Romance*.
3. See Máximo Pacheco's book on the actual events, *Lonquén*.
4. For an in-depth examination of this syndrome, see David William Foster's *Gay and Lesbian Themes in Latin American Writing*. Foster also provides for my discussion an illuminating account of the experiences of gay men and lesbians living under severe dictatorial regimes, most notably in his chapter "The Sociopolitical Matrix." On the problem of stereotypes in Allende's fiction, see Gabriela Mora, "Las novelas de Isabel Allende," where she argues that the stereotypes in Allende's novels perpetuate an ideology of fate, thus eradicating the possibility of agency for the women characters.
5. In this sense, the gay male is used as the medium of heterosexual bonding much in the same way as women are used in male homosocial bondings. Moreover, In *Of Love and Shadows*, the gay man plays the role usually ascribed to, and still expected of, women in conventional heterosexual love plots; both women and gay men are expected to support the reinscription of patriarchal interests.

6. See, for instance, Rachel du Plessis's *Writing beyond the Ending,* where she demonstrates how the female energies of the initial quest plot are absorbed by the romance/marriage plot.

7. Cliff's narrative tactics are outside the scope of this essay. For readers interested in this topic, I recommend Fiona R. Barnes, "Resisting Cultural Cannibalism: Oppositional Narratives in Michelle Cliff's *No Telephone to Heaven.*"

8. For an insightful account of the perceptions of homosexuality among Jamaicans, see Peter Noel with Robert Marriott.

9. On the ideologies of the courtship and marriage plots see Joseph Allen Boone's *Tradition Counter Tradition: Love and the Form of Fiction.*

10. In *Inventing AIDS*, Cindy Patton explains how Haitians were first labeled as a "risk group" because of researchers' "beliefs about voodoo religious practices" (17). On AIDS in Haiti, see Anne-Christine D'Adesky's *Advocate* cover story, "Silence + Death = AIDS in Haiti," Marie Marthe Saint Cyr-Delphe's "Haiti: Where Silence Reigns," and the indispensable writings of journalist Dan Coughlin.

11. A 1987 rule bars entry to the United States to foreigners who have tested positive to HIV.

12. Thomas L. Friedman reported in the *New York Times* that of the remaining Haitians detained at the Guantánamo Bay Naval base in Cuba, 143 were HIV-positive adults, 2 HIV-negative adults, and 13 minors who had not been tested for HIV. Earlier in the spring of 1993, the same U.S. federal judge, Sterling Johnson, Jr., ordered the release of about 50 people to the U.S. for medical treatment. See Thomas L. Friedman for further pertinent information.

13. See, for instance, Judith Butler's discussion of this type of proliferation in her essay, "The Force of Fantasy: Feminism, Mapplethorpe, and Discursive Excess."

14. I am excited by the essays in the second half of the anthology that begin to theorize emerging discourses of "tropicalizing of the North." My sense is that one way to reimagine stereotypes and appropriate "pre-tropicalized" signifiers is to focus on "local" interventions. That is to say that at this critical moment in U.S. culture, interventions that service one U.S. "minority" community—geographical, cultural, ethnic, or sexual—may not work for the specific dynamics of other communities. Thus the concept of the local—and with it, its affiliate, the vernacular—offers some possible fields for re-tropicalizations. On the idea of the vernacular, see Cindy Patton.

Works Cited

Allende, Isabel. *Of Love and Shadows.* Translated by Margaret Sayers Peden. Knopf: New York, 1987.

Almaguer, Tomás. "Chicano Men: A Cartography of Homosexual Identity and Behavior." *differences* 3 (1991): 75–100.

Barnes, Fiona R. "Resisting Cultural Cannibalism: Oppositional Narratives in Michelle

Cliff's *No Telephone to Heaven*." *Journal of the Midwest Modern Language Association* 25:1 (1992): 23–31.

Boone, Joseph Allen. *Tradition Counter Tradition: Love and the Form of Fiction*. Chicago: University of Chicago Press, 1987.

Butler, Judith. "The Force of Fantasy: Feminism, Mapplethorpe, and Discursive Excess." *differences* 2 (1990): 105–25.

Cliff, Michelle. *No Telephone to Heaven*. Vintage Books: New York, 1989.

———. "Conference Presentation." In *Critical Fictions: The Politics of Imaginative Writing*, edited by Philomena Mariani, 66–71. Seattle: Bay Press, 1991.

Clum, John. "'The Time Before The War': AIDS, Memory, and Desire." *American Literature* 62 (1990): 648–67.

Colás, Santiago. "Latin America and the Problem of Resistance Culture." *Polygraph* 4 (1990): 92–110.

Coughlin, Dan. "Victory at Guantanamo." *QW*, June 21, 1992: 14.

———. "Age of AIDS." *The Village Voice*, August 25, 1992: 18.

———. "HIV Detention Camp Erupts." *QW*, September 20, 1992.

———. "Political Blood." *PWA Newsline*, March 1993, Issue No. 85.

———. "AIDS: Words From the Front." *Spin*, July 1993: 67–68.

D'Adesky, Anne-Christine. "Silence + Death = AIDS in Haiti." *Advocate*, May 21, 1991.

du Plessis, Rachel Blau. *Writing beyond the Ending: Narrative Stategies of Twentieth-Century Women Writers*. Bloomington: Indiana University Press, 1985.

Foster, David William. *Gay and Lesbian Themes in Latin American Literature*. Austin: University of Texas Press, 1991.

Friedman, Thomas L. "U.S. to Release 158 Haitian Detainees." *New York Times*, June 10, 1993: A6.

Galeano, Eduardo. "In Defense of the Word: Leaving Buenos Aires, June 1976." In *Multi-Cultural Literacy*, edited by Rick Simonson and Scott Walker. Saint Paul: Graywolf Press, 1988.

Gordon, Ambrose. "Isabel Allende on Love and Shadows." *Contemporary Literature* 28 (1987): 530–42.

Harlow, Barbara. *Resistance Literature*. New York: Methuen, 1987.

Monette, Paul. *Afterlife*. Avon Books: New York, 1990.

Mora, Gabriela. "Las novelas de Isabel Allende y el papel de la mujer como ciudadana." *Ideologies and Literature* 2 (1987): 53–61.

Noel, Peter, with Robert Marriott. "Batty Boys in Babylon: Can Gay West Indians Survive The 'Boom Bye Bye' Posses?" *Village Voice*, January 12, 1993; 29–35.

Pacheco, Máximo. *Lonquén*. Santiago, Chile: Ed. Aconcagua, 1980.

Panos Institute. *The 3rd Epidemic: Repercussions of the Fear of AIDS*. London: Panos Publications, 1990.

Patton, Cindy. *Inventing AIDS*. New York: Routledge, 1990.

———. "Safe Sex and the Pornographic Vernacular." In *How Do I Look?: Queer Film and Video*, edited by Bad Object-Choices. Seattle: Bay Press, 1991.

Radway, Janice. *Reading the Romance: Women, Patriarchy, and Popular Literature*. Chapel Hill: University of North Carolina Press, 1984.

Retamar, Roberto Fernández. *Caliban and Other Essays*. Translated by Edward Baker. Minneapolis: University of Minnesota Press, 1989.

Rich, Adrienne. "Compulsory Heterosexuality and Lesbian Existence." In *The Signs Reader: Women, Gender, and Scholarship,* edited by Elizabeth Abel and Emily K. Abel. Chicago: University of Chicago Press, 1983.

Saldívar, José David. *The Dialectics of Our America: Genealogy, Cultural Critique, and Literary History.* Durham: Duke University Press, 1991.

Saint Cyr-Delphe, Marie Marthe. "Haiti: Where Silence Reigns." In Panos Institute, *The 3rd Epidemic: Repercussions of the Fear of AIDS.* London: Panos Publications, 1990, 168–72.

III

**Relocating Hegemony:
Tropicalizing Cuba from the United States**

María Teresa Marrero

Historical and Literary *Santería*: Unveiling Gender and Identity in U.S. Cuban Literature

One of the sharpest childhood memories I have of Cuba is this: I am very small and inside a cavernous church. The walls are made of rough white-washed stones. I look up and the cramped space is covered with glass eyes; crucifixes dangle, passport-sized photographs glued at the crux; small plastic arms and legs as well as life-sized ones hang on the walls. Full-sized crutches float in midair. The statue of a hunched saint (St. Lazarus/Babalú Ayé) is draped in white rags, and two dogs stand by, licking his bloody sores. I am transfixed with awe and fear and cannot take my eyes off the images.[1]

As a child growing up in the 1960s in a Southern California middle-class, beach neighborhood I knew that we Cubans were deeply and fundamentally different from the *norteamericanos*. But how? For one, our way of looking at life, death, and the relationship with things of the "other" world could not be more dissimilar. In my youthful imagination I concluded that Cubans were primarily different from the Anglos because we could "talk" with the saints and they responded. Our relationship with the supernatural was common-place. We were on familiar "*tú*" terms with a wide number of saints instead of the "thees" and "thous" of the American Catholic church. We had home altars. We didn't need a priest in order to arrange for someone's life to be spared from an accident or illness. The Cuban and Spanish-born women in my white, working-class family seemed to know how to arrange for miracles directly. My maternal grandmother was buried in the orange-and white-gingham cloth of La Virgen de la Caridad del Cobre, in fulfillment of a promise for sparing her only son's life. On her knees, my mother crept up the pyramidal steps of the Oriente province cathedral to the same virgin for sparing my life. While we didn't practice Santería per se, we certainly didn't practice standard

Catholicism either. I could find nothing analogous in my U.S. cultural surroundings, so I resolved my dilemma by keeping my beliefs a secret. It was not until graduate school that I came to realize that my childhood concerns constituted a legitimate field of study. It was not until then that I came to realize the full extent of the African influence upon our beliefs. It is this which makes Cuban "Catholicism" so different from the American version. This is not, however, a uniquely Cuban experience. It is present anywhere in the Americas where the enslaved Yoruba, Fon, Congo, Dahomey, and other African peoples took root (the Caribbean islands and many coastal regions of South America, Brazil, etc.).

In simplest terms, Santería, properly known in Cuba as *La Regla de Ochá*, is derived from the descendants of Yoruba (Nigeria, West Africa) slaves shipped to Cuba between the sixteenth and nineteenth centuries. Santería is cumulative in the sense that African beliefs of the *orishas* or deities are blended with the physical and psychological attributes of Roman Catholic saints; thus the name *Santería* (Castellanos 9–113). It permeates all aspects of Cuban life, including the more orthodox white Catholic practices. In secular life, the drum rhythms of the Cuban *danzón*, the rumba, the mambo, the cha cha chá, the Brazilian samba, the Puerto Rican bomba, the plena, the Jamaican calypso, and reggae all owe their syncopated rhythmic patterns to the West African "talking drum," a sacred (and equally profane) instrument. Singer Harry Belafonte has documented the trajectories of these musical styles from Africa to the Caribbean and then to the United States in the early 1900s with Edison's newly invented recording cylinder (Belafonte, *Routes of Rhythm*, 1990). Subsequently, for decades the particularity of the West African legacy has been influencing American musical life, whether it is generally acknowledged or not.

It is my intent to contextualize Santería as a particularly Cuban social and literary manifestation that has historically transcended its geographic demarcations. Subsequently, I place the three U.S. Cuban literary texts to be considered squarely within two traditions: first, as part of a long-standing *Cuban* literary tradition; secondly, as part of the newer field of Latino ethnic literature in the United States.

My introductory narrative carries within it the bi-cultural factors present in my subsequent discussion of Santería in the work of novelist Cristina García (*Dreaming in Cuban*, 1992), and of playwrights Dolores Prida (*Botánica*, 1991) and Caridad Svich (*Brazo gitano/Gypsy's Arm*, 1990). It uncovers an "I" related by gender, race, and cultural background to the authors who write in English and/or Spanish about the personal concerns of identity and culture. Second, my introductory narrative reveals a shared inclination toward centering the ethno-religious as a locus of *cultural identity*, which is tied, but does not restrict itself, to notions of *racial identity*. And third, it reveals that I, along with the authors, was not raised within the hegemonic enclave of the Miami

Cuban community. I suggest that these elements are significant in the current arena of identity-formation dynamics of first- and second-generation Cuban Americans. The practice of incorporating Santería in works of fiction by Cubans and Latinos in the United States, I believe, addresses more than literary tropicalization. More urgently, it suggests the creation and negotiation of a new cultural space for Latino self-identity (Flores and Yúdice 57–84).

As an underlying tenet I entertain the concept that the Yoruba Lucumí religious practices need to be considered both as a *worldview* and as a cultural practice of political and gender significance. I propose that this worldview is being rearticulated currently by white U.S. Cuban women writers (and other Caribbean writers of both sexes) in order to express their *cultural identity* within the context of life in urban areas such as New York, Miami, and Los Angeles. This idea first touches upon general issues that deal with Cuban Americans as part of a larger cultural group of Latinos who have to negotiate issues of acculturation and assimilation like other ethnic minorities in this country. As such, Santería, like salsa music, food, and other forms of popular culture, represents the perceived threat of the "tropicalization" of U.S. culture. Santería's popularity among non-Cubans across racial and cultural borders points towards its potential as a multi-cultural phenomenon (Murphy 2). However, there are issues which address the Cuban American exile community specifically. The representation of Santería by Cuban American writers challenges notions of the hegemonic, predominantly white, politically conservative Cubans to define identity politics for all Cubans in the U.S.

The Permanence of *La Regla de Ochá*

Santería's proper Cuban name is *La Regla de Ochá*. It proceeds from the Yoruba people of southeastern Nigeria (known in Cuba as Lucumí) who were imported to Cuba as slaves between the sixteenth and the mid-nineteenth centuries. Santería owes its name to the incorporation of the images of Catholic saints as syncretic expressions of the Lucumí/Yoruba deities, the *orishas*: Eleguá/San Antonio, Obatalá/Nuestra Señora de las Mercedes, Changó[2] /Santa Bárbara, Yemayá/La Virgen de Regla, Ochún/La Caridad del Cobre, Oyá/La Virgen de la Candelaria, Babalú-Ayé/San Lázaro, to name a few (Castellanos 18–125). Each *orisha* represents a natural force and is in charge of certain aspects of human life. As Wole Soyinka, the 1987 Yoruban Nobel laureate from Nigeria, has written in *Myth, Literature and the African World,* the deities have the same human frailties as their devotees. This relationship is quite unlike the Judeo-Christian tradition and is best exemplified by the Yoruba saying *Bi o s'enia, imale o si* ("If humanity were not, the gods would not be," Soyinka 10).

While Santería is by no means the only Afro-Cuban religion practiced on and off the island,[3] it is one of the most widespread. It is similarly practiced in Bahia in northeast Brazil, where Yoruban slaves also survived, under the name *Candomblé*. According to anthropologist William Bascom, "Second only to Bahia until recently, Yoruba religion probably was retained purest in form in Cuba, and particularly in Havana . . . [by] descendants of Yoruba slaves known as Lucumí" (Bascom 13).

To a number of cultural anthropologists—including Roger Bastide, William Bascom, and Joseph Murphy—as well as to scholars Fernando Ortiz, Lydia Cabrera, Mercedes Cros-Sandoval, Julia Cuervo Hewitt, Jorge and Isabel Catellanos, Roberto Lima, Jorge Emilio Gallardo, Fernando García Cambeiro, Barbara Bush (no relation to the former First Lady), and Roberto González Echeverría, the permanence of this historical and literary expression constitutes a manifestation of strong resistance towards acculturation and subjugation of the Afro-Cuban and Afro-Caribbean diasporic peoples.

Santería's specificity as a dynamic social process challenges the indiscriminate classification of Latino texts as "magical realist" if they exhibit elements of the "magical."[4] Is it possible for Latinos to incorporate vital elements of a West African tribal, pantheistic religion without "exoticizing" ourselves? Santería incorporates deities who display human frailties, who posses or "mount" the human devotee, who demand animal sacrifice and dance during a ceremony. Ontologically, there is no distinction between levels of experience usually called "real" and the metaphysical. To uninitiated others—Anglos or Latinos—these beliefs may be "exotic," mysterious, or even dangerous indeed.

A close historical look at slave resistance practices will reveal that, in part, the present image of Afro-Caribbean religions as dangerous, mysterious, and feared is not only a construction of the contemporary imagination but squarely grounded historically. It was an image created by the slave/master dynamics and it benefited the slaves to perpetuate it, particularly the women. For this important reason, any discussion of Santería in a volume that deals with the titillation of "exoticity" requires a historical reading.

Women, Fear, and Magic

Contact between the African and the European can be viewed as a two-way street: not only were Africans' lives deeply affected by their contacts with the Europeans, but the Europeans were also affected by their contact with Africans. The contact was infused with cruelty and violence; however, white society did not get by untouched.

British political scientist Barbara Bush's study on *Slave Women in Caribbean Society 1650–1838* offers an insightful look into the European's fear of the powerful combination of women and magic. She quotes from *Narrative of a Five Year Expedition against the Revolted Negroes of Surinam, 1772–1777* by John Stedman, published in London in 1796:

[The slaves] also have amongst them a kind of Sybils, who deal in oracles; these sage matrons [are found] dancing and whirling round in the middle of an assembly with amazing rapidity until they foam at the mouth and drop down convulsed. Whatever the prophetess orders to be done, during this paroxysm is most sacredly performed by the surrounding multitude which renders these meetings extremely dangerous, as she frequently enjoins them to murder their masters, or desert to the woods. (Bush 74)

The Greco-Roman allusion to sybils, oracles, and dionysian frenzy clearly violates the restraint of eighteenth-century British mentality. It is suggested that the danger of these African sage matrons lies in their ability to give free rein to their animal instincts ("foam at the mouth") and tap into some sort of diabolic power which can be harnessed to provoke a subversion of order. Not only is it suggested that the African "sybils" can stir men to revolt, but also that these women are responsible for such actions. The power attributed to them as individuals supersedes that of the "multitude."

Bush comments that there are similar reports from the French Caribbean, where grand voodoo priestesses had an important ritual role and gave "superhuman courage to insurgents" (74). Bush mentions that whites feared them not only because of their potentially subversive elements, which held a sinister association with poison and secrecy, but also because their beliefs were incomprehensible to them (75). In particular, she mentions the West African belief of a hidden and pervasive energy (a spiritual power called *ashé* in Santería and Candomblé) that could be harnessed and used by humans. To European Christianity then and now, this worldview smacks of witchcraft and witches, whose persecution has been inscribed into numerous misogynist chapters of world history. Furthermore, in Spanish America the legacy left by the not-so-holy Inquisition is also long and no less grotesque than that left by slavery.

Magic afforded slaves one of the few viable resources of cultural survival during centuries of imposed cruelty. According to former Cuban slave Esteban Montejo's autobiography, one of their resources was fear: "The overseers were really impressed by African sorcery, they didn't dare take their eyes off the Negro magic men for a second, because they knew that if the Negros wanted they could split their skulls open" (Montejo 26). But what was the basis of this perceived "power"? According to Montejo, it was twofold. The women's knowledge of medicinal and poisonous plants (42) and the ability of some of the old Africans (he mentions the Congolese) to perform sorcery (turn themselves into animals and fly, to call up spirits and make them materialize) (140).

The image of slave women as active historical agents is foregrounded in revisionist accounts of slave resistance. The self-respect and empowerment needed for a positive sense of identity were elaborated through their belief systems, shielded by secrecy, and expanded through legends shrouded in mystery and fear. Taken from the oral tradition, Montejo's words are witnesses to generalized beliefs, which held strong sway over the popular imagination, in spite of the problematic autobiography's meta-fictional character (see both Said and Taussig on this topic). Taken from an Afrocentric rather than a Eurocentric perspective, the image of the feared and secretive "sorceress" became a survival weapon with strong politically subversive overtones such as slave rebellions and maroonage, which threatened the core of plantation societies.

Enter the Whites into Afro-Cuban Secret Societies

How did whites penetrate secret Afro-Cuban societies, and why? As it appears, whites did not "penetrate" in the aggressive sense of the word; they were "allowed" in. The best-recorded case of a concerted effort to induct whites into black secret societies in Cuba was recorded by Lydia Cabrera, who according to Jorge and Isabel Castellanos is the only one to have recorded this phenomenon (Castellanos 181). The *regla* or society that produced such a unique mix was *La Regla Kimbisa del Santo Cristo del Buen Viaje,* headed by a light-skinned and handsome mulatto, Andrés Facundo Cristo de los Dolores Petit, from the city of Guanabacoa. Petit was born during the first half of the nineteenth century. He embodied a wide array of syncretic beliefs which characterize the integration and metamorphosis of African-derived worldview within Cuban popular culture. These include such disparate elements as Catholicism, Congolese and Yoruban *reglas*, spiritism, and masonry (Castellanos 181). Petit's *regla* was founded upon a deep faith and dedication to the ideals of charity and kindness. This kindness, extended to the whites, was deliberately well thought out. His saying was *"Por el cuero del chivo todos los hombres pueden ser hermanos"* [Through the goat's hide all men can become brothers] (203). Equality based upon blood ritual made brothers out of mulatto, black, and white men, something unattainable during the mid-nineteenth century by other social means. Petit apparently commanded great respect: not only was he a member of the Third Order of Franciscans (a secular, mendicant order for the poor), but he was also a *babalawo* (priest) in *La Regla de Ochá* (Santería) and a *ñáñigo* (priest) in *La Sociedad Secreta de Abakuá* (a feared secret society of male sorcerers from Calabar, Nigeria). Cabrera and Catellanos consider Petit a powerful force in the spread of Afro-Catholic religious practices in Cuba due to his tremendous popularity and the racial-cultural mix of his cult. While Castellanos attributes to him the "whitening" of the African *reglas*, the flip side of the coin is that Petit also Africanized white Catholicism.

The Battleground:
Cuban Cultural Identity in the Early Twentieth Century

In spite of the steady spread of Santería and other African-derived forms of popular culture (i.e., music and dance), over the eighteenth, nineteenth, and twentieth centuries, there is relatively little recorded historically about the literary work of black or mulatto Cubans. Enrique Noble's *Literatura Afro-hispano-americana* (1973) makes the necessary distinction between the *literatura negra* and *literatura negrista* (literature written by blacks versus that about blacks).[5] A particularly important figure is Rómulo Lachatañeré (1910–52), an Afro-Cuban who collected stories from the African oral tradition. The best known is Nicolás Guillén, a mulatto who put Afro-Cuban diction on the literary map. In the category of the autobiography, Esteban Montejo's *Autobiography of a Runaway Slave*, as recorded by Miguel Barnet in the early 1960s, narrates the life of a centenarian former Cuban-born slave as a *cimarrón* (runaway slave) in the late 1800s.

The bulk of anthropological knowledge about black culture in Cuba was written by white scholars who worked with black informants (Ortiz and Cabrera) or by white creative writers whose imagination re-creates black representations, as the well-known case of Alejo Carpentier. To Fernando Ortiz, the issue ultimately became one related to the transcultured nature of the Afro-Spanish Cuban national identity. The concept was first elaborated by Ortiz in an essay called "Del fenómeno social de la 'transculturación' y de su importancia en Cuba" (About the Social Phenomenon of "Transculturation" and its Importance in Cuba), originally published in the *Revista bimestre cubana* (1940). It subsequently became part of his major work, *Contrapunteo cubano del tabaco y el azúcar* (1940) (Pérez Firmat 169). Transculturation, according to Ortiz, creates a cultural configuration which encompasses the loss of original cultural elements, the absorption of new ones, and their fusion or synthesis into yet a third, and different, element.[6]

Ortiz's first publication, however, reflects the white imagination's projection of black popular culture. With his studies of the street culture of lower-class Afro-Cubans in *Hampa afro-cubana: Los negros brujos* (1906) Ortiz depicts the black "witches" under the overwhelming influence of a Positivist, racist vocabulary. By the mid-1940s, the "conqueror is conquered" and Ortiz ends up affirming Afro-Cuban culture in later works. His ethnographic studies of Cuba's secret religious societies played an important role in the intellectual integration of the African into Cuba's literary life. Though this exchange was uneven in power, this two-way movement was termed *transculturación* by Ortiz, and it signals an important historical development in the discourse about Cuban national identity between 1900 and the 1950s. Devoid of an aboriginal culture (native Tainos, Ciboneyes, and Caribs were decimated), all Cubans are, by definition, immigrants (Spanish, Africans, Chinese, Jews, and people from the Middle East). We are, as Ortiz described and Pérez-Firmat recently echoed, "un ajiaco," a stew, of many flavors.

Paris Becomes Fascinated with Our Black Culture, Why Aren't We?

Lydia Cabrera first published a volume of Afro-Cuban tales entitled *Contes negres de Cuba* (1936) in Paris—not Cuba. It was translated into Spanish in 1940. Along with Afro-Chinese-Cuban Surrealist painter Wifredo Lam, writer Alejo Carpentier and Cabrera had spent some years in Paris during the 1930s and were quite familiar with, and, in the case of Lam, personally involved in, the Surrealist movement (Herzberg, 1990: 23). According to art historian Julia P. Herzberg,

André Breton . . . was active on Lam's behalf beginning in 1942 . . . The Surrealists claimed the Cuban-born Lam as one of theirs out of their attitude that embraced the art and myths of the non-European peoples (Asian, African, Oceanic, and Native American). In their view these people "lived in a perpetual communion with the essence of things" [Nadeau, 1965: 340], thereby providing an antidote for the rational, materialistic, beautiful, and normal of the west [Clifford, 1982: 546]. (Herzberg 24)

While Paris was "burning" with desire to duplicate and re-create an idealized African "essence" from decontextualized objets d'art, Lam returned to Cuba to find a profoundly racist society, in spite of the work of the *afrocubanistas*. Afrocubanism as a literary movement lasted approximately from 1928 to 1938. In Havana, between 1937 and 1940, members of the Association of Afrocuban Studies, writers and intellectuals, began to investigate issues concerning the African diaspora in Cuba and other Latin American countries. However, the lingering legacy of Positivism left deep, racist marks in white Cuba's intellectual history. In spite of Europe's turn-of-the-century fascination with the "exotic" and "essential" African, in Cuba, we can count on one hand the names of those whose well-known work led toward the valuation and representation of Afro-Cuban cultural contributions: Fernando Ortiz, Lydia Cabrera, Nicolás Guillén, Alejo Carpentier, and artist Wilfredo Lam. All were born within a few years of each other, between 1900 and 1904 (twenty to twenty-four years after the abolition of slavery). Of the above-mentioned, it was Alejo Carpentier's *Ecué-Yamba-O* (1933) and *El reino de este mundo* (*The Kingdom of This World*, 1949) which first "showed that the presence of Blacks in Latin America was an important historical difference and force that had to be reckoned with in any writing or rewriting of Latin American history" (González Echevarría 584). I'd like to extend this perception to the literature being written in the United States by Cuban Americans.

A Postmodern Dramatic Aesthetic: Miami as Idea

Unlike Afro-Cuban plays such as Pepe Carril's *Shangó de Ima* (1969) and José R. Brene's *La fiebre negra* (1965), none of the texts under consideration here are "about" Santería per se. Only Svich's *Brazo gitano* personifies the *orishas* (deities) and allots them an active role in plot development. It was Svich's Master's project at the University of California at San Diego, where it was produced. Svich has written numerous plays and has been a participant at New York's INTAR Playwrights in Residence Laboratory headed by the Obie-winning Cuban American playwright María Irene Fornés.

Brazo gitano is not an easy play to read or to stage. *Brazo gitano*'s spiral structure, the multiplicity of characters who function on various levels simultaneously, and the lack of a focused dramatic conflict contribute to its difficulty. However, from the opening scene the characters make it clear that the geographic and psychological epicenter of the text is Miami ("Little Havana"). It is not so much the palpable, criollo Miami of *la Calle Ocho*, however, as it is a virtual space created by an ensemble of attitudes, ideas, and characters: Miami as an idealized locus. Thus, this Miami exists in the liminality of "betwixt and between," somewhere inside and outside of the "real" Miami and that created through the characters' attitudes about the exile culture. *Brazo gitano*'s Miami does not exist through references to absolute geographical coordinates such as street names, buildings, or other identifiable cultural landmarks (la Calle Ocho, Hialiah, etc.).

Brazo gitano's de-centered, non-linear aesthetic falls within the canons of postmodern drama, which Rodney Simard describes as "a new form of existential realism, wherein reality is displayed as subjective, and what may be seen as a plurality in form is actually a singularity in purpose" (Simard, xi). It curiously also fits quite well within descriptions of West African ritual drama as described by Yoruba playwright Wole Soyinka: "The act undertaken on behalf of the community, and the welfare of that protagonist is inseparable from that of the total community" (Soyinka 42). In *Brazo gitano* we do not find the focus on individuality usually found in Western European dramas. We see some characters who are economically well off and others who are beggars. Nevertheless, as a community, both seem to be dislocated and lost in their land of promise, Miami, USA.

The dramatic action begins with a polyphonic speech. The *orisha* characters open the play to the rhythm of the local bum, Santoyo's, silhouette dancing a solo rumba. Woman one, two, and three double as the *orishas*, Oyá,
Ochún, and Yemayá:

WOMAN ONE: (*As if from a travel brochure*) Miami.
SANTOYO: They say there's a park in Miami full of Cubans.
WOMAN ONE: Nature's Greatest Wonder.
SANTOYO: Can I take a bus from here and get there? I keep changing buses.
WOMAN ONE: Tropical Paradise.
SANTOYO: Of course, in Miami, no one needs buses.
WOMAN ONE: Promised Land.
SANTOYO: You see, without ladies, I am not well. Without ladies, I do not feel well.
WOMAN ONE: Land of Destiny.
SANTOYO: All I need is a park. They say there's a park in Miami full of Cubans.
WOMAN ONE: Magnet Whose Climate Will Bring the Human Flood.
SANTOYO: Can I take a bus from here and get there?
   (Playscript, 2)
   [This dialogue is repeated two more times, once with each of the *orishas*/women.]

The poetic, rhythmic, and communal quality of much of the dialogue
emerges immediately. As the three women/*orishas* and Santoyo establish the
rhythmic pattern of speech, they also establish an idealized place. But the idealization of place is not a fixed framework, since the Miami-as-paradise
metaphor achieves the opposite of what the words (signs) suggest: the construct of "paradise" is continually dissipated through irony. In its deconstruction of Miami-as-physical-space and in its reconstruction of Miami-as-idea,
Brazo gitano makes an implicit double claim: that Miami does not exist as
place locatable through absolute coordinates, and (possibly therefore) a relative description of how to "get there from here" is also unattainable.[7] The location alluded to in the text, then, is a state of mind. Without the restriction of
the time-space continuum, the characters possess the freedom to roam various
levels of perception simultaneously; thus, the *orishas*, Oyá, Ochún, and
Yemayá, can be divine and human. While place-as-idea seems to demarcate
the range of dramatic tension, one cannot pinpoint a central conflict as a key
referent. Rather, the construction of the dramatic action deconstructs a number
of circulating, cliché ideas about Cuban Miami. In this sense, *Brazo* typifies a
postmodern aesthetic.

The *orishas* evoke the truth from the characters in a syncopated rhythm
characteristic of the African call-and-response technique. Within the Western
tradition the function of the three *orishas*/goddesses form a chorus. In *Brazo
gitano* the chorus-like quality of the *orisha*'s speech serves to counterpoint

stereotypically acceptable cultural norms. This strategy is revisionist, I believe, because it reflects the attitude of an "outsider," one who can see particular cultural practices through the critical eyes of someone who does not "belong." Nostalgic retrospection as an emotional anchor is virtually absent. This allows the juxtapositioning of disparate elements (a monologue which literally should have a nostalgic charge is set within a dispassionate frame). It also places the text in the interstice between inside/outside, yet not statically so, because of its rhythmic, shifting movement.

The option suggested textually of contemplating a possible return to Cuba is neither constructed as a nostalgic longing nor as a patriotic exile invasion to "free the Island." Returning while Castro is still in power is not a viable option for most anti-Castro exiles. For whom, then, is this solution viable? Taking the example of Pilar in *Dreaming in Cuban*, it is an option for the generation who left the island as children in the 1960s and '70s and have grown up with the deprivation of familial and cultural loss and the longing to return as a way of filling the emptiness.

Given the contempt with which the hegemonic exile community holds those who participated in the Antonio Maceo student troops in Cuba, and anyone who is perceived as "soft" on communism, the textual perspectives in *Brazo* and in *Dreaming* present themselves as decidedly antithetical to that majority. These voices, then, place themselves on the periphery of their own dominant cultural nucleus. Women, as "transmitters" of cultural values through religious practices and attitudes are thus, in this context, constructed as navigators between the center and the margins.

The indictment against Miami as a virtual and physical paradise suggests disenchantment. The fact that Santoyo is the local street bum, and therefore outside Cuban middle and upper class ideology, indicates clearly that for his social class, this paradisiacal ideal place does not work. It does not work for the poor. This play's *Weltanschauung* addresses a sector of the Cuban community which is willing to assume a critical view of the way in which the dominant Cuban community of Miami attempts to define "Cubanness" in the United States. As appropriated by white culture, Santería here is seen as a fertile arena in the discussion of identity and political issues.

Botánica

Dolores Prida's play *Botánica* is constructed along the more familiar lines of the situation comedy, in which the action develops at a quick and lineal pace. It was first published by Arte Público Press in an anthology of Prida's work called *Beautiful Señoritas and Other Plays* (1991), edited by Judith Weiss. It was written in Spanish, evidently targeted at New York Spanish-speaking audiences. *Bótanica* has been a popular, long-running part of Repertorio Español, both in Spanish and in an English translation. Repertorio Español is run by Cubans René Buch and Gilberto Saldívar, and its season characteristically includes the production of plays in both languages.

Prida has been the subject of attack by the Miami Cuban enclave as a "Castro agent" on Spanish-language radio, and in 1985 her *Coser y cantar* was dropped from Miami's Hispanic Theater Festival (Morales 52). In the introduction to *Beautiful Señoritas* Judith Weiss states that:

> Alienation of a different kind can pose a serious political problem within the Cuban community. If one is perceived as being too liberal or—heaven forbid—a radical, the personal situation of the artist and writer becomes quite complicated. The pressure from the right-wing Cuban exiles can be pitiless. When a group of young Cubans who were raised in the U.S. and Puerto Rico established a dialogue with the Cuban authorities in 1979, two were assassinated and others (including Prida) have been periodically subjected to death threats. And it is usually impossible for a Cuban artist or intellectual who falls into this category to present his or her work in "anti-Castro" territory (Miami, or parts of New Jersey). (Prida 12)

Although Prida is Cuban-born, she has spent a number of years both in Puerto Rico and in New York City. Her characters in *Botánica* show the cultural mix of her own cross-cultural life. The protagonist, Millie, is estranged from her Cuban father. Her mother is Puerto Rican. The premise is fairly simple: the plot revolves around the lives of three generations of Puerto Rican women (grandmother, mother, and daughter) who survive in the Bronx by selling Santería herbs and magic love potions. The botánica shop belongs to the grandmother, and the action begins with Millie's graduation as a business major from a fancy East-coast school:

> In the first scene of *Botánica*, the *pasteles* that Millie's mother and grandmother are lovingly preparing for her graduation party are, for Millie, the concrete reason why she did not tell her family exactly when she was graduating. Those plantain and pork tamales would have been an invasion of the WASP space in which she had learned to survive by quietly denying her roots under peer pressure; the very smell of *pasteles* would have thrown her back four years, when as a frosh, she was first confronted by her classmates' racist prejudice. Rejecting the *pasteles* and keeping her family away from her college campus on graduation weekend means rejecting her grandmother's world. (Weiss, in Prida 15)

Her grandmother's world is the botánica, the Afro-Caribbean with which Millie does not identify:

MILLIE: No logro hacerles entender que no soy parte de esto. Estas imágenes, estas
creencias, han sido parte del equipaje de otras generaciones . . . del Africa al

Caribe, del Caribe a Nueva York . . . pero yo soy de aquí, yo nací aquí. Esto no es parte de mi equipaje . . . you know what I mean . . . (ibid. 164).

[I'm not successful in making you understand that I am not part of this. These images, these beliefs have been part of the baggage of former generations . . . from Africa to the Caribbean, from the Caribbean to New York . . . but I am from here, I was born here. This is not part of my baggage . . . you know what I mean . . .]

Millie's rejection of her Caribbean roots quickly falls apart when her grand-mother becomes ill and is hospitalized. She even considers selling the old building to developers. It is here that Rubén, a neighbor, warns her not to sell, because "Gentrification is coming to El Barrio, Mila" (165). The grand-mother's ill health prompts Millie to seek a miracle. Millie's reentry into her Puerto Rican identity occurs through the doors of Santería, specifically through the recognition/remembrance of the saints'/*orishas*' prayers that her grandmother had taught her. The comic sense that Santa Bárbara (Changó) does not speak English and that people only think of her/him when there is thunder is a culturally coded inside joke. One of the characteristics of "ritual" humor is that its function is directed at the members of the clan, and that it pro-vokes an acknowledgement of group identity (Bricker xiv).

San Lázaro responds to Millie's request by letting her know that he will do his best, but she has to make a promise, because, as he says, in a most Angli-cized voice, "Business is business" (167). Instead of a promise, Millie makes him a deal, which the audience is not privileged to hear. Through the denoue-ment it becomes evident that her grandmother's life is spared because of Mil-lie's "deal" with San Lázaro. Millie computerizes the botánica's books, gives the store a face-lift, and stays in the neighborhood.

Millie's archetypical heroic journey takes her psychologically far away from home, where she loses her identity by internalizing Anglo society's per-ception of her Puerto Ricanness as an inferior Other. Her symbolic return is not ontological: instead she transculturates both her Anglo and her Caribbean sense of self in a social and politically coded manner through Santería. As Rubén states:

RUBEN: . . . Pues . . . pa' mi ser de aquí . . . pues . . . es mango y strawberries . . . al-capurrias y pretzels . . . Yemayá y los Yankees . . . Yo no veo la diferencia. What's the big deal? Eso es lo que somos: brunch y burundanga, quiche y arroz con habichuelas, Chase Manhattan y la bolita . . . Todo depende de cómo empaques tu equipaje . . . (164)

[. . . Well . . . for me to be from here . . . well . . . it's mango and strawber-ries . . . fritters and pretzels . . . Yemayá and the Yankees . . . I don't see the difference. What's the big deal? That's what we are: brunch and stew, quiche and rice and beans, Chase Manhattan and the numbers . . . It all depends on how you wrap your baggage . . .]

Flores and Yúdice have elaborated the "interlingual" as a border voice which fends off the duality imposed by the "conflicting pressures toward both exclusion and forced incorporation" (Flores and Yúdice 57–84). In *Botánica* the struggle is interlingual and intercultural: it is informed by the triad of Puerto Rican, Cuban, and Anglo cultures. It is also informed by the topic of gentrification, one which affects the under-represented, regardless of ethnicity.

Dreaming in Cuban Both Inside and Outside the Island

There is an important difference between the two previous texts and *Dreaming in Cuban* (1992), a novel by Cristina García. Plays are events while novels are products. Plays are written to be produced and performed as figurative embodiments of a situation. For live theater the potential audience is smaller than that for a film or a novel. In the publishing world, it is a given that novels sell, plays (like poetry) do not.

Of the authors considered here, Cristina García's work has had the quickest and widest public exposure. Her novel was published by Alfred A. Knopf, a major publisher whose distribution networks are quite extensive. Arte Público Press, Prida's publisher, while the largest and oldest publisher of Hispanic literature in the United States, has a maximum circulation of 5,000.[8] Therefore it is reasonable to assume that *Dreaming in Cuban*, while most likely not written for a majority audience, is certainly marketed to one.

The novel's narrative structure is straightforward, yet the polyphony of the voices narrated makes *Dreaming in Cuban* quite as complex as *Brazo gitano*. *Dreaming* narrates the stories of three generations of Cuban women, both in Cuba and in the United States. The time span runs from Celia the grandmother's flashbacks, set in the 1940s, to the narrative "present" at the end, which takes place during the invasion of the Peruvian Embassy by Cubans who demand political asylum. Pilar (the granddaughter) grows up in New York City thinking about what it might have been like to have stayed in Cuba, and listening—telepathically—to an inner voice, which is that of her grandmother Celia, who stays in Cuba along with Felicia, Celia's second daughter. Felicia introduces the Afro-Cuban elements in the narrative. She marries a black man and has three children; she turns to Santería for salvation and eventually goes through a Santería initiation. Her good friend Herminia, the daughter of a "blue black" Yoruban father, who is a *babalawo* (Santería priest), describes Herminia as the "only person I've known who didn't see color. There are white people who know how to act politely to blacks, but deep down you know they're uncomfortable" (García 185).

Pilar, on the other hand, deals with questions of acculturation and assimilation as a Hispanic in the United States. Ideologically she represents the generation of Cuban children who were taken off the island due to their parents' fear of communism. While Cuban American children generally are raised to despise Castro and the communist regime, there were some from this generation who opted to see Cuba and its people for themselves. This includes those who went to Cuba with the Maceo brigades in the 1970s and 1980s. As adults some Cuban-born scholars, writers, and artists continue to engage in dialogue with and travel to Cuba in spite of the embargo. Some have been victimized by this choice. Quite outside the ironclad anti-Cuba position of the Republican Miami enclave, Cuban Americans who support the normalization of U.S.-Cuba relations (while Castro is still in power) are seen as outsiders by the politically well-organized Dade County hegemony.[9] Therefore, *Dreaming in Cuban*'s unique contribution lies in its opening up the ideological, literary, and political forum to reflect the complexity and diversity of perspectives articulated by three generations of Cubans in the United States. Significantly, women are the harbingers of this historically important discussion.

For me, it is difficult to give an "outsider's" reading of this novel. The novel appeals strongly to the "insider" cultural complicity it evokes from me. Simultaneously, it makes me feel uneasy, wondering how, say, Felicia's "craziness"—which is tightly associated with Santería—might be perceived by readers totally unfamiliar with the tradition. The representation of a play offers the playwright or director a measure of control over the created image on stage; a novel leaves the reader free to create his or her own mental images regardless of authorial intent.

Felicia's mental instability is partially explained by her syphilitic condition, with which she was infected by her philandering husband, who is black. Felicia can be described as a liminal character. She lives on the periphery of normalcy, psychologically and socially. Although this action takes place after the revolution, she does what white women usually don't do: she marries "down." Her father's rejection of such a union bespeaks an antagonistic attitude toward the marriage. Celia, her mother, detests the "hocus pocus" of Santería, and goes so far as to desecrate the images on Felicia's altar. Therefore, while Felicia's life unfolds in post-revolutionary Cuba, the judgment of her actions by her family is heavily coded with the prejudices of a pre-revolutionary, racist bourgeoisie. Felicia's open embrace of Afro-Cuban culture is specifically coded as an interracial act. In *Botánica*, we do not know if the characters are white, black, or mulatto. The same holds true for *Brazo*.

During Felicia's serious and extreme psychological states she turns to Herminia to take her to La Madrina (Santería "godmother"). However, Felicia's problems are not definitively solved through Santería; they are solved through her own death. The text suggests that while Felicia is within the accepted protection of her black Santería family, she is fine. However, when she finishes her initiation and returns to her own home, she finds her children and her mother unaccepting. It is this final rejection that she attempts to overcome, to no avail. Felicia is a culturally and racially liminal character: a white woman living as a member of a traditional Afro-Cuban religious sect. Her death suggests that she does not fit into either world, and subsequently her problems can only be resolved by death.

Felicia has an exceptional emotional range not commonly attributed to female characters of popular novels: she is victim as well as victimizer. She allows herself to be victimized (by her renegade and abusive husband). She victimizes others by being violent and cruel (she sets fire to her abusive husband); she can be spiteful (she burns Graciela Moreira's hair on purpose); she frees herself forcefully of an undesired element in her life by taking the opportunity when she sees it (by pushing her other husband off the roller coaster). As an archetype, this character exhibits a full psychological range; Felicia is not "nice." She is not bound by restrictive social conventions; she is a "wildish woman," however unsuccessful she may be at living "happily ever after" (Pinkola Estés 3–22).

While Felicia is one of the strongest fictional characters depicted in Latino literature currently, she may not be representative of post-revolutionary Cuban racial politics. Felicia is the construction of an American-educated imagination. The values and consequences of her choices are the values of U.S. literary conventions and not necessarily those of post-revolutionary Cuban perspectives. It is feasible to imagine Felicia as a Cuban fictional character, in Cuba, with options other than death to resolve her cultural and racial cross-over.

Pilar, who grows up in New York with the supernatural, hears her grandmother's voice within her. It is this that helps her counteract her mother Lourdes's rabid hatred of Castro and, by association, Castro's Cuba. Pilar's positioning of herself with the supernatural is the creation of an alliance with the Cuban, specifically the Afro-Cuban Santería: "I enter a botánica on upper Park Avenue. I've passed the place before but I've never gone inside. Today, it seems, there's nowhere else for me to go" (García 199). Because of Pilar's choice of a necklace of red and white beads, the elderly attendant recognizes Pilar as a daughter of Changó.

To Pilar, her necessary visit to Cuba resolves the lifelong questioning which many of us who were brought to the United States early in our lives go through: Would it not have been better to stay in Cuba and grow up with a strong cultural identity rather than grow up in another country, confused about one's place within its society? Pilar's answer is a self-defining clarification: "I'm afraid to lose all this, to lose Abuela Celia again. But sooner or later I'd have to return to New York. I know now it's where I belong—not *instead* of here, but *more* than here" (216). Pilar resolves her identity questions, her loyalties, and her sense of place in the world, in parallel with her reaffirmation of her own "supernatural" powers related to Santería. She belongs "more" in New York than in Cuba, yet what she recognizes as most Cuban in her—her strong bond with her grandmother, her own connection with Santería—diffuses the possibility of complete cultural assimilation. Pilar works out her identity in the battleground of her mother's anti-revolutionary politics and her grandmother's fervid pro-revolutionary stance.

Subsequently, the importance of Cristina García's novel is its masterful and honest portrayal of the dilemma that has marked the lives of three generations for thirty-four years. Politically and intellectually it is extremely timely for those who argue in favor of a sustained dialogue with Cuban intellectuals. García's novel and Caridad Svich's play address "Cubanness" as a trans-revolutionary issue. That is, it transcends, yet takes into account, the politics of geography. As in *Botánica* and *Brazo gitano/Gypsy's Arm*, women continue to be portrayed as the key historical agents of change who play important roles in the articulation of urgent socio-cultural concerns.

Last Thoughts

Foregrounding the role of Santería in contemporary U.S. Cuban literature punctuates the continuing role that this African religious tradition has played in the development of a Cuban cultural identity. It is a historical and cultural dynamic that offers a relatively unexplored avenue in the field of Latino ethnic studies. It implies that similar strategies of cultural retention may be taking place within some U.S. Latino Caribbean groups.[10]

In part the image of Santería as a mysterious, "exotic," and powerful African tradition served the enslaved as an instrument of cultural survival. In Cuban postcolonial society, politicians and intellectuals have used Africanity for a number of political purposes throughout Cuba's history. Its current rearticulation by U.S. Cuban writers is not surprising, if their work is taken as part of a uniquely Cuban tradition which precedes immigration into the United States. As such, I believe, it forms part of a thrust towards a mediated and selective cultural retention. It signals a growing ethnic awareness by Cuban Americans to navigate through the lure of total "Americanization," the alienating impulse to perceive Self as an exotic Other.

These works suggest moving beyond the hitherto prevalent notions of exile, loss, and nostalgia, which are emotionally bound with vengeance and reactionary politics. And while gender is not dealt with as an issue independent of cultural identity, it is nevertheless Cuban American women writers who are voicing the issues. White writers continue to serve as brokers of historically black culture. But perhaps this model is one constructed by my segregated, American consciousness. Perhaps in post-revolutionary Cuba, where the black and white lines are not so distinct, this framework may not apply.

Notes

1. It is the Capilla de San Lázaro (Chapel of Saint Lazarus) in La Habana during the late 1950s, and all the amulets symbolize promises made by sick people who successfully entrusted themselves or their loved ones to the saint's care. Later, I learned the saint's Afro-Cuban Lucumí name, Babalú-Ayé patron of illnesses, and his particular influence over the pantheon of beliefs which permeate all Cuban life and culture, inside and outside the Island (Castellanos and Castellanos 57–59).
2. The reader will see "Changó" also spelled Shango and Xangó. The first is the Spanish, the second the English, and the third the Portuguese version of the same *orisha*. (The "c"/"s" switch also occurs with *orisha/oricha*.)
3. Other important *reglas* or socio-religious systems are: the *reglas congas* (from the former Congo), of which among the most important are the Regla de Palo Monte of Mayombé and the Regla Kimbisa del Santo Cristo del Buen Viaje (which will also play an important role, as we will later see); and the Sociedad Secreta de Abakuá, which is a *regla carabalí*, whose origins may be traced back to the Efik and Ekoi peoples of the Calabar region (Castellanos and Castellanos 11–17).
4. Antonio Planells quite capably traces the debate on defining magical realism in "El realismo mágico ante la crítica," *Chasqui, revista de literatura latinoamericana* XVII, 1 (May, 1988): 9–23.
5. Some of the writers mentioned by Noble are: Juan Francisco Manzano (1797–1854), a slave whose sonnet "Mis treinta años" (My Thirty Years) inspired white critics and writers of the *tertulia* led by critic Domingo Del Monte to purchase his freedom for 850 pesos (Noble 15–16); Felipe Pichardo Moya (1892–1957), a mulatto poet whose *Canto de isla* (1942) is considered a precursor to the *negrista* movement (83); Gabriel de la Concepción Valdés (1809–44), a mulatto who under the pseudonym of Plácido wrote romantic poetry; and Regino Pedroso (1896–?), a mestizo of working-class Chinese and African parents who wrote extensively about the subject of social justice and anti-imperialism between 1919 and 1955 (113).
6. According to Ortiz, the circulating anthropological term of the time, *acculturation,* was inadequate because it informed a process in a partial manner. Acculturation depicts the acquisition of a new culture by an outsider who is required to shed the culture of origin. The host culture is privileged through this perception; it is complete, static, and predatory, waiting to absorb all foreign matter.
7. Theories of cognitive mapping offer basic referents here. For instance, one of the components of being able to solve spatial geographic problems concerns one's

ability to imagine the location of a place and how to get there. *Absolute coordinates* or *state descriptions* (like longitude, latitude, street names, etc.) help locate places. In the absence of absolute coordinates or state descriptions—and sometimes in conjunction with them—*relative* or *process descriptions* are thought to be always possible, particularly when absolute descriptions are unavailable: directions given by someone who knows the terrain can usually help us "get there from here" (Downs and Stea 46).

8. This number is an approximation based upon my year of work as coordinator of Recovering the U.S. Hispanic Literary Heritage Project at Arte Público Press during 1992.

9. Estela Bravo's 1992 documentary entitled *Miami/Havana*, although histrionic at times, offers a glimpse of some key figures in the debate. She films a pro-Cuba (anti-embargo) march in Miami and interviews pro-Cuba personalities such as José Cruz, president of the Cuban-American Coalition, and Francisco Aruca, director of Radio Progreso in Miami and host of the highly controversial talk show "Ayer en Miami." Bravo also interviews Mas Canosa, the Republican founder of the Cuban American Foundation, a powerful and well-financed group that favors the continuation of the embargo.

10. *Self-Representation in Chicana and Latino Theater and Performance Art*, unpublished doctoral dissertation, University of California, Irvine, 1992.

Works Cited

Bascom, William. *Shango in the New World*. Austin: University of Texas, Afro and Afro-American Research Institute, 1972.

Bastide, Roger. *The African Religions of Brazil, Towards a Sociology of the Interpretation of Civilizations*. Translated by Helen Sebba. Baltimore and London: Johns Hopkins University Press, 1978.

Bush, Barbara. *Slave Women in Caribbean Society 1650–1838*. Bloomington: Indiana University Press; Kingston: Heinemann Publishers; and London: James Currey Publisher, 1990.

Brene, José R. *Teatro*. La Habana: Ediciones Unión Contemporáneos, 1965.

Bricker, Victoria Reifler. *Ritual Humor in Highland Chiapas*. Austin: University of Texas Press, 1973.

Cabrera, Lydia. *La sociedad secreta Abakuá*. Miami: Editorial C.R., 1969.

———. *El monte*. Miami: Editores Universal, 1975.

Carpentier, Alejo. *La música en Cuba*. La Habana, 1946.

Carril, Pepe. "Shangó de Ima." In *Totem Voices, Plays from the Black Repertory*, edited by Paul Carter Harrison. New York: Grove Press, 1989. Premiered in Cuba, 1969.

Castellanos, Isabel, and Jorge Castellanos. *Cultura afrocubana vol. 3, Las religiones y las lenguas*. Miami: Ediciones Universal, 1992.

Clifford, James. "On Ethnographic Surrealism." In *The Predicament of Culture*. Cambridge, Mass., and London: Harvard University Press, 1988.

Cros-Sandoval, Mercedes. *La religión afrocubana*. Madrid: Playor, 1975.

Cuervo Hewitt, Julia. "Ifa: Oráculo Yoruba y Lucumí." *Cuban Studies/Estudios Cubanos* 13, 1 (Winter 1983).

Cuervo Hewitt, Julia, and William Luis. "Santos y santería: conversación con Arcadio, santero de Guanabacoa." *Afro-Hispanic Review* 6, no. 1 (January 1987).

Downs, Roger M., and David Stea. *Maps in Minds, Reflections on Cognitive Mapping*. New York, Hagerstown, San Francisco, London: Harper & Row, 1977.

Flores, Juan, and George Yúdice. "Living Borders/Buscando América," *Social Text* 24: 57–84.

Freedberg, David. *The Power of Images*. Chicago and London: University of Chicago Press, 1989.

Gallardo, Jorge Emilio, and Fernando García Cambeiro. *Presencia africana en la cultura de América Latina, vigencia de los cultos afroamericanos*. Buenos Aires: Colección Estudios Latinoamericanos, 1986.

García, Cristina. *Dreaming in Cuban*. New York: Alfred A. Knopf, 1992.

González Echeverría, Roberto. "Socrates Among the Weeds: Blacks and History in Carpentier's *Explosion in the Cathedral*." *Massachusetts Review*, Autumn 1983.

Herzberg, Julia. "Wilfredo Lam." *Latin American Art Magazine*, Summer 1990.

Lima, Roberto. "The Orisha Changó and Other African Deities in Cuban Drama." *Latin American Theater Review*, Spring 1990.

Montejo, Esteban. *The Autobiography of a Runaway Slave*. Edited by Miguel Barnet. New York: Pantheon Books, 1968.

Morales, Ed. "Muzzled in Miami." *American Theater Magazine*, May/June 1993.

Murphy, Joseph. *Santería, An African Religion in America*. Boston: Beacon Press, 1988.

Nadeau, Maurice. *The History of Surrealism*. New York: Macmillan, 1965.

Noble, Enrique. *Literatura afro-hispanoamericana, poesía y prosa de ficción*. Lexington, Mass., and Toronto: Xerox College Press, 1975.

Ortiz, Fernando. *Hampa afro-cubana, los negros brujos*. Madrid: Editorial América, 1917.

———. *Contrapunteo cubano del tabaco y del azúcar*. La Habana, 1940.

Pérez Firmat, Gustavo. *Literature and Liminality*. Durham: Duke University Press, 1986.

———. *The Cuban Condition*. Cambridge: Cambridge University Press, 1989.

Pinkola Estés, Clarissa. *Women Who Run with the Wolves*. New York: Ballantine Books, 1992.

Planells, Antonio. "El realismo mágico ante la crítica." *Chasqui* v. xviii, no. 1 (May 1988).

Prida, Dolores. *Beautiful Señoritas and Other Plays*. Houston: Arte Público Press, 1991.

Said, Edward. *Orientalism*. New York: Pantheon Books, 1978.

———. *Joseph Conrad and the Fiction of Autobiography*. Chicago: University of Chicago Press, 1985.

Simard, Rodney. *Postmodern Drama, Contemporary Playwrights in America and Britain*. New York and London: University Press of America, 1984.

Soyinka, Wole. *Myth, Literature and the African World*. Cambridge: Cambridge University Press, 1976.

Svich, Caridad. *Brazo gitano*. Unpublished playscript, 1990.

Taussig, Michael. *Shamanism and the Wild Man, a Study in Terror and Healing.* Chicago and London: University of Chicago Press, 1987.

Verger, Pierre Fatundi. *Orixás. Deuses Iorubás na Afríca e no Novo Mundo.* Salvador, Brasil: Editora Corrupio Comércio Ltda., and Círculo do Livro S.A., 1981.

Whitten Jr., Norman E., and Arlene Torres. "Blackness in the Americas." *Report on the Americas, The Black Americas 1492–1992.* NACLA v. xxv, no. 4 (February 1992).

Silvia Spitta

Transculturation, the Caribbean, and the Cuban-American Imaginary

Edmundo Desnoes once observed that the Caribbean had, since 1492, existed only in terms of a single Manichean political, economic, and discursive opposition which was repeated ad nauseam. This opposition, paradise/hell, noble savages/cannibals, has persisted to this day, but now it reads: friendly natives/hostile guerrillas. The West, therefore, has consumed or repressed the Caribbean depending on whether it was perceived as useful or as dangerous.[1] Given the limitations placed on any discourse on the Caribbean, it is not surprising that Cuban-Americans, when writing either about a homeland from which they have been exiled to the United States, or about their assumed identity as Cuban-Americans, either inadvertently reproduce the tropicalization of the Caribbean in/from the U.S. or parodically engage the very terms with which the West has delimited and limited the Caribbean.[2] That is, they self-tropicalize themselves *ad absurdum* and thereby attempt to deconstruct stereotypical constructions of the Cuban-American.

My aim here is to analyze what happens to the theory of transculturation when it is appropriated by Cuban-American critics to write both about Cuba and about the newly emerging Cuban-American ethnicity. The route is circuitous within the insularity of the Caribbean: from Fernando Ortiz's early formulations in the 1940s, transculturation is today being redefined from the perspective of U.S. Cuban-American critics such as Gustavo Pérez Firmat and Antonio Benítez Rojo, who read Cuba as a nostalgic "there" and see it through the eyes/I's of a "here" that is only now being accepted as residence and no longer as utopia (i.e., no place) of exile.[3] As a specifically Cuban response to North American theories of the melting pot, Ortiz's theory of transculturation emphasizes the two-way cultural interchanges that take place in any situation where different cultures come into contact with one another. Cuban-American critics are, on the one hand, returning to Ortiz yet re-inscribing transculturation with precisely those very connotations of as-similation that the theory was meant to combat; on the other hand, they take transculturation further in terms of creating a theory of the bicultural U.S. minority subject.

This essay will therefore be divided into three sections that reflect the three moments the theory of transculturation is undergoing in its move north: the first will consist of an analysis of transculturation as a *specifically* Cuban theory; the second will examine how Cuban-American critics imagine Cuba— particularly how they write about transculturation—from "here"; and the last section will deal with how these critics construct a Cuban-American culture and identity as a U.S. "ethnicity."

Transculturation: A Cuban Theory

Coined by the Cuban anthropologist Fernando Ortiz, the term "transculturation" was a specifically Latin American reading, or a culturally motivated misreading, of the ideological metatext of the term "acculturation" which was coming into vogue among North American anthropologists in the 1940s.[4] Whereas the theorists of acculturation had envisioned it as the process of interaction and mutual influence between cultures, Ortiz understood it from a Latin American perspective as the theory of the one-way imposition of the culture of the colonizers.[5] He created the neologism "transculturation" to undermine the homogenizing impact implicit in the term "acculturation," which in his view obfuscated the true dynamics at work in colonial situations. Instead, Ortiz insisted on understanding inter-cultural dynamics as a two-way *toma y daca* (give and take).[6]

Ortiz defined transculturation in Cuba as a three-fold process: the partial loss of culture by each immigrant group, the concomitant assimilation of elements from other cultures (European, African, Asian), and finally, the creation of a new, "Cuban," culture.[7] Since foreign influences always were and are invariably present, the "new" culture is never achieved: it is forever deferred and forever in the making. The "new" could be said to refer to the distance that mediates between an African in Africa and a Cuban of African-European-Asian descent. It is therefore an explanation of *difference from* the originary cultures rather than a descriptive term. As Ortiz explains, employing the biological terms so prevalent at the time: "la criatura siempre tiene algo de ambos progenitores, pero también siempre es distinta de cada uno de los dos" [the child always inherits something from both parents, but is also always different from each one of them].[8]

Ortiz's *Contrapunteo cubano del tabaco y del azúcar* [*Cuban Counterpoint; Tobacco and Sugar*, trans. Harriet de Onis, 1947] situates the discussion of transculturation within the social and economic dynamics that arise out of the production of tobacco and sugar in Cuba. Tobacco: indigenous, dark, and gendered male by Ortiz, is a labor-intensive crop traditionally grown on small farms along the banks of rivers and usually tended by one family. Sugar: imported, white, and gendered female, is a product grown on immense *latifundios* (plantations) and requiring large amounts of labor at peak times. Sugar, an exogenous product, a white product—literally and figuratively—was the reason why African slaves were imported to Cuba and why African culture became preponderant in Cuba.[9] The two crops, according to Ortiz, give rise to two very different types of social and economic conditions on the island: tobacco is grown on a small scale, usually by one family, using few or no machines, and requires continual, year-round care. The production of sugar, on the other hand, is highly centralized, mechanized, and depersonalized. Tobacco is one of the few vestiges of the original island culture, whereas sugar is imported and stands for foreignness; it is the "agricultural equivalent of empire".[10] The tension or counterpoint between them gives rise to and at the same time characterizes Cuban culture.[11] At a more general level, the history of each product is also the history of transculturation: sugar, a white import, has changed the landscape of Cuba while tobacco, a native Cuban crop, has changed the leisure habits of the rest of the world. Together with alcohol (rum), sugar and tobacco form the holy trinity of Cuban exports of pleasure and indulgence (Ortiz, *Contrapunteo* 88).

It is no accident that Ortiz used the term "counterpoint" as a synonym for transculturation, since he was interested in showing that African and European elements stand in an equal relation in the shaping of "Cuba." Since the term counterpoint "comes from the Latin *contrapunctus*, properly *punctus contra punctum*, meaning 'note against note' or, by extension, 'melody against melody,'" it was a fitting symbol for the process Ortiz wanted to underline.[12] The reason critics follow Ortiz in using music as a referent for the intercultural dynamics of/in Latin America is perhaps due to the fact that the processes of transculturation are most clearly evident and most easily pinpointed in music. Furthermore, the *difference between* cultures is often most readily seen in the different ways different cultures shape bodies and their rhythm.

The use of "counterpoint," however appropriate it is to Ortiz's overall project, becomes problematic when understood from the perspective of the musicologist, given that counterpoint pertains to western polyphonic music, particularly the compositions of Palestrina and Bach. It therefore sounds odd when Ortiz writes of polyrhythmic Afro-Cuban music in terms of counterpoint. As with his gendered metaphors—which assume the sexes are equal—so, too, Ortiz's use of "counterpoint" implies the equality of the musical notes or melodies that through their tension fuse into a musical composition. Ortiz's use of the term can be justified only if it is understood that he transculturated it to refer to the subtextual tension of any musical composition and cultural configuration in Cuba. For, as Stuart Hall points out,

Africa, the signified which could not be represented directly in slavery, remained and remains the unspoken, unspeakable "presence" in Caribbean culture. It is "hiding" behind every verbal inflection, every narrative twist of Caribbean cultural life. It is the secret code with which every Western text was "re-read." It is the ground-bass of every rhythm and bodily movement. *This* was—is—the "Africa" that "is alive and well in the Diaspora."[13]

The "counterpoint" then does not actually allude to the "note against note" structure of contrapuntal musical compositions, but rather to an African subtext and rhythm in a more general contrapuntal relationship to all of western music and culture. In the end, it is this expanded, transculturated notion of "counterpoint" that operates in Ortiz's texts.

Likewise, Ortiz's deployment of gendered metaphors is problematic since, in his appeal to the family and to relations between the sexes as the model for transculturation, he assumes that the mother/women and the father/men are equal. Women and men may be considered equal yet physiologically different, but they are never equal when it comes to power—particularly in a colonial context based on the violence of one race over another and one gender over the other. Modern Latin America is not—as Ortiz assumes—the product of a happy marriage of differences. It stems, as the myth of La Malinche shows, from the rape of the native woman by the Spaniard. "Culture" is therefore implicitly gendered as *male*, even though theorists such as Ortiz mobilize gendered metaphors to describe its components.

Although Ortiz proposed that his theory could explain any encounter between two cultures,[14] therefore making claims for its universal validity, we need to understand it as a specifically *Cuban* theory. In fact, Cuba, and the Antilles more generally, are a special phenomenon within Latin America not only because of their insularity but also because there the indigenous populations were completely wiped out in the early years of the Conquest. Their populations consist almost exclusively of immigrants: Europeans, African slaves, Asians, and North Americans.[15] This is a significant point that needs to be stressed, because even though the term "transculturation" can be useful in describing the dynamics of cultural contact very generally, it has to be continually redefined for specific contexts.[16] The Andean nations,[17] for example, where the population still is mainly Indian, provide a context very different from that of Cuba, as do marginalized cultures in the United States today, such as those of African-Americans, Native Americans, Latinos, and Asian-Americans.

Cuban Blues: Cuba and Ortiz Viewed from "Here"

The need to contextualize the theory of transculturation has acquired renewed urgency today, when so many Cuban-American critics are writing about transculturation from a U.S. perspective and adopting Ortiz's term to denote a very different cultural transfer. Critics Gustavo Pérez Firmat and Antonio Benítez Rojo both take Ortiz as their point of departure and source of inspiration to write about Cuban, Caribbean, and Cuban-American literature. In the process of transplanting Ortiz's theory to the United States, however, as Cuban-Americans they begin to theorize Cuba and the Caribbean from the hyphen that both connects the Cuban to the "American" and separates the Cuban from the "American."[18] As a result, "transculturation" as theorized by Ortiz, José María Arguedas, and Angel Rama is replaced by terms such as "translation" and "chaos" respectively.

Gustavo Pérez Firmat's *The Cuban Condition: Translation and Identity in Modern Cuban Literature* (1989) and Antonio Benítez Rojo's *La isla que se repite. El Caribe y la perspectiva posmoderna* (*The Repeating Island: The Caribbean and the Postmodern Perspective*, 1992) both displace transculturation from the Caribbean to the United States.[19] The works, though very different in nature, are similar in their theorization of a "Cuban"—and in the case of Benítez Rojo a "Caribbean"—literature and in their use of Ortiz's theory of transculturation. As the title suggests, *The Cuban Condition: Translation and Identity in Modern Cuban Literature* is the elucidation of what Pérez Firmat calls the "translational rather than foundational" nature of Cuban literature and culture—particularly that of the criollist/creole writers of the 1940s (Pérez Firmat, *The Cuban Condition* 8). *La isla que se repite*, dedicated to Fernando Ortiz, Benítez Rojo's "distant master," is in turn an attempt to postulate the overarching *identity* of the whole Caribbean using Cuba—or what Benítez Rojo, following Ortiz's discussion of sugar plantations, calls the "Plantation machine"—as paradigm.

For Pérez Firmat, transculturation is translation. The reason critics often resort to the term translation as a synonym for transculturation is that it lends itself better to use as a verb: "to translate" is less awkward than "to transculturate." Translation also etymologically implies the carrying over, dis-placing, and transferring of meaning from one language into another and is therefore particularly appropriate in referring to geographical, linguistic dis-placements. As Pérez Firmat writes: "translation [is] displacement. The intralingual translator is someone who knows that in order to pick his words, he has to keep his distance" (5).

In *The Cuban Condition*, translation figures as a positive, creative endeavor. It is the process whereby Cubans take the language of the colonizer—

Spanish—and infuse it with African and Asian elements, creating "cubanismos," or a vernacular "Cuban" different from peninsular Spanish. As Pérez Firmat suggests, Cuban writers such as Nicolás Guillén, Fernando Ortiz, Carlos Loveira, and Alejo Carpentier write in the vernacular. In doing so, they use language to stake out their distance from the mother tongue and the motherland ("la Madre Patria") and thus inscribe "Cuban Spanish" as a national language. They do the same at the literary level: while they gain their inspiration from Spanish literature, they re-create it, or, what amounts to the same thing, they creatively translate and dis-place it into what becomes "Cuban literature." The most visible example of this process is Nicolás Guillén, who is known for his radical use of the vernacular in poetry. The titles of some of his poems (e.g., "Sensemayá") and of his seminal collection of Afro-Cuban poems, *Sóngoro cosongo,* signal this move. As Pérez Firmat points out, however, Guillén also uses "learned" forms such as the sonnet and the madrigal and transculturates them into mulatto madrigals and mestizo sonnets (68). In the poem "El abuelo" he addresses a woman in true courtly fashion: "¡Ah, mi señora!" and follows the European tradition dictated by classical rhethoric of directing the male gaze from the woman's head downward to her torso. But Guillén "blackens" the content of the poem by referring to the woman's African blood—embodied in her long-gone African grandfather—that underlies her European appearance (71). In this sense her grandfather, "el que te rizó por siempre tu cabeza amarilla" [the one who put the curls in your golden head] is the grandfather of most Cubans.

For Pérez Firmat then, translation—both linguistic and literary—is always *intralingual* (from Spanish to Cuban and from the Spanish literary tradition to a Cuban literary tradition). It is never passive or literal but rather creative. To avoid too great a closeness to the source, a collapsing of the "copy" with the "original," the translator must deviate from the original "in perceptible ways" (5). It is in this sense that Pérez Firmat affirms that Cuban culture is characterized by a "translation sensibility"—and, skirting a discussion of loaded terms such as "original," "copy," and "intertextuality," he concludes that Cuban literature is translational rather than foundational (4).

I insist on haggling over terminology because the choice of "translation" over "transculturation" is problematic, given the negative associations the term "translation" invariably elicits. As Willis Barnstone recently wrote in his *The Poetics of Translation: History, Theory, Practice* (1993), in which he tries to valorize and redeem translation as a creative endeavor, "the shame of translation is real, alas, universal, even though superficial and absurd, more real and more traumatic than Harold Bloom's related 'anxiety of influence' (a similar dialogical battle between authors in a tradition)."[20] Not only is translation a negatively loaded term, but within the parameters Pérez Firmat establishes in *The Cuban Condition,* Spanish literature implicitly functions as "foundational" and "non-translational" whereas Cuban literature is derivative. As Willis Barnstone points out, all literatures are translational, and to argue that one text is a translation whereas another is an "original" is to "obey a feudal principle of originality" (Barnstone, *The Poetics of Translation* 13). Furthermore, given that questions of authenticity, originality, derivativeness, and imitation-as-degeneration are all issues that have plagued Latin American literary and artistic histories, I think it is in our interest—as Latin American critics—to keep Ortiz's "transculturation" as the two-way, multi-level cultural interchanges, borrowings, displacements, and re-creations characteristic of both Latin American *and* European literatures, languages, and cultures.

Although Pérez Firmat insists that Cuban literature is receptively creative, his privileging of the term "translation" over "transculturation" is unfortunate also because translation, like language, has served as the handmaiden of empire. Translations of the Bible into Quechua were used to evangelize the Indians in the Andean nations, and priests learned Quechua to gather information that was used in the attempt to eradicate the native religion more effectively. Moreover, translations of European literary texts in Latin America served to acculturate the literate elite to a European tradition. For the monocultural and monolingual reader, translation tends to reduce the "Other" to the familiar and effaces the text's difference, moving it into the territory of the reader.[21] When understood in these terms, translation loses its implied innocence and pretensions of equality, since the dis-placement and the transfer of meanings has then to be situated within an uneven, unequal, and ultimately exploitative and violent context. Moreover, in claiming an always-epigonic position for the Cuban writer—the "translational" rather than "foundational" status of Cuban literature—Pérez Firmat's argument undoes Ortiz's claim that culture contact is never uni-directional. "Transculturation" is a term we should keep, since it describes the dynamics of the colony *from* the space and the perspective of the colonized.

Antonio Benítez Rojo, in *La isla que se repite: El Caribe y la perspectiva posmoderna*, expands the margins of the discussion. Using Cuba as paradigm, he attempts to delimit "the Caribbean" as an entity with a singular identity. Even though colonized by different powers (Spain, Holland, Britain, France, Portugal) and therefore not only culturally but also linguistically divided, the Caribbean, he argues, is nevertheless a meta-archipelago of sorts, not only because it functions as a way-station between North and South, but also because it shares an African inheritance and the socioeconomic structures of the Plantation (sugar plantations) everywhere. Again using Ortiz as point of departure, Benítez Rojo argues that even though the Plantation serves as common denominator, regional differences have to be attributed to the different rates of institutionalization of the Plantation in the Caribbean. Thus Spain, for example, due to its slower rate of industrialization in relation to the rest of Europe, did not institute a system of sugar plantations in Cuba until well into the eighteenth century. African slaves and freed Africans were better integrated into Cuban society and therefore were an active presence in the Africanization of Cuba. In contrast, in British colonies such as Barbados and Jamaica, where the Plantation was instituted very early on, the islands were far less Africanized even though, paradoxically, the majority of the population (over 90 percent) were African slaves. On these islands the slaves were isolated on the plantations, and since the islands served the sole purpose of exporting sugar, they were organized accordingly. Cities in their own right such as La Habana did not come into being until recently.[22]

Benítez Rojo derives the impetus for his study from a postmodern reading of—or a search for the postmodern elements in—Ortiz's *Contrapunteo*. He argues that not only does Ortiz's counterpoint between tobacco and sugar refer to these products but that, in fact, it also sets in motion a much larger metaphorical field: between myth and history, blacks and whites, slaves and plantation owners, art and machines, small rural landholdings with labor-intensive crops and huge plantations, quality and quantity, national and foreign capital, independence and dependence, sovereignty and intervention, desire and repression, the discourse of power and that of resistance, the revolutionary and the reactionary (Benítez Rojo, *La isla que se repite* 178). In the end, however, for Benítez Rojo, Ortiz's whole scheme can be reduced to the counterpoint between "las fábulas de legitimación propias de los Pueblos del Mar y de Occidente" [the fables of legitimation set forth respectively by the Peoples of the Sea (the Caribbean) and by the West], that is, to the coexistence and interplay between modern and premodern elements in the Caribbean.[23] And it is this counterpoint that in turn takes precedence throughout *La isla que se repite* and is used to affirm the identity of the Caribbean. The institutionalization of sugar plantations—what Benítez Rojo calls the Plantation machine—is the single most important economic factor in the shaping of the Caribbean. Benítez Rojo transforms the counterpoint between tobacco and sugar into the counterpoint between the west's and modernity's master narratives and discourses of scientific legitimation on the one hand and the praxis of premodern orality and immanence in Cuba on the other.[24] The dichotomy between the modern and the primitive, the cooked and the raw, the west and the rest, is reelaborated within a postmodern context—not of binary oppositions but of counterpoints—where fragmentation, instability, lack, noise, and chaos are emphasized over totality, synthesis, acculturation, and miscegenation (xxxv).

For Benítez Rojo, however, the counterpoint between modernity's narratives of legitimation and those of premodern, oral cultures ultimately revolves around two different conceptions and functions of *rhythm*. For the West, rhythm has become the one-two, one-two of imperialism, militarism, and scientific knowledge (xxxiii). For premodern, oral cultures such as those that persist in Cuba, rhythm is carnivalesque, polyrhythmic (and resistant to notation), intimately tied to a religion/cosmology that pervades every aspect of life that endows the Word with the effectiveness and power it possesses in oral cultures. It is this typically Caribbean *rhythm* that for Benítez Rojo creates a regional unity across the diversity of languages, cultures, races, histories, and economies prevailing in the area. Under the impact of that rhythm, the imperialism of rock or big-band music, for example, is transformed into the mambo, the cha-cha-cha, the bossa nova, the bolero, salsa, reggae. That is, "la música del Caribe no se hizo anglosajona sino que ésta se hizo caribeña dentro de un juego de diferencias" [Caribbean music did not become Anglo-Saxon but rather the latter became Caribbean within a play of differences] (Benítez Rojo, *The Repeating Island* 21). To avoid the pitfalls of binary oppositions, Benítez Rojo always insists on the "play of differences" or the counterpoint—in Ortiz's terms—between elements that are usually seen as opposed. Therefore, if something as elusive as rhythm can be seen as an underlying common thread that could be used to affirm a Caribbean identity—albeit tenuously—it nevertheless operates in a field that is always in danger of being torn asunder by its cultural and linguistic differences. For Benítez Rojo, it is the tension between one and the other, between centripetal and centrifugal forces, between modernity and premodernity, which could be said to define the Caribbean—and at the same time to create the undefinability of the Caribbean embodied in a rhythm that defies notation and ultimately eludes his own attempt to define it.

For Benítez Rojo, there is neither synthesis nor syncretism, only an ill-defined "supersyncretism." It is a supersyncretism created by a process whereby

el significante de *allá*—el del Otro—es consumido (leído) conforme a códigos locales, ya preexistentes; esto es, códigos de *acá*. Por eso podemos convenir en la conocida frase de que la China no se hizo budista sino que el budismo se hizo chino. En el caso del Caribe, es fácil ver que lo que llamamos cultura tradicional se refiere a un *interplay* de significantes supersincréticos cuyos "centros" principales se localizan en la Europa preindustrial, en el subsuelo aborígen, en las regiones subsaharianas de Africa y en ciertas zonas insulares y costeras de Asia meridional. (Benítez Rojo, *La isla que se repite* xxxiv)

the signifier of *there*—of the Other—is consumed ("read") according to local codes that are already in existence; that is, codes from *here*. Therefore we can agree on the well-known phrase that China did not become Buddhist but rather Buddhism became Chinese. In the case of the Caribbean, it is easy to see that what we call traditional culture refers to an interplay of supersyncretic signifiers whose principal "centers" are localized in preindustrial Europe, in the sub-Saharan regions of Africa, and in certain island and coastal zones of southern Asia. (Benítez Rojo, *The Repeating Island* 21)

The "supersyncretism" mentioned above refers to all the extraterritorial, cultural significations embodied in one Cuban symbol or sign. Thus, for example, la Virgen de la Caridad del Cobre, patroness of Cuba (Benítez Rojo's privileged example), has her origin in three cultures: European (as Virgin of Illescas, a Spanish virgin with Byzantine origins), native American (containing elements of the *taino* deity Atabey or Atabex), and African (deriving from Ochún, a Yoruba deity).[25] Yet only someone with a vast knowledge of the flow of intercultural influences would know this. For the vast majority of people she is a *Cuban* virgin. But here the term "Cuban" erases the long trajectory of intercultural signification embodied in the virgin.

What we see taking place in Benítez Rojo's argument is the inversion of what took place in most Latin American nations during and after independence and in the era of nationalism. Then, words such as "Cuban," "Chilean," etc., reduced nationality to one factor: creole consciousness and desire. They tended to exclude the disenfranchised majority from that definition. Here, we see the opposite move at work: that is, the term "Cuban" is being opened up to all its different roots and possible significations. It becomes an inclusive term—a term that breaks down national boundaries and situates "the native" in the exogenous and vice versa. It is in this context that we have to understand Benítez Rojo's statement that the term la Virgen del Cobre, "Virgen cubana," is an impoverishing term because it erases all the different elements that constituted her. It is in this sense too that "the Caribbean" as a region unified by a common Plantation machine and an underlying rhythm is also and at the same time a region of differences, discontinuities, and unstable identities.

Benítez Rojo's analysis, with its emphasis on chaos, discontinuities, fragmentation, counterpoint, and diversity, can be understood as a postmodern reading of Ortiz and the Caribbean. Benítez Rojo, however, is adamant in disclaiming any continuity with postmodernism because it has excluded Latin American/Caribbean forms of knowledge and therefore has to be seen as embodying specifically North American and European sensibilities. For Benítez Rojo, there is a postmodernism implicit in Ortiz and in all Caribbean ways of life that is very different from, and unrelated to, Eurocentric theories of postmodernism.[26] He writes:

me interesa el *Contrapunteo* porque pienso que es uno de los libros más consecuentes con las dinámicas de lo caribeño que se han escrito alguna vez—lo cual hago extensivo a Ortiz y al resto de su des-ordenada obra—, y también, sobre todo, porque provee el método para conducir una lectura del Caribe que resulta diferente a las de la modernidad y posmodernidad, al fin y al cabo perspectivas estrictas de Occidente, lecturas estrictas de Occidente. (Benítez Rojo, *La isla que se repite* 158)

I am interested in the *Contrapunteo* because I think that it's one of the most revealing books ever written about the dynamics of the Caribbean—a judgement that I extend to Ortiz himself and the rest of his (dis)ordered work—and also, especially, because it offers a method by which one can conduct a reading of the Caribbean that has an outcome different from any that might have been done from the perspectives either of modernity or of postmodernity, which are, finally, strictly Western perspectives and Western readings. (Benítez Rojo, *The Repeating Island* 156–57)

In other words, he discovers in the Caribbean a postmodernism *avant la lettre*. It should be pointed out, however, that even if Benítez Rojo distances himself from a Eurocentric postmodernism and implicitly posits the concept "transculturation-as-counterpoint" as a Latin American alternative to postmodernism, he nevertheless cannot quite stake out his terrain without having his discourse taken over by postmodern elements. This is not only his problem, but the problem that all Latin American critics confront today. For, if "postmodern" elements can be traced in Latin American literature and culture all the way to the colony, one has to ask: what is "postmodernism" when studied in a Latin American context? Is it something that has always been there—and in every other culture, including North America and Europe—and that we are only now identifying because postmodernism itself provides us with the language to see and name these processes? Or does postmodernism have nothing to do with Latin America and an uneasy and equivocal overlapping takes place? Or—and this is the option I favor—is postmodernism yet another unacknowledged western cannibalization of the "Third World"? And if I insist on the third option, where does that leave Benítez Rojo's argument, indebted as it is to postmodernism, and coming as it does from a very specifically Cuban context *in* the United States?

It is not my intent here to attempt a resolution of the issue of postmodernism in/of Latin America, but it is a problem that needs to be discussed in connection with the question of transculturation and popular culture. That is, many of the processes of transculturation also entail negotiations very similar to those seen in popular culture and its precarious balance—and tension—between some sort of integrity, ethnic resistance, creative reception, and passive consumption. If, to take an example discussed above, the Virgen de la Caridad del Cobre, patroness of Cuba, is a Virgin who has her origins in—at least— three very different cultures and systems of signification, and if, nevertheless, she is assumed to be "Cuban," she is still and always will be, in Benítez Rojo's words, an "uneasy composite of differences." That is, anyone with an interest in the matter will be able to detect in the color of her skin or in her attributes the different cultures and elements from which she derives. Since a label such as "Cuban" tends to stress unity over diversity, it becomes the trace of a long history of erasure of the different—particularly African—roots of Cuban culture. The term "Cuban" therefore becomes the privileged sign espoused by hegemonic centripetal forces afraid of dissolution and intent on maintaining a grip on the definition of the nation and the national.

Finally, we need to consider the significance of the fact that Ortiz's theory has been bypassed for over forty years and, aside from certain Latin American exceptions,[27] is only now being mobilized by Cuban literary critics residing in the United States. For, even if Pérez Firmat and Benítez Rojo start out from Ortiz, they nevertheless dis-place transculturation into translation or chaos. Africa, even though written in as trace or desire, nevertheless remains absent as signifier and diaspora. With his choice of "chaos" and privileging of rhythm, Benítez Rojo constructs an ever-vanishing Caribbean, a nostalgic mirage of everything that the United States is not and can never be for a Cuban academic living here, now.[28] For, to quote Stuart Hall

Who can ever forget, when once seen rising up out of that blue-green Caribbean, those islands of enchantment. Who has not known, at this moment, the surge of an overwhelming nostalgia for lost origins, for "times past"? And yet, this "return to the beginning" is like the imaginary in Lacan—it can neither be fulfilled nor requited, and hence is the beginning of the symbolic, of representation, the infinitely renewable source of desire, memory, myth, search, discovery.[29]

With migration to the United States, the Caribbean is lost for the enunciating "I" of *La isla que se repite*. It is reconstructed as an ever-vanishing and elusive entity, forever the object of yearning and desire, forever the repository of all that is experienced as absent and lacking in the "here" of the enunciation. This brings us to the deeply ambivalent yet unproblematized and assumed "here" of *La isla*. Where is the "here" for a displaced Cuban in the United States? To complicate the issue even further, and to use Benítez Rojo's own words, is the Caribbean of chaos and rhythm, the "Other" that is "there," being read with the codes of an ambivalently experienced "here"?

For Pérez Firmat the ambivalence of the "here" of the enunciation is manifested in the desire to trace a continuity of "hyphenated thinking" between himself and Ortiz. He situates Ortiz as an "ethnic" writer and argues that the *trans* in Ortiz's "transculturation" is first and foremost the *trans* of the transitory nature of Cuban identity. "Mr. Cuba [Ortiz] also thinks in hyphens," Pérez Firmat asserts.[30] In a very general sense this is true of every one of us. Nonetheless, to think in hyphens for a Cuban and to think in hyphens for a Cuban-American are two different things. For Pérez Firmat, to think in hyphens means to claim descent from Ortiz *as well as* from Desi Arnaz, that is, to situate himself in a here/there that informs his interpretation of Cuba, and is informed by a reaction to a certain North American stereotyping or tropicalization of Latino men that limits and delimits the possibility of Latino self-definition and self-representation in this country.

Transculturation in/from the United States

What divides Ortiz's theorization of transculturation and contemporary re-workings of the term like those of Benítez Rojo and Pérez Firmat is, then, not only the distance of forty or more years, but also the gap that separates an anthropologist situated in Cuba and literary critics situated in the United States who begin to theorize from the hyphen that both separates the Cuban from the "American" and links the Cuban to the "American." The attempt to theorize transculturation from the United States has today become an attempt to expand the borders of the national to include the Cuban *in* the United States—as in Pérez Firmat's most recent study of the latinization (read Cubanization)[31] of U.S. culture and literary tradition[32]—or to expand the margins of the Caribbean as in Benítez Rojo's studies—to include cities as far north as New Orleans and as far south as Montevideo.[33] Despite their differences, these two critics share the realization that borders are conventions subject to change. Both also argue that the Caribbean has come to the United States, that this country is increasingly becoming tropicalized, and that, as Gloria Estefan sings, "The rhythm is going to get you."

Since the "here" of the enunciating Cuban-American is always split between the desire to acculturate "here" and the nostalgia for a Caribbean "there," which is experienced as a lost paradise and conflated with a lost paradisiacal childhood, the "I/eye" of the Cuban-American is also split. Identity, which was defined hand in hand with a sense of belonging, a sense of place, and a tie to the land that "I" cultivate, can no longer be assumed.[34] "I" am no longer defined and contained by the place where I live. In fact, for bilingual, bicultural subjects, the "here" of my enunciation often carries within it a "there" from which I have been displaced. As we could say in a post-Freudian sense: I am where I am not. Or, as Pérez Firmat so aptly put it in his poem "Díptico de la Identidad," "SOY YOS,"[35] which he translates in an essay on Cuban-American literature as "In sum: we are two."[36]

The space of the hyphen, the doubleness of being, is the space of contradictions. As Gloria Anzaldúa would say, Latinos speak with a forked tongue; or as Pérez Firmat writes, the Cuban-American man, being bilingual, is a "cunning lingual."[37] Likewise, in Cuban-American poetry two mutually exclusive positions are espoused simultaneously: the longing for "home" and the realization that there is no going home. Responding to Heberto Padilla's poem "Postcard to USA," which asks how Cuban-Americans can continue living with two languages, two houses, two nostalgias, Pérez Firmat writes in "Carolina Cuban":

> Y yo te respondo, Heberto, talmúdicamente:
> ¿cómo no seguir viviendo con dos
> lenguas casas nostalgias tentaciones melancolías?

Porque no puedo amputarme una lengua
ni tumbar una casa
ni enterrar una melancolía.
Quisiera, al contrario,
singularizar lo indivisiblemente dividido,
hacer de dos grandes ojos una sola mirada.[38]

And I answer you, Heberto, talmudically:
How not to continue living with two
languages houses nostalgias temptations melancholies?
Because I cannot amputate one tongue
nor destroy one house
nor bury one melancholy.
I would like, on the contrary,
to singularize what is indivisibly divided,
to make of two big eyes one single look.

The doubleness of the Cuban-American is lived both as nostalgia for whole-ness, closure, singularity *and* the celebration of doubleness, multiplicity, and homelessness. In "Bilingual Blues" Pérez Firmat writes: "Soy un ajiaco de contradicciones" [I am a melting pot of contradictions]. By adopting Ortiz's transculturation of the concept of the melting pot into the Cuban *ajiaco* or stew, Pérez Firmat makes contradiction tasty, the space and spice of the Cuban-American.[39]

At the academic level, the space of contradiction from which critics such as Pérez Firmat and Benítez Rojo write informs their discourse in "hyphenated" ways. For Benítez Rojo, the challenge is to think the Caribbean in three differ-ent—impossible—ways at once: a premodern, modern, and postmodern space; a space both inside and outside the United States; a space that can be concep-tualized even as it resists conceptualization.[40] That is, he attempts to conjugate the Caribbean as a verb in three tenses simultaneously. As I showed above, he has called that conjugation "chaos"; his stance is theoretically rigorous yet chaotically playful. For Pérez Firmat, "hyphenated" academic thinking has be-come the attempt to tropicalize academic discourse in three different ways: first, by exceeding academia with poetry and fiction; second, by carnivalizing the position of the critic and critical discourse, particularly with respect to Cuban-American literature and culture (see the difference in "levels" of his writings in *The Cuban Condition* and his most recent writings on the Cuban-American imaginary *Life on the Hyphen*); and third, by embodying the worst stereotypes that the U.S. mainstream and Anglo academics have of Latino men in his roles as poet, writer, and character in his own poems and fiction. That is, he represents and/or performs himself as the "tropicalized Other" in the U.S. imaginary even as he argues for the increasing tropicalization, latinization, and

musical transculturation of this country. And "self-tropicalization" is never innocent or naive. It is a double mimicry, a parody of mainstream tropicalizations of the Caribbean.

The most clear example of this "self-tropicalization" can be found in the
narrative stance Pérez Firmat adopts in the story "My Life as a Redneck." The
chair of the department is a Cuban man, a Pisces whose birthday is March 2,
"like Desi Arnaz."[41] Tired of his wife, who, like all Cuban women, is a
"mother," he leaves her for the department secretary, "the *Americanita* of [his]
dreams" (Pérez Firmat, "Redneck" 225). The scenario, then, is stereotypical:
Cuban man meets his Lucy: "In my eyes Catherine and I became the protagonists of the great Cuban-American love story, a Lucy and Ricky for the
nineties" (226, 228). As Pérez Firmat never tires of repeating in one way or another, and as he writes in "My Life as a Redneck," the best fate that can befall
a (Cuban-American) man is to marry an American paradigm (read Anglo
woman),[42] that is, to repeat the Ur-story at the basis of Cuban-American culture and to marry Lucy.[43] The price the Cuban man pays for marrying Lucy is
Lucy[ing] his name: the actor Desiderio Arnaz becomes Desi and as a character he becomes "Ricky" Ricardo. The diminutive of his name serves as a
marker for his "Hispanic" ethnicity.[44] At the same time as he points this out,
however, Pérez Firmat overlooks the fact that the "y" in Lucy, in turn, serves as
marker of *her* gender.

"My Life as a Redneck" becomes even more oppressively stereotypical
when the chair characterizes himself as a typical Latin lover: "I stashed con-
doms in the tenure files," "her ass became my barometer"; and manifests the
symptoms of infatuation: "My pants bulged. My pecs grew. I began to strut"
(226, 228). If the role of Latin lover is ridiculed, the flip side of that role—that
of the misogynist macho—is also taken to an extreme when the chair's women
colleagues tell him that they feel uncomfortable with the goings-on in the
office. He relates the episode as follows:

When some of my fallow feminist colleagues complained that they felt uncomfortable
around the Department, I quit the chairmanship. Fucking and feminism make uneasy
bedfellows, and I have to admit that my plan to hold a beauty pageant and pick Miss
Literary Theory of 1990 may have been a bit too much. The throne might have gone va-
cant anyway. My legacy to the Department was a three-year subscription to *GQ*. (232)

The chair of the department becomes the embodiment of the worst fears and
stereotypes many Anglo-American feminists have of Latino men.

The strategy in "My Life as a Redneck" is to perform U.S. tropicalizations
and thereby show the reader how constraining mainstream constructions of the
internal other actually are. In this story, and in Pérez Firmat's critical writings,
Cuban-American identity is informed both by the tension between "here" and

"there" and by the constant confrontation with devastating stereotypes. The parameters of the possible and the "real" that the story establishes are completely limited and delimited by U.S. tropicalizations of Latino men. The story merely stages these and shows how Latino men have no other "out" than to carnivalize the whole situation, that is, to take mainstream tropicalizations to their extreme and hence reflect back to the mainstream the poverty of their naming. The Cuban-American subject then "is" not; he exists only as negativity and becomes a masquerade of himself. The chair ends the story thus: he lives his life *as* a redneck, that is, in Cedar Key—"redneck Riviera"—and he passes: "But since I don't look particularly Cuban and since Catherine looks especially American, I felt anonymous rather than out of place. It was wonderful. We were happy that night, Catherine and I, a spic and his paradigm dancing the night away" (234). Elsewhere Pérez Firmat writes "I am myself a somewhat odd coupling of North and South, of Carolina and Caribbean, spic and hick in equal parts."[45]

How does transculturation function in this context? On the one hand, culture contact becomes the redirection of Cuban male desire away from Cuban wife/mothers and onto Anglo women/Lucys—that is, assimilation. Writing about a Nuyorican musical group's song "Bailando pegaito," Pérez Firmat asserts that the Latino band has "transculturated [and] ghettoized" the Irving Berlin standard "Cheek to Cheek." In the Latino version, "a Puerto Rican kid from the *barrio* tries to get a sophisticated anglo girl to dance." However, there is a double move here: on the one hand the ghettoization of a popular American song; on the other, the attempt of a Puerto Rican kid to move out of the barrio by seducing an Anglo girl. By writing only about music and the musical/rhythmical transculturation taking place in the United States today and not about the minority status and disenfranchisement of the Latino community, Pérez Firmat overlooks that double move and the fact that if the border is the space of a cheek to cheek it is also a war zone. The tension between claiming the latinization of the United States (the rhythm is going to get you) while arguing, at the same time, for the transmutation of Cuban exiles into Cuban-Americans (or 1.5's, as he later calls his own, transitional, generation in *Life on the Hyphen*) is never resolved. And in a sense this contradiction cannot ever be resolved because it is what characterizes the move of culture in general. Centripetal and centrifugal forces create a field of tension that allows for both the latinization of a culture and the assimilation of Latinos into that culture. "We tend to act as if identity were a fixed given and needfully forget that it is not an essence but a 'production' which is never complete, always in process, and always constituted within, not outside, representation."[46] Hence the vertiginous—alienated and alienating—play of tropicalization and self-tropicalization is the play that signals the impossibility of living life both other than as nos/otros (us/others) and other than *as*.[47]

Beyond that—and more importantly—what we are seeing is the development of two distinct yet at times overlapping modes of conceptualizing the border. The first is oppositional, explosive, politically engaged (i.e., the border is a war zone where dancing the mambo together will not erase the racism, xenophobia, and ethnocentrism of our time);[48] the second corresponds to the internationalization of the border (i.e., it attempts to systematize the consciousness of displacement) where, as Guillermo Gómez-Peña writes, any encounter between people of different cultures constitutes a "border experience."[49]

Notes

All translations are mine unless otherwise stated.

1. Edmundo Desnoes, "El caribe: paraíso/infierno," *Literatures in Transition: The Many Voices of the Caribbean Area*, ed. Rose S. Minc (Gaithersburg: Ediciones Hispamérica, 1982).
2. Carolina Hospital points out that many Cubans born in the U.S. nevertheless have grown up with a consciousness of exile. Cf. Carolina Hospital, "Los hijos del exilio cubano y su literatura," in *Explicación de textos literarios*, 15, 2.
3. Cf. Gustavo Pérez Firmat, "Transcending Exile: Cuban-American Literature Today," Paper published as Dialogue #92 by The Latin American and Caribbean Center, Florida International University, December 1987.
4. "Acculturation" was first defined systematically by Redfield, Linton, and Kerskovits in the 1930s. They defined it as follows: "Acculturation comprehends those phenomena which result when groups of individuals having different cultures come into continuous first-hand contact with subsequent changes in the original cultural patterns of either or both groups . . . Under this definition acculturation is to be distinguished from culture-change, of which it is but one aspect, and assimilation, which is at times a phase of acculturation." Cf. *International Dictionary of Regional European Ethnology and Folklore* (Copenhagen: Rosenkilde and Bagger, 1960) 19, 236.
5. Ortiz's critique of the term is corroborated when the editors of the *International Dictionary* write that "acculturation," even if used by Herskovits to mean the process of mutual modification and adaptation of cultures that come into contact with one another, actually ends up by being used in the more narrow sense of "assimilation" of the dominated group into the culture of the dominant. In the *Dictionary*'s definition of "transculturation" Ortiz is mentioned, and Malinowski, who in the preface to *Contrapunteo cubano* enthusiastically endorsed Ortiz's use of the term, is criticized for not having made use of the concept in his own publications. Even a general Spanish dictionary definition shows that Ortiz had reason to be

suspicious of the term. "Acculturation" is defined as: "s. civilización, instrucción, educación, transmisión de cultura [civilization, instruction, education, transmission of culture]." Emilio M. Martínez Amador, *Standard English-Spanish and Spanish-English Dictionary* (Barcelona: Editorial Sopena, 1958).

6. Bronislaw Malinowski's enthusiastic endorsement of the term "transculturation" and critique of "acculturation," in his introduction to Ortiz's *Contrapunteo*, reads as follows: "Aparte de su ingrata fonética (suena como si arrancara de un hipo combinado con un regüeldo), la voz *acculturation* contiene todo un conjunto de determinadas e inconvenientes implicaciones etimológicas. Es un vocablo etnocéntrico con una significación moral. El inmigrante tiene que 'aculturarse' (*to acculturate*); así han de hacer también los indígenas, paganos e infieles, bárbaros o salvajes, que gozan del 'beneficio' de estar sometidos a nuestra Gran Cultura Occidental" [Aside from its harsh phonetics (it sounds as if it started off from a hiccup combined with a belch), the term "acculturation" implies a whole set of specific and inconvenient etymological implications. It is an ethnocentric word with a moral signification. The immigrant has to "acculturate"; as well as the natives, the pagans and infidels, the barbarians and savages, that enjoy the "privilege" of being subjected to our Great Western Culture]. Bronislaw Malinowski, "Introduction," in Fernando Ortiz, *Contrapunteo cubano del tabaco y el azúcar* (La Habana: J. Montero, 1940) xii. Cf. also Fernando Ortiz, *Cuban Counterpoint; Tobacco and Sugar*, Trans. Harriet de Onis (New York: A. A. Knopf, 1947).

7. Ortiz's definition of transculturation reads as follows: "Entendemos que el vocablo *transculturación* expresa mejor las diferentes fases del proceso transitivo de una cultura a otra, porque éste no consiste solamente en adquirir una cultura, que es lo que en rigor indica la voz anglo-americana *aculturación,* sino que el proceso implica también necesariamente la pérdida o desarraigo de una cultura precedente, lo que pudiera decirse una parcial desculturación, y, además, significa la consiguiente creación de nuevos fenómenos culturales que pudieran denominarse *neoculturación.*" We understand the term *transculturation* to better express the different stages in the process of transition between one culture and another, because this process does not consist exclusively in acquiring a culture—which is what the Anglo-American term *acculturation* really means—the process also necessarily implies the loss or uprooting of an originary culture, which could be termed a partial deculturation as well as the consequent creation of new cultural phenomena which could be described in terms of a *neoculturation.* Cf. Fernando Ortiz, *Contrapunteo cubano.*

8. Ortiz, *Contrapunteo cubano*, 103.

9. For an interesting historical study of the transculturation of agricultural products, see *Seeds of Change: A Quincentennial Commemoration*, ed. Herman J. Viola and Carolyn Margolis (Washington, D.C.: Smithsonian Institution Press, 1991).

10. I thank Lois Parkinson Zamora for bringing this book to my attention. Cf. Gustavo Pérez Firmat, *The Cuban Condition. Translation and Identity in Modern Cuban Literature* (Cambridge: Cambridge University Press, 1989) 56.

11. Ortiz's use of the term "counterpoint" is a resemantization of a European musical term usually used to refer to Bach's compositions and transplanted to Cuba to refer to Cuba's Afro-latin rhythms.

12. Willi Apel and Ralph T. Daniel, *The Harvard Brief Dictionary of Music* (New York: Pocket Books, 1960) 72.

13. Stuart Hall, "Cultural Identity and Diaspora," *Identity, Community, Culture, Difference,* ed. J. Rutherford (London: Lawrence and Wishart, 1990) 222–37, 236.

14. Ortiz himself emphasized the African over the Asian in his studies of Cuba. As far as I know, the Asian elements in Cuban culture have not yet been studied.

15. Likewise, Françoise Lionnet, who uses the term "métissage" in much the same way as Ortiz uses transculturation, bases her definition on the history of the island of Mauritius which was uninhabited and settled by successive waves of immigrants. She writes: "This is why a word like *métis* or *mestizo* is most useful: it derives etymologically from the Latin *mixtus*, 'mixed,' and its primary meaning refers to cloth made of two different fibers, usually cotton for the warp and flax for the woof: it is a neutral term." I disagree with her here, finding that in most cultures today racial mixture is viewed ambivalently, to say the least. For Latin America, however, *mestizaje* or miscegenation, often used synonymously with transculturation and/or translation, carries precisely those sexual connotations absent in the latter terms and yet crucial to explain the dynamics of cultural and sexual "encounters." However, I still opt for "transculturation" since mestizaje, regardless of Lionnet's claims, carries with it negative connotations—particularly of the suppressed rape of Indian women by Spanish colonizers at the base of Latin American culture.

16. I develop this point further in my book *Between Two Waters: Narratives of Transculturation in Latin America* (Houston: Rice University Press, 1996).

17. Cf. the works of José María Arguedas, *Formación de una cultura nacional indoamericana,* ed. Angel Rama (México: Siglo veintiuno, 1975) and *Señores e indios: Acerca de la cultura quechua,* ed. Angel Rama (Buenos Aires: Arca Editorial, 1976); and Angel Rama, *Transculturación narrativa en América Latina* (México: Siglo Veintiuno [1982] 1985).

18. The "theory of the hyphen" stems from Mexican-American studies. Juan Bruce-Novoa, one of the first to use and develop the term, argues that the Chicano literary space is neither Mexican nor American, but the hyphen *between* Mexican-American. Chicano literature stems from "the intercultural nothing of that space"; it is constantly pushing and expanding that space apart while creating its own reality *and* at the same time creating strong bonds of "interlocking tension that hold the two in relationship." Cf. Juan Bruce-Novoa, "The space of Chicano Literature," *De Colores* 1, 4 (1975): 22–42, 27.

19. Antonio Benítez Rojo, La isla que se repite. El Caribe y la perspectiva posmoderna (Hanover: Ediciones del Norte, 1989). All translations stem from James Maraniss's translation The Repeating Island: The Caribbean and the Postmodern Perspective (Durham: Duke University Press, 1992).

20. Willis Barnstone, *The Poetics of Translation: History, Theory, Practice* (New Haven: Yale University Press, 1993) 9.

21. Cf. Susana Jakfalvi-Leiva, *Traducción, escritura y violencia colonizadora: un estudio de la obra del inca Garcilaso* (Syracuse: Maxwell School of Citizenship and Public Affairs, 1984).

22. Antonio Benítez Rojo, *La isla que se repite. El Caribe y la perspectiva posmoderna* (Hanover: Ediciones del Norte, 1989) 39–65.

23. Benítez Rojo, *La isla que se repite* 171, 184. This same counterpoint is at work in Ortiz's text where African beliefs appear next to and alongside western ones and are given an equal explanatory power and validity as scientific ones. It is for this reason that Ortiz's work has been so easily dismissed by modern anthropologists and critics who see it as unorthodox and unscientific. Ortiz himself situated his work as always unfinished, always in process, just like a fugue that could go on endlessly and lead nowhere, and where the lines of the counterpoint keep changing with the changing times.

24. "la práctica narrativa de los Pueblos del Mar es muy distinta a la del relato de legit-imación de Occidente, pues en ésta el problema de la legitimidad es el referente de un dilatado proceso de indagación, verificación y comentario, mientras que en aquélla el relato provee su propia legitimidad de manera instantánea, al ser emitido en presente por la voz rítmica del narrador, cuya competencia reside sólo en el hecho de haber escuchado el mito o la fábula de boca de alguien." *La isla que se repite* 175, xxiii.

25. For a complete tracing of her origins see Benítez Rojo, *La isla que se repite* xviii.

26. Jean Franco's very timely proviso also addresses this issue: namely, that the post-modern is a European and North American phenomenon and that while much Latin American fiction may appear postmodern to the foreigner, it has a very different genesis: "Hybrid genres," she writes, "have always abounded in Latin America. Thus, both 'national allegory' and postmodern [*sic*] imply an impoverishment for they overlook an entire culture history in which essay, chronicle, and historical document have been grafted onto novels, a history of rereadings and rewritings which give rise to voluminous compendia . . . that defy categorization . . . Such texts may seem 'postmodern' because of a sum of characteristics—pastiche, nos-talgia, and the like—and because they reflect the dissolution of any universal sys-tem of meaning or master discourse." However, postmodernism "cannot ade-quately describe those texts that use pastiche and citation not simply as style but as correlatives of the continent's uneasy and unfinished relationship to modernity." Cf. Jean Franco, "The Nation as Imagined Community," *The New Historicism*, ed. H. Aram Veeser (New York: Routledge, 1989) 204–12, 210–11.

27. Arguedas, Rama.

28. This critique is indebted to a discussion I had with Alberto Sandoval after hearing a talk delivered by Benítez-Rojo (Dartmouth College, Hanover, May 1992).

29. Stuart Hall, "Cultural Identity and Diaspora," *Identity, Community, Culture, Differ-ence,* ed. J. Rutherford (London: Lawrence and Wishart, 1990) 222–37, 236.

30. Gustavo Pérez Firmat, "From Ajiaco to Tropical Soup: Fernando Ortiz and the Definition of Cuban Culture," Dialogue #93, Published by the Latin American and Caribbean Center, Florida International University, Miami, 1987, p. 13.

31. Gustavo Pérez Firmat, "Life on the Hyphen," lecture delivered at Pomona College, November 1992.

32. Gustavo Pérez Firmat, "Introduction: Cheek to Cheek" in *Do the Americas Have a Common Literature?* ed. Pérez Firmat (Durham: Duke University Press, 1990).

33. Antonio Benítez-Rojo, Dartmouth lecture.

34. Cf. Néstor García Canclini, "Escenas sin territorio: Estética de las migraciones e identidades en transición" (*Revista de crítica cultural* 1, 1): 9–14.

35. Gustavo Pérez Firmat, *Equivocaciones* (Spain: Editorial Betania, 1989) 31.
36. Gustavo Pérez Firmat, "Transcending Exile: Cuban-American Literature Today" *Occasional Paper Series Dialogues* (Florida International University: Latin American and Caribbean Center, December 1987) 12.
37. Gustavo Pérez Firmat, "Transcending Exile: Cuban-American Literature Today," in Dialogue #92, The Latin American and Caribbean Center, Florida International University, 1987, p. 10.
38. *Triple Crown: Chicano, Puerto Rican, and Cuban-American Poetry* (Arizona: Bilingual Review Press, 1987) 159.
39. *Triple Crown: Chicano, Puerto Rican, and Cuban-American Poetry* (Arizona: Bilingual Review Press, 1987)164.
40. Antonio Benítez-Rojo, "La literatura caribeña y la teoría del caos," in *Latin American Literary Review* XX, 40 (July–December, 1992): 16–18.
41. Gustavo Pérez Firmat, "My Life as a Redneck," in *Iguana Dreams: New Latino Fiction*, ed. Delia Poey and Virgil Suárez (New York: Harper, 1992) 224.
42. See "My Life as a Redneck," in *Iguana Dreams: New Latino Fiction*, ed. Delia Poey and Virgil Suárez (New York: Harper, 1992).
43. Gustavo Pérez Firmat, "Life on the Hyphen," lecture delivered at Pomona College, November 1992.
44. Gustavo Pérez Firmat, "Life on the Hyphen," lecture delivered at Pomona College, November 1992.
45. Gustavo Pérez Firmat, "Spic Chic: Spanglish as Equipment for Living," in *Caribbean Review* XV, 3 (Winter 1987): 20–22 and 36–37.
46. Stuart Hall, "Cultural Identity and Diaspora," in *Colonial Discourse and Post-Colonial Theory: A Reader*, ed. Patrick Williams and Laura Chrisman (New York: Columbia University Presss, 1994) pp. 392–403.
47. See my *Between Two Waters: Narratives of Transculturation in Latin America* (Houston: Rice University Press, 1996), 213.
48. Cf. Guillermo Gómez-Peña, "From Art-Maggedon to Gringo-Stroika," in *High Performance* 55 (Fall 1991): 20–27.
49. Guillermo Gómez-Peña, "An Open Letter to the National Arts Community," in *High Performance* 47 (Fall 1989): 18–28.

IV

**Si(gh)ting *Latinidad*:
Tropicalized Cultural Locations**

Juan Flores

The Latino Imaginary: Dimensions of Community and Identity

Hispanics? Latinos?
What do we call them? What do they want to be called?
What do they call themselves?
What do they call us? What do we want to be called?
What do we call ourselves?

What difference does it make? We all know who we're talking about. You know, Spanish people.

You mean from Spain?

No, you know, Spanish-speaking people.

You mean they don't speak English?

Yeah, they do, some of them anyway, but, you know, they have Spanish names, they're from Spanish families.

So they *are* from Spain.

No, they're Mexicans, Puerto Ricans, Cubans, you know, like that.

So people in Mexico, Puerto Rico, Cuba, and other Latin American countries are Hispanics or Latinos?

No, I mean here, in the United States.

Ah, so that's what we're talking about: people from Latin America, or of Latin American background, living in the United States.

Right, just what I said!

Where I come from, in New Mexico, nobody uses Latino, most people never even heard the term. We're Mexicanos, Chicanos, Mexican-Americans, Raza, even Hispanic, but never Latino. Anyone who comes around talking about Latino this and Latino that is obviously an outsider, and is most likely trying to push something.

Hispanic? For me, a Hispanic is basically a sell-out, *un vendido*. Anyone who calls himself Hispanic, or refers to our community as Hispanic, just wants to be an American and forget about our roots.

183

Bits of conversation like these point up the range of contention over the choice of words to name a people, a culture, a community. Behind the war of words, of course, there lurks the real battle, which has to do with attitudes, interpretations, and positions. In the dismissive indifference of many Americans there is often that undertone of annoyance which, when probed a little further, only turns out to be a shield against other, submerged emotions like ignorance and fear. The gaps among Latinos or Hispanics themselves can be as polarized as they appear here, with one usage thoroughly discrediting the other. But usually the options are more flexible, operational, and mediated by a whole span of qualifying terms, tones, and situations. And over against those who use the words at all, there are many Mexican-Americans, Puerto Ricans, Colombians, Cubans, and Dominicans, who have no use for any such catch-all phrases and would rather stick to distinct national designations.[1]

Yet this disparity over nomenclature, sharp as it is in the case of Latinos, should not be mistaken for a total lack of consensus or collective identity, nor as proof that any identification of the group or "community" is no more than a label imposed from outside, and above. Regardless of what anyone chooses to name it, the Latino or Hispanic community exists because for this whole stretch of history, and multiplying geometrically the closer we approach the present, people have moved from Latin America to the United States. Along with their increase in numbers there has also been an intensification of their impact, real and potential, on the doings and, yes, the destiny of this country.

It is becoming clear that any discussion of the "American community" must be inclusive of Latinos and cognizant of the existence of a "Latino community" intrinsic to any historical discourse about U.S. culture. The real challenge, though, is that the Latino presence makes it necessary to recognize that the very meaning of the word, the concept "community" itself, is relative according to the perspective or position of the group in question: there is both a "Latino community" and a "community" in the Latino sense of the word.

"Comunidad," "común"-"unidad": the Spanish word, even more clearly than the English, calls to mind two of the key terms in the conceptualization of this notoriously elusive idea. What do we have in "common," and what "unites" us, what are our commonalities and what makes for our unity? It is important to note that though the two terms point in the same direction they are not synonymous, and their apparent coupling in the same word, "comunidad," is not a redundancy. For while "común" refers to sharing those aspects in the cultures of the various constitutive groups that overlap, the sense of "unidad" is that which binds the groups above and beyond the diverse particular commonalities. The point I am making with this rather willful deconstruction is, once again, that the Latino "experience," the group's demonstrable reality and existence, includes but is not co-terminous with its self-consciousness: "común" stands for the community *in* itself, while "unidad" refers to the community *for* itself, the way that it thinks, conceives of, imagines itself.

The "Latino community" is an "imagined community"—to summon Benedict Anderson's well-worn though useful phrase—a quintessential present-day example of a social group etched and composed out of a larger, impinging geopolitical landscape.[2] The role of the social imagination and the imaginary in the self-conception of nationally, ethnically, and "racially" kindred groups is of course central, but must always be assessed with a view toward how they are *being* imagined, from the "outside," and to what ends and outcomes. Distinguishing between interior and exterior perspectives is thus a necessary step, and given that in the case of Latinos the outside representation is the dominant one, any instance of cultural expression by Latinos themselves may serve as a healthy corrective to the ceaseless barrage of stereotypes that go to define what is "Latino" in the public mind.

But the marking off of "us" and "them," though the foundational exercise in "imagining" communities, has its own limits, as it becomes evident that there is as much blurring involved as clear and meaningful bounding. Vexing questions like who is Latino and who is not, and what kind of Latinos/as we are talking about, quickly press in on any too facile dichotomy. Beyond the issue of names and labels, and even who is using them, there are differing levels or modes of meaning simultaneously at work in the very act of apprehending and conceptualizing the "community" in question. "Latino" or "Hispanic" not only mean different things to different people; they also "mean" in different ways and refer to different dimensions of collective social experience.

I would suggest that by distinguishing between a *demographic,* an *analytical,* and an *imaginary* approach to Latino unity and diversity it is possible effectively to complicate and deepen our understanding of cultural expression, identity, and politics without becoming paralyzed by the sheer complexity and contradictoriness of it all. Whether Latinos or Hispanics are thought of as a numbered aggregate of people, an analytically differentiated set of constituent groups, or a historically imagined cultural "community" is at the core of ongoing debates and confusions.[3] Not that these diverse approaches are mutually exclusive, or that they are to be considered in any mechanically sequential or hierarchical way. On the contrary, as I seek to describe them it will be obvious that all three are equally necessary, and that they are complementary; they are really different emphases rather than discrete forms of explanation. But scrutinizing them in hypothetical isolation not only helps understand their interrelation, but may also enhance our analysis and appreciation of the images and voices of Latino art.[4]

. . .

The demographic conception of Latinos, or of a "Latino community," refers to an aggregate of people whose existence is established on the basis of numerical presence: count them, therefore they exist. Here Latinos—or, more commonly at this level, Hispanics—comprise not so much a community as a "population," a quantifiable slice of the social whole. Shallow though such a means of identification may seem, it is nevertheless the dominant one, serving as it does both government bureaucracies and corporate researchers in setting public taste and policy. This definition of the Hispanic community by official measurement is of course inherently instrumental, since the immediate goal is really to identify, not so much social groups or lines of cultural diversity, but voting blocs and consumer markets. From this perspective, Latinos appear as a homogeneous, passive mass, a "target" public, with any concern for internal differentiation or possible social agency itself geared toward those same incremental goals of electoral or commercial utility.[5]

But it is not only campaign managers and ad writers for whom Latinos are, first of all, numbers. The labels and tallies they arrive at for their convenience—be it Hispanic or Latino, at whatever percentile—are made visible, credible, "real," by means of a whole sensorium of images, sounds, and smells. The demographic label thus aims not only to "buy" the Hispanic package but to "sell" it; it "targets" not only potential customers but merchandise, or even movers of merchandise. Whatever the particular purpose, though, the means and result are the same—stereotypes: distorted, usually offensive, and in any case artificial, portrayals of Latino people.[6] And these are the only images of Latinos that most people in the United States, and around the world, are ever exposed to, which makes it difficult to test their accuracy. It is important to recognize them as products not just of opportunist politicians or greedy salesmen but of the demographic mentality itself. Numbers call forth labels, which in turn engender stereotypes. According to the same logic, holding economic and political power relies on the work of both the census-taker and the cameraman.

. . .

The process of adding up is accompanied by the need to break down, to identify not the sum total but the constituent parts. The analytical approach—the business, above all, of social scientists—is bent on de-aggregation; it presumes to move closer to Latino "reality" by recognizing and tabulating the evident diversity of Latino groups and experiences. Such varying factors as country of origin, time in the United States (generation), region or place of settlement, occupation, sex, and race move into focus as the only meaningful units or angles of analysis with any cohesion among Latinos referred to only in the plural: typically, there are only Latino "populations," groups, or at best "communities."

This analytical account of Latino multiplicity is indeed often helpful in counteracting stereotypes and monolithic categories, but it is still close kin to the demographic approach. Even the census evidences an increasing official need to break the composite down, with "Hispanics" now grouped into Mexican, Puerto Rican, Cuban-origin, Central and South American origin, and "Other Hispanic." (It would be interesting to determine how many in the latter category, which numbers more than any but the first two, are Dominicans, and why they don't yet warrant their own label.) Commercially geared demographics are even further along in their analytical enterprise, having persuasively charted both a "pan-Hispanic" as well as regionally differentiated Los Angeles, Miami, and New York–centered markets.

To this extent, and in most social scientific "studies," the pluralizing "analysis" of Latino reality is still dealing with a community "in itself," constructed in terms of relatively inert categories with their appropriate labels and stereotypical representations.

Yet Latinos are not just passive objects in this analyzing process, and do not tend to sidestep the task of "telling Hispanics apart." Consciously and intuitively, personally and collectively, Puerto Ricans, Mexicans, Cubans, Dominicans, and each of the other groups project their own respective national backgrounds as a first and primary line of identity and on that basis, fully mindful of differences, distances, and particularities, negotiate their relation to some more embracing "Latino" or "Hispanic" composite. Here the force of analysis, rather than an extension of demographic aggregation and labeling, stands in direct opposition to it, an instinctive reaction against instrumental measuring and its pernicious consequences. Of course there are interests involved here too, but in this case they are the interests of the "object" of analysis itself, the Latino peoples and communities.

From a Latino perspective, analysis is guided above all by lived experience and historical memory, factors which tend to be relegated by the dominant approach as either inaccessible or inconsequential. Rather than as slices or cross-sections, the various groups and their association are seen in dynamic, relational terms, with traditions and continuities weighing off subtly against changes and re-configurations. Differences are drawn among and within the groups not so as to divide or categorize for the sake of more efficient manipulation, but to ensure that social identities, actions, and alliances are adequately grounded in the specific historical experiences and cultural practices that people recognize as their own.

. . .

It is this critical, historically based analysis of diverse and changing Latino realities that underlies and sustains the Latino "imaginary," as I call it, another notion of pan-group aggregation that is too often and too easily confused with the official, demographic version. Not that calculation is itself foreign to an "imagined" Latino community; in fact it is from this perspective that the very act and the authority of counting and measuring become issues of vital social contestation. The "imaginary" in this sense does not signify the "not real," some make-believe realm oblivious to the facts, but a projection beyond the "real" as the immediately present and rationally discernible. It is the "community" represented "for itself," a unity fashioned creatively on the basis of shared memory and desire, congruent histories and meshing utopias.

The Latino historical imaginary refers, first of all, to home countries in Latin America, the landscapes, lifeways, and social struggles familiar, if not from personal experience, at least to one's family and people, and in any case indispensable to Latinos in situating themselves in U.S. society. Mexico, Puerto Rico, and Cuba are very different points of imaginative reference, to be sure, and again, it is always through their particular national optics that Latinos tend to envision some generic Latin America or Latino "We." But the features of José Martí's "nuestra América" do stand out in the Latino historical unconscious in that long narrative of Spanish and North American colonial conquest, the enslavement and subjugation of indigenous and African peoples, the troubled consolidation of nations under the thumb of international power, and the constant migratory movement of peoples, cultures, and things which has been attendant to all aspects of the Latino saga. For Latinos in the United States the passage to, and from, "el Norte" assumes such prominence in the social imaginary that migration is often confounded with life itself, and any fixity of the referential homeland gives way to an image of departure and arrival, the abandoned and the re-encountered.

This nomadic, migratory dimension of the Latino imaginary is anchored in the historical reasons for coming here, and in the placement assigned Latinos in U.S. society. Unlike earlier waves of European immigrants, Latinos move to this country as a direct result of the economic and political relationship of their homelands, and home region, to the United States. However much Cuba, Mexico, and Puerto Rico may differ in status and social arrangement—and if we add the Dominican Republic and Colombia the range could hardly be wider in present-day geopolitics—huge portions of their respective populations have come to live in the United States because of the gravitational pull of metropolitan power and dependency at work in each and all of their histories. Since World War II, its economy on a course of shrinkage and transition rather than unbridled expansion, the United States has been tapping its colonial reserves to fill in its lower ranks, and its Latin American and Caribbean neighbors have proved to be the closest and most abundant sources at hand.

Colonial relations of hemispheric inequality underlie not only the historical logic of Latino migration, but also the position and conditions of Latinos here in this society. Differential treatment is of course rampant, as is most dramatically evident these days in the contrasting fates of Cubans and Haitians arriving on the same rafts from their beleaguered home islands. And today even many Cuban-Americans, recent arrivals and long-standing citizens, are finding the red carpets and gold-paved streets mythical at best, and increasing numbers are coming to resent being cited as the exception to the rule of Latino disadvantage. For the Latino imaginary, even when the relatively "privileged" Cubanos are reckoned in, rests on the recognition of ongoing oppression and discrimination, racism and exploitation, closed doors and patrolled borders. Whether sanguine or enraged, this recognition structures the negotiated relations among Latinos, between Latinos and the dominant culture, and with other groups such as African Americans and Native Americans.

Memory fuels desire; the past as imagined from a Latino perspective awakens an anticipatory sense of what is, or might be, in store. The alarmist hysteria over the prospect of "America's fastest-growing minority" overrunning the society is directed not only at Latino people themselves, but at the ground shift, however imaginary, in power relations implied in that new calculus. For the desire that these demographic trends awaken in Latinos is directed first of all toward recognition and justice in this society, but wider, hemispheric changes always figure somewhere on the agenda. The Latino imaginary infuses the clamor for civil rights with a claim to sovereignty on an international scale; retribution involves reversing the history of conquest and subordination, including its inherent migratory imperative. A full century after its initial pronouncement, Martí's profile of "nuestra América" still looms like a grid over the map of the entire continent, with the northern co-optation of the name America demanding special scrutiny and revision.

But Latino memory and desire, though positioned as a challenge to prevailing structures of power, are not just reactive. The imaginary articulates more than a reflexive response to negative conditions and unfavorably weighted relations which, though oppositional, is as a response still ultimately mimetic and confined to extrinsically set terms. It is important to recognize that the Latino imaginary, like that of other oppressed groups, harbors the elements of an alternative ethos, an ensemble of cultural values and practices created in its own right and to its own ends. Latinos listen to their own kind of music, eat their own kind of food, dream their dreams, and snap their photos not just to express their difference from, or opposition to, the way the "gringos" do it. These choices and preferences, though arrived at under circumstances of dependency and imposition, also attest to a deep sense of autonomy and self-referentiality. Latino identity is imagined not as the negation of the non-Latino, but as the affirmation of cultural and social realities and possibilities inscribed in their own human trajectory.

. . .

The conditions for the emergence of a Latino cultural ethos were set around mid-century, as it began to become clear that these "new immigrants" filing in from the southern backyard constituted a different kind of social presence than that constituted by European arrivals of earlier years. Of course the histories of each of the major U.S. Latino groups extend much further back than that: Cubans and Puerto Ricans to the later nineteenth century, when colonies of artisans and political exiles formed in New York and Florida, while today's "Chicanos" were "here" all along, for centuries before the fateful year 1848 when the northern third of their nation was rudely moved in on and annexed by the bearers of Manifest Destiny. In fact, in the long historical view the literary and cultural presence of Spanish-speaking people in the territory now called the United States actually precedes that of the English. And if we add to that the indigenous, "Native American" perspective of "nuestra América," a full-scale revision, or inversion, of the national history results, with the supposed "core," Anglo-Saxon culture appearing as the real intruder, the original illegal alien.

It is a serious fallacy, therefore, to think of Latinos in the United States as "recent arrivals." But despite their long-standing, constitutive role in North American history, sheer demographic growth and diversification point to a markedly new structural positioning and cultural dynamic for Latinos in the second half of the twentieth century. Now more than ever, in the present, "postcolonial" era, Latinos are here as colonial migrants, whose very locations and movements are defined by the status of their "home" countries within the system of transnational economic power. Rather than an ethnic minority or immigrant group, those trusty old concepts of cultural pluralism, Latinos may now be more accurately described as a diasporic community or, more suggestively, a "world tribe." But the term I like best to characterize the social and cultural space occupied by Latinos is "delocalized transnation," of whom it is also said that they "become doubly loyal to their nations of origin and thus ambivalent about their loyalties to America."[7]

Social consciousness and cultural expression of this new geopolitical reality burst out in the late 1960s. Inspired by the Civil Rights movement and the Cuban Revolution, countless movements, causes, and organizations rallied thousands of Mexicans and Puerto Ricans to the cries of "¡Viva la Raza!" and "¡Despierta Boricua!" The political momentum of the Latino imaginary was set in those spirited movements, and found vibrant artistic expression in such diverse forms as wall murals, bilingual poetry and street theater, and hybrid music and dance styles like salsa and Latin soul, Joe Bataan and Santana. *Talleres* and *conjuntos*, readings and *actos* proliferated, lending voice and vision to the fervent political struggles of Latino and Latin American peoples.

By our time, in the 1990s, that heyday is long past, no longer even a living memory for young Latinos. But the Brown Berets and the Young Lords Party, the Chicano Moratorium and the Lincoln Hospital takeover are still an inspiration, a model of militancy and righteous defiance for the present generation of Latinos of all nationalities as they sharpen their social and political awareness. For although the immediacy, intensity, and cultural effervescence has no doubt waned in the intervening decades, Latinos in the United States have just as assuredly continued to grow as a social movement to be reckoned with, nationally and internationally, in the years ahead. This is true demographically in the striking (for some startling) multiplication in their numbers, and analytically in the equally striking diversification of their places of origin and settlement, and as a more differentiated site of intersecting social identities, especially along sexual, racial, and class lines.

But the persistence and expansion of the Latino social movements are most prominent as a cultural imaginary, a still-emergent space or "community" of memory and desire. In the present generation Latino youth from all backgrounds played a formative role in the creation of hip-hop, and its inflection toward Latino expression and experience; though not explicitly political in intention, the Latino contribution to contemporary popular music, dance, performance, and visual imaging has accompanied important signs of social organization and self-identification among young Latinos in many parts of the country. In the case of the "casitas" in the New York barrios—another favorite example from recent Latino experience—entire neighborhoods across generational and many other lines are drawn together by way of sharing in the enactment of collective cultural memory.[8]

· · ·

Hispanic? Latino? Settling on a name never comes easy, and in the case of an embracing term for Mexicans, Puerto Ricans, Cubans, Dominicans, Colombians, Salvadorans, Panamanians, and a dozen other Latin American peoples in the United States, consensus does not seem to be near at hand. But the search for a name, more than an act of classification, is actually a process of social imagination. And in that sense the search for Latino identity and community, the ongoing creation of a Latino imaginary, is also a search for a new map, a new ethos, a new *América*.

Notes

The opening citations are slightly dramatized renderings of statements I have heard in the course of conversations or interviews or in newspaper accounts. Examples of the abundant published discussion of the terms Hispanic and Latino may be found in Suzanne Oboler, *Ethnic Labels, Latino Lives: Identity and the Politics of (Re)Presentation in the United States* (Minneapolis: University of Minnesota, 1995); Earl Shorris, *Latinos: A Biography of the People* (New York: Norton, 1992); and *Latin American Perspectives* 19: 4 (Fall 1992). See also my essay "Pan-Latino/Trans-Latino: Puerto Ricans in the 'New Nueva York,'" *Centro Journal* (1996), xxxx.

1. Documentation of this widespread preference for national designations may be found in Rodolfo O. de la Garza et al., "Latino National Political Survey," as published in *Latino Voices* (Boulder: Westview, 1992). For a response see Luis Fraga et al., *Still Looking for America: Beyond the Latino National Political Survey* (Stanford Center for Chicano Research, 1994).

2. Benedict Anderson, *Imagined Communities: Reflections on the Origin and Spread of Nationalism* (London: Verso, 1983).

3. The range of theoretical accents from strictly quantitative to comparative to ideological is evident in the growing published literature on "Hispanics" or "Latinos," as cited in note 2 above. See in addition writings like Marta Tienda and Vilma Ortiz, "Hispanicity and the 1980 Census," *Social Science Quarterly* 67 (1986): 3–20; Ilan Stavans, *The Hispanic Condition: Reflections on Culture and Identity in America* (New York: Harper Collins, 1995); Félix Padilla, *Latino Ethnic Consciousness: The Case of Mexican Americans and Puerto Ricans in Chicago* (Notre Dame: University of Notre Dame, 1985); Rebecca Morales and Frank Bonilla, eds., *Latinos in a Changing U.S. Economy* (Newbury Park: Sage, 1993).

4. The present essay was originally intended as a general introduction to the projected catalogue of "Latino Voices," the first international festival of Latino photography, which opened in Houston in November, 1994. The idea of conceptualizing and circumscribing a "Latino imaginary" arose while pre-viewing slides of images by Chicano, Puerto Rican, and Cuban photographers included in that historic exhibition and figuring out how to present their theoretical and cultural significance to a broad United States audience of the 1990s. The catalogue has not yet materialized, but I have presented the paper in a variety of settings across the country, incorporating insights as I went along.

5. The most extended discussion of these instrumental uses of the "Hispanic" label may be found in Oboler, op. cit., note 2 above, though I find the exchange between Fernando Treviño and David Hayes-Bautista in the 1987 *American Journal of Public Health* of interest as well.

6. For examples of "Hispanics" in advertisements and other commercial uses, see Flores and George Yúdice, "Living Borders/Buscando América: Languages of Latino Self-Formation," *Social Text* 24 (1990): 57–84.

7. Arjun Appadurai, "Patriotism and Its Futures," *Public Culture* 5 (Spring 1993): 411–29, 424.

8. On Latino rap, see my essays "Puerto Rican and Proud, Boyee!: Rap, Roots and

Amnesia," in *Microphone Fiends: Youth Music and Youth Culture*, ed. Andrew Ross and Tricia Rose (New York: Routledge, 1995), 89–98. For an interpretation of the casita phenomenon, see my "Salvación Casita: Puerto Rican Performance and Vernacular Architecture in the South Bronx," in *Negotiating Performance: Gender, Sexuality, and Theatricality*, ed. Diana Taylor and Juan Villegas (Durham: Duke, 1994), 121–36.

Frances R. Aparicio

On Sub-Versive Signifiers: Tropicalizing Language in the United States

> I am waiting for them to stop talking about the "other," to stop even describing how important it is to be able to speak about difference. It is not just important what we speak about, but how and why we speak. Often this speech about the "Other" is also a mask, an oppressive talk hiding gaps, absences, that space where our words would be if we were speaking, if there were silence, if we were there.
>
> —bell hooks, *yearning*

> Weather report: Green bananas have been reported falling from heaven in some parts of the city.
>
> —Víctor Hernández Cruz, *Tropicalization*

As bell hooks suggests above, when the dominant subject speaks about the "Other," these signifiers hide the very absence of the silenced group, of those oppressed by a lack of access to official discourse and language. Víctor Hernández Cruz's verse, as the above epigraph, embodies "that space where our words would be if we were speaking," that is, the voices of U.S. Latinos and Latinas who transform the U.S. landscape, urban life, and mainstream culture into realities informed and subverted by visual icons, cultural practices, texts, and language from the Hispanic Caribbean. Together, both epigraphs illustrate the tensions between the dominant discourse on Latinos and on *latinidad* emerging from mainstream United States, a hegemonic tropicalizing, and the voices of Latinos and Latinas who constantly appropriate this very same discourse, re-tropicalizing it with new, politicized, transgressive, and "trans-creative" meanings.[1] Attempting to go beyond a simplistic binarism that denounces the monologism of U.S. dominant constructs and thus positions Latinos as Other, as mute objects of discursive hegemony, my essay emphasizes, instead, the "processes of subjectification"[2] by which U.S. Latinos/as engage in discourse, recirculating particular "tropical" signifiers with newly invested meanings, at times liberatory, at others potentially oppressive in their ambiguity. Thus, U.S. Latinos/as wage a discursive war by resisting, opposing, rewriting, and subverting stereotypes. In this process, they tropicalize themselves—already tropicalized Others—assuming new discursive power as linguistic subjects. As Juan Flores and George Yúdice have stated, "language itself, of course, is the most obvious site of Latino inventiveness."[3] Here I will explore this struggle for discourse and language in the public spaces of mass media, popular music, and literature.

Recent trends in U.S. advertising, the mass media, the literary market, and the arts have revealed a Latino-mania obviously motivated by the potential financial benefits of the 1992 Quincentenary celebrations, although this is not necessarily a new phenomenon. The McDonald's incursion into Mexican food, with new "fa-hee-tas" and burritos, and the Arby's slogan "Different Is Better," are but two examples of fast-food publicity that unveils an attraction for what is not idiosyncratically American. Conga drums and Latin rhythms have become a staple as background music for TV advertising, from the now famous Anglo grandmother turned rumbera in a Duracell commercial to Edgar de León's group advertising the NBC-affiliate TV station in Detroit, Michigan. The 1990 Pulitzer prize was the first awarded to a U.S. "Hispanic" author, Oscar Hijuelos, for his novel *The Mambo Kings Play Songs of Love*, and the ensuing film *The Mambo Kings*—advertised as "hot and sizzling"—coincided with the resurgence of the "Mambo Craze" in New York City.[4] Advertising gimmicks capitalize on the discourse of multiculturalism implemented in the United States as a benign euphemism for diversity, that is, as deracialized difference. In the post–Cold War era, the United States has redirected its political and economic gaze toward the Middle East and the south, Latin America. While the Berlin Wall was being dismantled, the U.S.-Mexico border was being militarized. The Panama invasion of 1989, the Cuban embargo, the Puerto Rican plebiscite, NAFTA, and corporate globalizing trends have helped renew old sets of images, icons, and stereotypes of Latin America, "distributing" them throughout the mass media and literature and "elaborating"[5] in them revitalized meanings that articulate contemporary political relations and the unchanging agenda of the U.S. government and of corporate interests.

The increasing visibility of Latinos/as in the U.S. mainstream may be naively explained as a corroboration of America's diversity, as an example of this country's openness towards true multiculturalism. This recognition of Latinos also has economic motivations, capitalizing on the consumer power of an ever-increasing Latino/a population. Nevertheless, the cultural complexities of this mainstreaming process still need to be discussed in their contradictory ideological implications: "the critique of western idealism or logocentrism requires that there is a constitutive discourse of lack imbricated in a philosophy of presence, which makes the differential or deconstructionist reading possible, 'between the lines.'"[6]

Thus the growing visual, linguistic, and cultural presence of Latinos/as in the United States is concomitant to the historical and cultural crisis—ultimately epistemological—by which the United States has begun to recognize the failures of the dominant paradigms (American exceptionalism, individualism, democratic capitalism) that have "glued" this country together since its constitutional inception. The fact that certain Anglo sectors have begun to dismantle the homogeneous concept of American culture and now include "subordinate" cultural practices as part of their daily lives and social interaction is a positive, progressive step toward a more democratic and inclusive society. Yet this aperture is simultaneously an attraction toward Otherness, a cultural fixation that cannot be separated from the national *lack*: a gradual realization that the American Dream and the American self are beginning to sound hollow, that the values once held to be sacred, static, eternal, and universal are more a sign than a reality, more an absence than a fulfilling social and cultural praxis. Is this Latino-mania, then, another instance of cultural fixation on the Other, an attempt to displace the unsettled and unsatisfying paradigms of the internal self, as the men's movement fueled by Robert Bly has clearly evinced? Or is this phenomenon a direct consequence of the growing power, cultural contributions, and intellectual and artistic strengths of Latinos/as, a more democratic latinization of the United States from within? Is it neither or both?

In ideological contrast to a number of cultural studies interventions that turn into neocolonial voyages into Latino/a cultures,[7] Juan Flores and George Yúdice's essay "Living Borders/Buscando América: Languages of Latino Self-Formation" (1993 [1990]) theoretically explores the processes of forming a Latino subjectivity by foregrounding the voices and the literary and artistic production of U.S. Latinos, mainly Chicanos and Nuyoricans. Flores and Yúdice examine "how Latino identity is mediated and constructed through the struggle over language under such postmodern conditions" as "the welfare state" and "the permeation of representation by the consumer market and the media,"[8] two historical factors not present during the earlier European migrations into the United States.

Flores and Yúdice focus on the ways in which U.S. Latinos have developed an aesthetic that is not separated from everyday practices, an "ethos" textualized through the border trope that becomes ideologically powerful in its political deployment:

The trope of a border culture is thus not simply another expression of post-modern aesthetic indeterminacy, along the lines of Derrida's decontextualized frame or *parergon*, "the incomprehensibility of the border at the border," or a Baudrillardian simulacrum (*neither* copy *nor* original). The trope emerges, rather, from the ways in which Latinos deploy their language in everyday life. It corresponds to an ethos under formation; it is practice, rather than representation of Latino identity. And it is on this terrain that Latinos wage their cultural politics as a "social movement." As such, Latinos' aesthetics do not pretend to be separate from everyday practices but rather an integral part of an ethos which seeks to be politicized as a means to validation and self-determination. And it is precisely the projection of this ethos into the culture at large and into the political arena which threatens the dominant "Anglo" culture with loss of control of its physical and metaphorical borders.[9]

This extensive quote signals major differences between a neocolonial scholarship that privileges theory over the knowledge of subaltern cultures and of people's practices and voices, and that of Flores and Yúdice who, in their engaging analysis of Latino processes of constructing identity, manage to inform and enhance deconstructionist and postmodern theories by integrating the real, material, political, and everyday practices of Latinos/as into the analysis of the border trope.

Indeed, the contribution of Latinos/as to the emergence of "alternative public spheres"—through language, music, advertising, political organizations, and most concretely in the phenomenon of the *casitas*—is clearly illustrated by the shift from a discourse on rights (as in the Civil Rights movement) to one based on needs.[10] Thus this alternative public sphere blurs the public and the private spaces, inserting everyday practices into the political arena. Further evidence of this impact is revealed in the reactions of Anglos to Latino claims. As Flores and Yúdice state, "'Anglo insecurity' looks to the claims of Latinos and other minority constituencies for the erosion of the United States position in world leadership, the downturn in the economy and the bleak prospects for social mobility for the next generation."[11]

We have come full circle with respect to our discussion of Latino-mania and the Latinization of the United States. As suggested by Flores and Yúdice in "Living Borders," the internal impact that U.S. Latinos/as and other "minorities" are having on the public spaces of the country indeed fuel the accusatory stance of many Anglos toward minority claims. Thus the national *lack*—the failed myths of America—can only be accepted and read by Anglos as a projection on the Other, an egregious social construct that Fredrick Pike also foregrounds in his historical research on U.S.-Latin American relations.[12] That is, the inferior status imposed on U.S. minorities displaces the need for self-reflection at the national level, thus making Latinos the scapegoat for domestic problems. This is evident in the 1990s, as anti-immigration, anti–affirmative action and English-Only initiatives continue to target these populations.

Tropicalized Tropicalizers

The July 11, 1988, issue of *Time*, entitled "Magnífico: Hispanic Culture Breaks Out of the Barrio," signaled a new direction for cultural criticism in the United States. The series of articles on music, art, cinema, food, fashion, architecture, and language recognized for the first time in official, mainstream North American discourse the impact of the Latino presence in the United States. These pieces, however, are laden with signifiers that simultaneously undermine the power of Latinos/as as agents of their own cultural production and hinder their effect on social and cultural transformations at the national level. The overall celebratory tone throughout the *Time* volume is obfuscating, for it conceals the fact that the volume's signifiers, both visual and verbal, consistently objectify Latinos/as. Traces of primitivism ("Of ghosts and magic"), associations with passion and sensuality ("burning with passion," "TV's hottest minority," "shake your body"), and with "south of the border" imagery ("color and spice") abound in this issue of *Time* as much as in any mainstream discourse about Latinos/as, either past or present. This so-called "celebration" of Latino/a culture may be read as a subterfuge for the century-old strategy of objectification and co-optation. Underlying class and economic interests form the core of this recognition, contingent on two factors: first, that these "celebrated" Latinos, in one way or another, and despite their ideological diversity, have "made it" in society and thus are worthy of being publicly acclaimed as examples of the American Dream. Most, if not all, of the profiles are on actors, actresses, singers, artists, writers, and fashion designers. Second, the discourse by which these Latinos/as are glorified is not always their own, but rather that of the U.S. mainstream, a language and perspective still constructed from the very same linguistic and ideological elements that have "invented" Latin America since Columbus "discovered" us.

I propose, however, that within these hegemonic representations of *latinidad* the voices of Latinos/as assume those very same constructs, at times subverting them as strategies for empowerment: the tropicalized simultaneously become tropicalizers. Despite the facile dismissal of Chicanos and Nuyoricans, of the subaltern voices, by postmodern theory and cultural studies, the fact remains that the demographics of twenty-million-plus Latinos/as in the United States and the ensuing impact on literary, artistic, musical and cultural spaces have made possible a counterdiscourse simultaneously voiced—yet framed and at times contained—within mainstream representations. These sub-versive signifiers also appear as Spanish subtexts in the literature of renowned U.S. Latino and Latina writers who write in English.

Contemporary constructs of Latinos/as remain obedient to a long history of stereotypes of Latin America textualized through media, literature, historical texts, popular music, and folklore.[13] While we may not see any more Carmen Mirandas on film, the icon of the eroticized, tropicalized Latina informs a description of Maria Conchita Alonso in *Time*:

Vanity Fair had it right when it described this deliciously delirious Cuban Venezuelan as "half out of her mind, half out of her dress." When Maria Conchita Alonso talks, the accent is muy caliente. "We Latins have this fire inside us, in our hearts, in our skin, the flesh. You just go for it." Does she worry that her Spanish-flavored English may limit her roles? "Who cares? I know plenty of actresses who speak without accents. They're not working. I am." And she's working on a record album in her English too. So there.[14]

This short paragraph evinces the positional complexities of the multifarious processes that constitute tropicalizations. We listen here to three different voices—*Vanity Fair*'s, the journalist's, and Maria Conchita Alonso's—all of which merge at one point or another, mediating each other. Together they share a complicity with the mainstream's tropicalizing discourse. The Caribbean-born actress is described in terms of flavor (*sabor*)—including her "Spanish-flavored English"—and concomitantly as an object to be consumed (actress) and eaten (sexual object). She is also constructed as irrational and primitive ("half out of her mind"). However, the associations with the erotic are most specifically articulated by Alonso herself. While she defines her own body as a space of sensual pleasure for her consumers and fans, a construct geared toward publicity and further fame, she can only achieve this within the subject position of collectivity and auto-stereotyping: "We Latins have this fire inside us." Is this perhaps a superficial generalization on the part of a mindless actress? Or could it be a strategy of empowerment, a willed expression of a differential identity that allows Alonso herself to "go for it," whatever that "it" means—fame, fortune, success, or cultural or women's agency? Indeed, the final sentence, "So there," an utterance on the part of the journalist, also expresses Alonso's attitude toward herself and her language as a site of difference and of indifference to the normative, to Anglo leveling hegemony. Both utterances reveal Alonso's own process of signifying her difference for individual and economic empowerment. Despite—or because of—her accent and her difference, she is a sought-after actress, she says. She does not dismiss the possibility that her success may be based on her accent and difference, on the Anglo attraction for the exotic, erotic Caribbean woman-other.

An analogous strategic self-tropicalization is used by salsa singer and composer Willie Colón in his 1990 song "Color americano." In the text, he accuses the United States of being a country divided by racial tension, cultural dualities, and hegemony. However, Colón simultaneously scripts himself as a Latino commodity, an exotic other attractive to the Anglo gaze:

con mi color
color café
voy causando sensación en New York
con mi color
color café . . .
[with my coffee-
colored skin
I am causing a sensation in New York
with my coffee-
colored skin . . .]

While Colón racializes himself as a dark, Latino male whose difference is, in fact, what makes him a desired other, he simultaneously plays an important role as cultural subject. The title of the song, "American Color," is ideologically transformed as we listen to the lyrics. If the color of America is dark, *café con leche* [coffee with milk], then this America is not only Anglo, white America but a more inclusive one, a plural America: North, South, Central, and Caribbean America, the Americas of *mestizaje* and *mulatismo*, the geocultural space that José David Saldívar has proposed as a new paradigm for American Studies in *The Dialectics of our America*.[15] Through this discursive repositioning, whites become the other, the minority. As a famous Salsa singer, along with other Latino poets and artists, Willie Colón participates here in a proactive radicalizing of cultural signifiers, a semiotic problematizing that responds to historical, demographic, and cultural changes in the United States and globally. At the same time, he engages in a process of racializing himself, of self-tropicalization. By willfully defining and constructing himself as a dark Latino, he subverts previous negative constructs of *latinidad* and of the Latino male. He empowers himself with these re-coded signifiers as part of his discursive possessions and allows himself to revel in the power of being a *desired* Latino because of his racial difference. By consciously objectifying himself as a desired (and desirable) other, he assumes power in gender relations. He invests dark-colored skin with positive attributes rather than with the social connotations of the lazy Puerto Rican on welfare or as a criminal element dangerous to society.

Both Alonso and Colón tropicalize themselves in order to vindicate the image of the Puerto Rican "brown" male in the latter case, and to make visible and render desirable the Caribbean female as professional (actress and singer) in the case of Alonso. As problematic as these self-tropicalizations are with respect to gender politics, both Alonso and Colón dialogize the hegemonic tropicalizing of U.S. mainstream discourse. They unsettle the monologic discourse on Latinos by positioning themselves as linguistic subjects, rendering invalid and displacing their status as cultural objects. These two instances of tropicalized tropicalizers exemplify the complex interweaving of voices and the simultaneous ideological forces played out in popular culture and the mass media.

Tropicalizing English

In *Time*'s presentation of Maria Conchita Alonso, the journalist recognizes the construction of difference when she or he defines Alonso's English as "her English." By distinguishing Anglo English (unaccented), from Alonso's "Spanish-flavored English," the viability of an-Other English is proposed. Latino English, in fact, may be defined as a tropicalized linguistic locus that is listened to/read "differently." In Alonso's case, while her English is being described as marginal, the Latina actress also participates in this tropicalizing gesture.

Quite far from Alonso's postmodern Hollywood world of fleeting images and appearances, Latino poetry in the United States has been the site of a new English that can be read ideally through the eyes and ears of a bilingual, bicultural reader. The early interlingual Latino poetry produced since the late 1960s and early 1970s—Alurista, José Montoya, Miguel Algarín, Pedro Pietri—exhorted a new "American" ideal readership who would recognize itself in the code-switching praxis of U.S. working-class Latino communities. Much of this poetry, unfortunately, has remained outside the margins of the literary canon, virtually unread by an English-speaking audience.

The linguistic tropicalization that interests me here, however, is located in the Latino fiction and poetry written entirely or almost entirely in English. Since the early 1980s, works by U.S. Latinos/as have emerged as monolingual texts, and while this linguistic trend may be interpreted as assimilationist, or as an indication of Latino/a literature's mainstreaming, this literary English is a differential one, a language tropicalized from within. It constitutes, in its rich variations, a transformation and rewriting of Anglo signifiers from the Latino cultural vantage point. As such, it becomes a textual *diferencia* from the linguistic repertoires of Anglo U.S. authors. Latino/a writers like Sandra Cisneros, Gary Soto, Helena Maria Viramontes, Pedro Pietri, Judith Ortiz Cofer, Aurora Levins Morales, and others write in English because that has been the language of their education and intellectual formation, proof that the cultural conquest has had its consequences. Yet a close reading of their lexicon and syntax reveals the underlying presence of Spanish in most of their works. As Helena María Viramontes has observed about her own writing, Spanish language and Latino cultural texts constitute the intertexts and subtexts that inform her work in English: "Sometimes my mistakes turn out to be my best writing. Sometimes I think in Spanish and translate . . . I still say that if my works were translated into Spanish, they would somehow feel better. More, more, what's the word? At home."[16]

What prescriptive linguists, editors, and authorities in education deem a deficit—the so-called interference of Spanish in English—a hybrid, Latino-centered approach values as positive, creative contributions to literature. Indeed, the most important contributions of these writers to U.S. literature lie not only in the multiple cultural and hybrid subjectivities that they textualize, but also in the new possibilities for metaphors, imagery, syntax, and rhythms that the Spanish subtexts provide U.S. literary English. Needless to say, this transformation is not contained within the level of the signifier only, because the implications it proposes for reading and readership are inevitably clear. What on the surface appears to be a praxis that signals cultural assimilation may be defined also as a subversive act: that of writing the Self using the tools of the Master and, in the process, infusing those signifiers with the cultural meanings, values, and ideologies of the subaltern sector. Subversive also in a literal sense: the Hispanic and Caribbean subtexts that permeate Latino fiction and poetry are only present to those readers who can recognize the underlying intertextuality veiled by the Other language. My thesis, however, needs further clarification, since it seems redundant to speak of Latino literature's bicultural texture. Works written before the Chicano movement of the late '60s and early '70s have been characterized by a stance of *cultural ambivalence*. Many authors wrote in English, eager to be accepted by the Anglo mainstream readership. Affirmation of the Latino self went hand in hand with an ambiguous discourse of cultural distancing, shame or stereotyping. As Gloria Treviño has defined it, "cultural ambivalence expressed the central dilemma of the Chicano who is conscious of being a product of both Mexican and American cultures. [It] characterizes the dual consciousness of Chicanos as they mediate between the values of the dominant culture and those of the minority group."[17] She adds that "it is important to understand that Chicanos have not chosen to be ambivalent but that cultural ambivalence has primarily been a result of their socio-historical position in a society which subordinates minority groups both economically and culturally."[18]

In my view, this ambivalence is articulated through the "verbo-ideological" world to which the texts conform.[19] In these earlier works when Spanish appears, if it does, it is usually translated into English or subsumed under the principal discourse in English. It is explained through an apologetic and culturally alienated perspective. The novel *Pocho* (1959), by José Antonio Villarreal, is an excellent illustration of this linguistic ambivalence.[20] While it has been criticized by many Chicano critics as a text that promotes the assimilationist paradigm for young Chicanos, at the same time the author/narrator judges his characters from a traditionally Mexican male perspective in relation to gender issues, and to American social and moral values in general.

The language of Juan and Consuelo Rubio, parents of Richard Rubio, the protagonist, is partly constituted by linguistic *calques* from Spanish to English, that is, literal translations of Spanish idiomatic expressions. For example, "she has given light," "I have an ache of head," and others are English utterances born of Spanish phrases (*dar a luz*) and syntactic patterns (*dolor de cabeza*). As a device of linguistic verisimilitude, as instances of polyphony and heteroglossia, this strategy attempts to present to an Anglo reader the first generation's linguistic praxis as Spanish speakers. In a literary decision of pragmatic compromise, Villarreal silences and hides the Spanish behind the English signifiers. Rather than creating a bilingual text that would reaffirm the cultural and linguistic realities of Juan and Consuelo, Villarreal opts for the needs of the readership, using English to mask the Spanish of this first generation. Their Hispanicized, uneducated English establishes a rupture from the discourse of Richard and of the narrator, whose English is quite literate, formal, and very academic. Anticipating Richard Rodríguez's conscious choice of linguistic loss and cultural separation from his family, Richard Rubio in *Pocho* establishes a differentiation from his Spanish-speaking parents through English and reading, while Villarreal uses English to silence Spanish. In this context, the novel is an ambivalent articulation of internalized colonialism.

A second group of authors, whose poetics and literary discourse are shaped at the height of the Chicano movement, employ Spanish within English in an effort to contest the silencing of Spanish by previous Latino writers and by the American social and educational machinery. True to the militant reaffirmation of Chicano identity politics, authors such as Saúl Sánchez, in *hay plescha lichans tu di flac*,[21] Alurista, in *Spik in Gliph?*[22] and José Antonio Burciaga in *Weedee Peepo*,[23] create an English that conforms to the phonetic system of Hispanics. In a vindicatory linguistic act, these titles are examples of English written and spoken according to the graphic and phonetic norms of Spanish, that is, according to the ways in which thousands of Hispanics struggle to pronounce English. Since pronunciation is the linguistic element most vulnerable to discrimination and shame,[24] this strategy inverts the negative values imposed by others on the Hispanic pronunciation of English. Socially unaccepted and ridiculed by many, this phonetic praxis is transformed into poetic discourse, obliging the reader to pronounce and read English under the phonetic and graphic system of Spanish. In contrast to the underlying, silenced Spanish of *Pocho*, in these works Spanish functions in a subversive mode. It inverts the center-margin axis between both languages, legitimizing the mis-pronunciation of English by Hispanics and creating signifiers that are derived from Spanish linguistic practices and norms.

The subversive presence of Spanish in English works has been further developed in Latino/a poetry and prose since the 1980s. In Sandra Cisneros's *The House on Mango Street*,[25] the use of the diminutive in English ("The Family of

Little Feet," "Mamacita") constitutes part of Cisneros's poetic voice while it semantically and culturally affects the reading of the English use of the diminutive. If "little" generally means small, and it may also imply either derogatory or affectionate connotations, in the works of Cisneros "little" is semantically saturated as a term of endearment, of "cariño," a function which is reaffirmed by the Latino cultural context and by the particular sociolinguistic praxis of Spanish. As many speakers from Latin America and the Caribbean know, the Spanish diminutives -ito, -ico remit us to an affective mode.

Víctor Hernández Cruz's poetic works are constituted by many phrases, images and metaphors in English that originate in linguistic *calques*, literal translations of colloquial phrases, proverbs, and even song lyrics from the Hispanic Caribbean. *Calques*, as traditionally defined, are unconscious linguistic utterances that exemplify the power of one dominant language over another. Many linguistic studies on Spanish in the United States or on bilingualism have focused on the influence of English over Spanish, thus reaffirming the position of the former as the dominant language. *Calques* are associated with so-called uneducated speakers, and illustrate the subordination of Spanish to English, perpetuating at the same time the stereotype of the Hispanic who is losing his/her mother language.

Yet so-called *calques*, a term that connotes lack of originality as an uncreative, involuntary mimetic act, may indeed be a very original literary strategy. As Jorge Luis Borges once commented on Biblical translations, literal renderings may be a very important vehicle for formulating new images and metaphors in a second language.[26] He illustrates his point by citing the "Song of Songs," an original Hebrew construction that exemplifies the absence of the superlative in that language. The literal transposition of the phrase onto European languages respected the syntactic structure of the original, thus offering European readers a much more poetic utterance than the expected English equivalent, "The Greatest Song." In literature, literal translations can possess an original and surprising value within the text and within the context of the second language whose literary tradition may be transformed or affected by the syntax, imagery, and lexicon of the first language.

Literal translations in Víctor Hernández Cruz's works invite the bicultural and bilingual reader to recognize those Hispanic sub-texts behind the English, under the surface structure. What in English may read as a funny, surrealist, or absurd metaphor, the "insider" reader perceives as repetition with a difference: an idiomatic phrase, a proverb, or a cultural reference from the Caribbean which originates in Spanish but is articulated twice through English signifiers. Thus a rupture is established between signifier and signified, for there is no correspondence between both as to linguistic source nor as to cultural field of reference. The following are examples of Cruz's play with *calques*:

Text In English	*Subtext from Spanish*
They put fire to the lata Flame to the can ("Financial Report")	"darle fuego a la lata" (colloquialism)
Put Seeds into the Maraca So That It May Sound (*By Lingual Wholes*)	Echale semillas a la maraca para que suene (Salsa song by R. Cortijo)
His ear stayed with it . . .	Se quedó con él
Good Water	Aguas Buenas (the poet's hometown)
The world could blow up *but you tranquil*	pero tú tranquilo (colloquialism)
Can he take the Can?	from "darle lata" (to give somebody a hard time)
You see . . . (as ending)	¿tú ves?
What doesn't kill gets you fat	lo que no mata engorda (proverb)
in the songs of love	canciones de amor (syntax)
again the factory of leather	fábrica de piel (syntax)

How do these images promote a tropicalization of North American poetic discourse? These utterances introduce new images and metaphors to English, while at the level of linguistic structure they propose new ways of manipulating lexicon and of inscribing the syntax and rhythms of Spanish within English. The "You see . . . ?," a mimicry of the "¿Tú ves . . . ?," criticized by many Spanish speakers as the use of a linguistic crutch (and quite predominant among Dominican speakers), infuses English with the rhythms and pauses inherent in Caribbean speech patterns. In the Mexican-American context, poet Gina Valdés suggests, in her aptly titled poem "English con salsa," that English in the voices of Latino immigrants necessarily becomes "English Surely Latinized." This is, to be sure, an ironic allusion to the educational dynamics of power in ESL courses whereby the disenfranchised Latino is deemed inarticulate and ignorant and is symbolically and literally muted by his supposed "lack" of knowledge and cultural competence. Valdes's poem is a celebration of the transculturation from below of the language, of imperialism, an English that she enumerates as "English refrito, English con sal y limón, English thick as mango juice, English poured from a clay jug, English tuned like a requinto from Uruapán, English lighted by Oaxacan dawns, English spiked with mezcal from Juchitán, English with a red cactus flower blooming in its heart."[27]

If tropical intertexts may transform poetic discourse in English, they also oblige the Latino/a bicultural reader to a more distanced re-reading of the original cultural text. Proverbs and idiomatic phrases, such as "darle fuego a la lata," once decontextualized, become the object of laughter and humor. Once the frozen-into-formula of a proverb is undone, it is free to propose a new expressive value characterized by its discrepancy within its new context, by that rupture between signifier and signified, by its displacement. Re-reading Caribbean proverbs in English implies returning them, transformed, to the literal value that they lose precisely because of their figurative and metaphoric nature.

The bilingual and bicultural texture of many U.S. Latino/a works—in its subversive location—privileges the ideal bilingual/bicultural reader as it simultaneously achieves a balance negotiating between an Anglo monolingual audience and a Latino bilingual readership. However, a monolingual reading can always at best only be a partial, limited one. When Roberto Fernández, the Cuban-American writer, translates literally into English the canonized works of Latin American authors, or when he refers to the famous Cuban musical group El Trío Matamoros as "The Moorkiller Trio," or alludes to the famous *merengue* "El negrito del batey" as "The Little Blackman from the Sugarmill,"[28] the monolingual, monocultural reader cannot revel in the pleasure created by the parodic literal translations. When Víctor Hernández Cruz refers to "Good Water," only readers who are familiar with Puerto Rican geography—whether puertorriqueños or not—will engage in the joy of this doubled recognition. However, this partial reading on the part of an outside reader does not dismiss the potential for new, creative readings of these utterances. Yet the politics of reading proposed by these tropicalized English works are clear. By metaphorically displacing the ideal monolingual American reader and by producing texts whose poetic and cultural signifying solicit crosscultural competency and complicity, contemporary U.S. Latino/a writers are marginalizing and perhaps even excluding the predominant ideal of the monolingual reader.

A Mangó Is Not a Mango: Tropicalizing Cultural Signifiers

> I dream with suitcases
> full of illegal fruits
> Interned between white
> guayaberas that dissolved
> Into snowflaked polyester.

As Víctor Hernández Cruz suggests in "Snaps of Immigration,"[29] the Spanish words of many Latino writers melt into the English of their otherness like the white guayaberas that have dissolved in the cold of snow and into the neutral homogeneity of polyester. However, the poet dreams of illegal fruits, mangoes, guavas, and plantains not allowed to enter the United States due to federal agricultural restrictions. These fruits—in the poet's fancy—reveal the absent presence of his Spanish, a language analogously restricted by linguistic racism and English Only laws. The forbidden, illegal fruits interned between the white guayaberas continue to "contaminate" them, to stain allegorically the English signifiers with signs of Caribbean and Latino cultural identity, as the Puerto Rican phrase *mancha del plátano* (the stain of the plantain) so succinctly expresses, and as Cruz's first verse, "I dream *with* suitcases," reveals in its Hispanicized use of the preposition.

While Latinos are prohibited from bringing our mangoes into the United States, Chiquita Brands has "kicked off a national consumer awareness campaign and has increased the volume of fruit it imports from Mexico" (*Ann Arbor News* 1990). As a result, "mango mania has hit mainstream America." Articles in the Food sections of local U.S. newspapers explain how to eat this "exotic" fruit and offer a "cram course in mango trivia" for those who are "mango illiterates." Not surprisingly, these suggestions, whose objectives are to increase sales and profit for Chiquita Brands, are entitled "It doesn't take two to mango."

The mango/tango *différance* evokes the Argentinian dance. It plays simultaneously with the lack of knowledge of the "average guy on the street" who, a decade ago, "wouldn't know whether you were talking about a tropical fruit or the latest dance craze from South America." The fact remains that, despite mango and tango crash courses, despite celebrations of Latino culture such as *Time*'s 1988 issue, most Anglo-Americans would not know the difference between a Spanish flamenco and an Argentinian tango. This mango/tango linguistic pun reveals the process by which cultural objects or products of Latin America are objectified, construed, and redefined according to the economic needs and interests of multinationals, capitalizing on the cultural ignorance of the mainstream-gringo consumer.

Contesting these dominant constructs, Víctor Hernández Cruz's long, surrealist narrative poem "The Man Who Came to the Last Floor" proposes a shifting semantics of the mango in the hands, eyes, and mouths of the Latino as writing subject and as agent of cultural awareness and change. The poem narrates the story of an older man who comes from Puerto Rico to New York, where he can only find a place to live on the top floor of a tenement building without an elevator:

> There was a Puerto Rican man who
> came to New York
> he came with a whole shopping bag
> full of seeds strange to the big
> city[30]

He spends his time looking down the window and throwing mango seeds down to the street below, one of which happens to fall on a policeman's head. The seed grows into a mango tree and the cop becomes a media sensation in the city:

> Surely he was going crazy he thought
> He could not go to work with a mango
> tree growing out of his head
> It soon got to be five feet tall
> and beautifully green
> He had to sleep in the living room
> His bedroom could no longer contain him
> Weeks later a young mango showed up
> hanging from a newly formed branch
> "now look at this" he told his wife
> He had to drink a lot of water or he'd
> get severe headaches
> The more water he drank the bigger
> the mango tree flourished over his head
> The people of the somewhere city heard
> about it in the evening news and there was
> a line of thousands ringed around his
> home
> they all wanted to see the man who
> had an exotic mango tree growing from
> his skull
> And there was nothing that could be done.[31]

The poem concludes with the Puerto Rican man sitting at the airport waiting for his flight back to the island. Reading the newspaper with his limited knowledge of English, he is taken by surprise not by the anomaly of the mango tree growing on the cop's head, but by the actual publicity:

> Qué cosa he said Wao
> Why write about a Mango tree
> There are so many of them
> and they are everywhere
> They taste gooooooooood
> Cómo eh.[32]

Within the context of tropicalizations, I read this poem as a political and cultural allegory of the struggles for discourse—and ultimately cultural and economic power—in which U.S. Latinos/as have engaged historically. The Puerto Rican man embodies the Latino/a writer, artist, and subject, and his/her role is to plant the seeds of a cultural consciousness in Latinos themselves as well as in others outside the community. This cultural "planting" includes the recuperation of history and the transformation of hegemonic structures (the policeman as a figure of authority and law) and of the marginalized location of Latinos. "Planting" moves us from cultural erasure to cultural power and presence, from the top floor as a site of the powerless to a top floor that becomes the positionality of those empowered. As Esmeralda Santiago narrates in *America's Dream*, working-class Latinas hold the potential to transculturate the children of the Anglo upper class, even if in small, everyday rituals such as serving asopao.[33] Cruz's Latino fantasy, as irrational and humorous as it is, proposes a way of mapping the historical attempts of the Puerto Rican communities to take into our hands the transformation of our own circumstances—physical, linguistic, educational, and social—changes needed to surpass the hegemonic tropicalizing that others impose on us as victims and to move on to a status as agents of our lives.

To throw mango seeds from the top floor is a poetic and symbolic act of reappropriating the Chiquita mango construed for mainstream consumption. More profoundly, to throw mango seeds onto a policeman's head and change his life *is* to displace the hierarchies of power; it means inverting the exotic Other/cultural subject dichotomy; it means redefining urban space and infusing it with icons from the rural homeland, as the *casitas* in the Bronx have achieved; it means reconceptualizing what it means to be "American" and dark-skinned from the position of the Latino male, as in Willie Colón's song; it ultimately means radicalizing English by rewriting its signifiers with Caribbean subtexts.

By engaging in a close reading of representations of Latinos in *Time* magazine, by tracing the presence of Spanish in Latino English, and by briefly examining the shifting semantics of the mango as a cultural signifier construed both by mainstream interests and by Latino writers, I have proposed multidirectional modes of engaging in the politics of representation. These readings have brought forth the voices of Latinos/as in these texts and as a central part of the processes of cultural negotiation in the United States. Through literature, language, and music, Latinos have subverted this tropicalizing discourse that has objectified us historically. Moreover, we are reclaiming the tropics as a cultural site of our own, rewriting and transforming "American" culture with our own sub-versive signifiers.

Notes

A brief version of this paper, titled "On Sub-versive Signifiers: U.S. Latina/o Writers Tropicalize English," appeared in *American Literature* 66:4 (December 1994): 795–801.

1. Juan Flores and George Yúdice, "Living Borders/Buscando America: Languages of Latino Self-Formation" in *Social Text* 24 (Fall 1990): 57–84. Reprinted in Juan Flores, *Divided Borders: Essays on Puerto Rican Identity* (Houston: Arte Público Press, 1993) 199–224. See especially pp. 217–18 in *Divided Borders*.

2. Homi K. Bhabha, "The Other Question: Difference, Discrimination and the Discourse of Colonialism" in *Out there: Marginalization and Contemporary Cultures* 71.

3. Flores and Yúdice, 219–20.

4. Oscar Hijuelos, *The Mambo Kings Play Songs of Love* (New York: Farrar, Straus, Giroux, 1989).

5. Edward Said, *Orientalism* (New York: Vintage Books, 1979), 12.

6. Bhabha, 73.

7. See our Introduction to this volume for such a critique.

8. Flores and Yúdice, 201.

9. Flores and Yúdice, 203.

10. Flores and Yúdice, 217. For informative essays on the casitas phenomenon, see Juan Flores, "'Salvación Casita': Puerto Rican Performance and Vernacular Architecture in the South Bronx," *Negotiating Performance: Gender, Sexuality, and theatricality in Latin(o) America*, ed. Diana Taylor and Juan Villegas (Durham and London: Duke University Press, 1994) 121–36, and Luis Aponte Parés, "What's yellow and white and has land all around it?: Appropriating place in Puerto Rican barrios," *Bulletin Centro de Estudios Puertorriqueños,* 7:1 (1995): 8–19.

11. Flores and Yúdice, 204–5.

12. Frederick Pike, *The United States and Latin America: Myths and Stereotypes of Civilization and Nature* (Austin: University of Texas Press, 1992).

13. Frederick Pike, *The United States and Latin America*.

14. *Time*, 72.

15. José David Saldívar, *The Dialectics of Our America: Genealogy, Cultural Critique, and Literary History* (Durham and London: Duke University Press, 1991).

16. Helena María Viramontes, "'Nopalitos': The Making of Fiction" in Horno-Delgado, Asunción, et al., eds., *Breaking Boundaries: Latina Writings and Critical Readings* (Amherst: University of Massachusetts Press, 1989), 33–38. See especially page 37.

17. Gloria Velásquez Treviño, "Cultural Ambivalence in Early Chicana Literature," in Genevieve Fabre, ed., *European Perspectives on Hispanic Literature of the United States* (Houston: Arte Público Press, 1988), 140–46. See especially page 140.

18. Treviño, 141.

19. N. M. Bakhtin, "Discourse in the Novel," in Michael Holquist, ed., *The Dialogic Imagination* (Austin: University of Texas Press, 1981), 270.

20. José Antonio Villarreal, *Pocho* (New York: Doubleday, 1959).

21. Saúl Sánchez, *Hay plescha lichans tu di flac* (Berkeley: Editorial Justa Publications, 1977).

22. Alurista, *Spik in Gliph?* (Houston: Arte Público Press, 1981).

23. José Antonio Burciaga, *Weedee Peepo* (Edinburg, Texas: Pan American University Press, 1988).

24. Ana Celia Zentella, "Linguistic Attitudes Among Hispanics in New York City,"

presentation at the Tenth Annual Conference on Spanish in the United States (Tucson, Arizona, October 1989).

25. Sandra Cisneros, *The House on Mango Street* (Houston: Arte Público Press, 1985).
26. Jorge Luis Borges, "Word-Music and Translation," Charles Eliot Norton Lectures, Harvard University, 1968.
27. Gina Valdés, "English con Salsa," in Lori M. Carlson, ed., *Cool Salsa: Bilingual Poems on Growing Up Latino in the United States.* New York: Fawcett Juniper, 1995, pp. 4–5.
28. Roberto Fernández, *Raining Backwards* (Houston: Arte Público Press, 1988).
29. Víctor Hernández Cruz, *Red Beans* (Minneapolis: Coffee House Press, 1991), 13.
30. Víctor Hernández Cruz, "The Man Who Came to the Last Floor," *Rhythm, Content, and Flavor* (Houston: Arte Público Press, 1989), 60.
31. Víctor Hernández Cruz, 1989, 64.
32. Víctor Hernández Cruz, 1989, 65.
33. Esmeralda Santiago, *America's Dream* (New York: Harper Collins, 1996). While I find this novel unsurprisingly sensationalist in its primitivist portrayal of the Puerto Rican male, the insertion of a working-class Puerto Rican woman into the privileged Anglo family as a nanny raises important questions about the asymmetries of power among women of different race, class, and ethnic locations.

Works Cited

Alurista, *Spik in Gliph?* Houston: Arte Público Press, 1981.
Aponte Pares, Luis. "What's yellow and white and has land all around it?: Appropriating place in Puerto Rican barrios." *Bulletin of the Center for Puerto Rican Studies* 7, 1 (1995): 8–19.
Bakhtin, M. M. "Discourse in the Novel." In *The Dialogic Imagination*, edited by Michael Holquist. Austin, Texas: University of Texas Press, 1981.
Bhabha, Homi K. "The Other Question: Difference, Discrimination and the Discourse of Colonialism." In *Out there: Marginalization and Contemporary Cultures*, edited by Russell Ferguson, Martha Gever, Trinh T. Minh-ha, and Cornel West, 71–87. Cambridge, Mass.: The MIT Press, 1990.
Borges, Jorge Luis. "Word-Music and Translation." Charles Eliot Norton Lectures, Harvard University, 1968.
Burciaga, José Antonio. *Weedee Peepo.* Edinburg, Texas: Pan American University Press, 1988.
Cisneros, Sandra. *The House on Mango Street.* Houston: Arte Público Press, 1985.
Colón, Willie. "Color americano." In *Color americano.* Miami: CBS Discos, Inc., 1990. DCC-80351.
Fernández, Roberto. *Raining Backwards.* Houston: Arte Público Press, 1988.
Flores, Juan. "'Salvación casita': Puerto Rican Performance and Vernacular Architecture in the South Bronx." In *Negotiating Performance: Gender, Sexuality, and*

Theatricality in Latin(o) America, edited by Diana Taylor and Juan Villegas, 121–36. Durham and London: Duke University Press, 1994.

Flores, Juan, and George Yúdice. "Living Borders/Buscando America: Languages of Latino Self-Formation." In *Social Text* 24 (Fall 1990): 57–84. Reprinted in Flores, Juan. *Divided Borders: Essays on Puerto Rican Identity.* Houston: Arte Público Press, 1993: 199–224.

Hernández Cruz, Víctor. *Mainland.* New York: Random House, 1973.

———. *Tropicalization.* New York: Canon, 1976.

———. *Rhythm, Content and Flavor.* Houston: Arte Público Press, 1989.

———. *Red Beans.* Minneapolis: Coffee House Press, 1991.

———. *By Lingual Wholes.* San Francisco: Momo's Press, 1992.

Hijuelos, Oscar. *The Mambo Kings Play Songs of Love.* New York: Farrar, Straus, Giroux, 1989.

Hill, Jane. "Junk Spanish." Paper presented at conference on "Fixation and Disavowal: Resistance and the Matrices of Desire." Humanities Research Institute, University of California, Irvine, June 10–12, 1993.

hooks, bell. "Choosing the Margin as a Space of Radical Openness." In *Yearning: Race, Gender, and Cultural Politics,* 145–53. Boston: South End Press, 1990.

"Magnífico: Hispanic Culture Breaks Out of the Barrio." *Time,* July 11, 1988.

Pike, Fredrick B. *The United States and Latin America: Myths and Stereotypes of Civilization and Nature.* Austin: University of Texas Press, 1992.

Said, Edward. *Orientalism.* New York: Vintage Books, 1979.

Saldívar, José David. *The Dialectics of Our America: Genealogy, Cultural Critique, and Literary History.* Durham and London: Duke University Press, 1991.

Sánchez, Saúl. *Hay plescha lichans tu di flac.* Berkeley: Editorial Justa Publications, 1977.

Santiago, Esmeralda. *America's Dream.* New York: Harper Collins, 1996.

Treviño, Gloria. "Cultural Ambivalence in Early Chicana Literature." In *European Perspectives on Hispanic Literature of the United States,* edited by Genevieve Fabre. Houston: Arte Público Press, 1988.

Valdés, Gina. "English con Salsa." In *Cool Salsa: Bilingual Poems on Growing Up Latino in the United States,* edited by Lori M. Carlson. New York: Fawcett Juniper, 1995.

Varkonyi, Charlyne. "Getting to Know Mangoes." In *The Ann Arbor News,* July 31, 1991.

Villarreal, José Antonio. *Pocho.* New York: Doubleday, 1959.

Viramontes, Helena María. "'Nopalitos': The Making of Fiction." In *Breaking Boundaries: Latina Writings and Critical Readings,* edited by Asunción Horno-Delgado, et al., 33–38. Amherst: University of Massachusetts Press, 1989.

Zentella, Ana Celia. "Linguistic Attitudes Among Hispanics in New York City." Presentation at the Tenth Annual Conference on Spanish in the United States, Tucson, Arizona, October 1989.

Juan León

Tropical Overexposure: Miami's "Sophisticated Tropics" and the *Balsero*

> This is Miami, more a dream and an idea than stark reality . . .
> Miami, a commentary on our American civilization . . .
> —"Miami" American Geographical Society, 1969

The Primitive Tropics

Borrowing a well-known term from Edward Said as a point of departure, we might say that in modern times the tropics have been "Orientalized," or, more properly, "tropicalized." They have become an imaginary as well as a geographical site, one with quite specific territorial characteristics and cultural valences. The tropics denote a horizontal band of the earth's surface demarcated to the north by the Tropic of Cancer and to the south by the Tropic of Capricorn, parallels between which the sun travels in its seasonal migration across the heavens.[1] Due to the bounds of that movement tropical latitudes receive more direct light than any others on the planet. But just as the Orient invokes much more than a global position relative to the West, so too the Tropics are more than a matter of sunny clime. Home to people that have in some ways lived quite differently from modernizing Euro-Americans, the tropics have been purposefully (if not always self-consciously) made into an unsettling version of modernity's antithesis.[2]

Historically, the tropics are identified for the West not only by their warmth but also by their primitiveness, their striking remoteness from the conditions of the developing modern state.[3] To read western commentators on the tropics from Montaigne onward is consequently to be informed that under tropical

213

conditions human living is least involved with modern social and material advances. In this interpretive tradition tropical societies tend to be described in terms of the sophistications they do not possess: "no manner of traffic; no knowledge of letters; no science of numbers; no name of magistrate or statesman" (Montaigne 206). Motivated in part by national self-interests, religious differences, and technological disparities between cultures, such a characterization has lent itself to the exploitation of tropical regions and of the people who live there. Feminized, racialized, and paganized, the "primitive" tropics have been subjected to the sometimes well-intentioned, frequently rapacious, attentions of modernizing Euro-America.

As much as the tropics are denigrated in the tradition associated with Montaigne, we should bear in mind that the tropics are also important to that tradition through their seeming simplicity, their constructed primitiveness. A world apart from Euro-America, the imaginary tropics provide a vantage from which the modern writer, artist, or citizen can fashion a critique of self and society. Montaigne speculated that Plato would have been forced to develop an entirely different political philosophy had he been able to meet with natives of the Caribbean (206). The writings of Herman Melville on the South Pacific, Joseph Conrad on the Congo, and D. H. Lawrence on Mexico, the South Seas of Gauguin, the adoption of African motifs by modernist artists, and the popularity of Tarzan novels and films all attest to the complex allure of a Tropics seen as the challenging, primitive alternative to modern civilization.

In contrast to existence within modernity, life in the tropics of the western imagination can promise certain harmonies. It can be free of artificial structure and attuned to the environment. In these tropics storms and tropical breezes complement human excitement and languor. The allure of ripe fruit complements the pleasures and satiations of the uninhibited life of the tropical body. Distant from things modern, these fanciful tropics can be many related things: places of recreation rather than work, feeling rather than intellection, spontaneity rather than planning, indulgence rather than self-restraint, fecundity rather than sterility, community rather than alienation. Most broadly, these tropics represent surrender to human nature and the natural world rather than (perhaps stifling) control over both.

In their primitive contrast to modernity the tropics can be alluring, but they can also be threatening places of ill-health, decay, and violence inhabited by ferocious savages. If in the tropics of Euro-American vision whites may find a city of gold, a rejuvenating fountain, a beautiful, dark-skinned lover, or a naturally virtuous humanity, they may also be lost in the overgrowth of a tropical jungle, consumed, literally, by cannibals or eaten away by diseases: malaria, typhoid, dengue fever. Whites may happily "go native" in the tropics, or they may lose their heads to demonic rituals and howling head-hunters. In keeping with such a cultural double vision, the people who live in the tropics can themselves appear to westerners as benign or dangerous, as our salvation or our undoing. In her landmark study of versions of the primitive constructed by modern Euro-America, Marianna Torgovnick has given eloquent expression to our fundamental ambivalence toward the people who live in an imaginary land: "They exist for us in a cherished series of dichotomies: by turns gentle, in tune with nature, paradisal, ideal—or violent, in need of control; what we should emulate or, alternatively, what we should fear; noble savages or cannibals (3).

Thus, the primitive stands as a necessary, two-faced Other to modernity. The primitive serves as a kind of potent cultural supplement, representing a life that one can escape to, or, alternatively, escape from, a life that can remake us or destroy us. Torgovnick goes on to suggest that in the primitive's radical supplementarity there may exist the elements of a constructive critique of modernity. It remains equally possible, she warns, that the disturbing Otherness of primitivism may become merely another flash in our post-modern play of images and ideas, a bit of color in an irresponsible "melange of us and them" (246, 41). These paired possibilities are given greater immediacy and complexity, I would add, when we consider an aspect of the primitive beyond the bounds of Torgovnick's work, when we look at the primitive tropics not as traveling philosophers, artists, scientists, or anthropologists have, but as modern U.S. tourists have.

What becomes of the primitive tropics when they are not only fantasized in the West but literally "Made in the USA"? This is the question we can begin by asking of Miami as we pursue the city's questionable tropicality, and we can frame our answer by noting that in Miami the tropics are doubly denatured. First, Miami does not lie within the tropical zone. It is not, geographically speaking, tropical but rather sub-tropical. Secondly, the city is not the ambiguously signifying Tropics of the Euro-American tradition, but rather a transformed version of it, a Tropics manufactured entirely by a modern state within its own borders and for its own purposes.

Tropical Exposure

Perhaps more than any other major city in the United States, Miami owes its development to sun-seeking tourists and retirees, to dreams of escape, relaxation, and recreation in the tropics. In this it is the product not only of a local but of a national fantasy. Miami's unique self-creation was accomplished by and for others. At the turn of this century Miami's founders—wealthy, educated investors from the North—built the city on top of the Everglades through massive drainage and construction projects. A city that came into being with few of the usual industrial or commercial justifications, Miami was always to be a vacation spot, and over the years Miami was to owe its continuing success to meeting national demands and aspirations for tropical relief from modern life. As the Chamber of Commerce put it in the 1940s:

Miami is not like any other place. Miami is America's only national playground city in the only U.S. tropics—built by Americans for all America—for people like you . . . Who did it? "We, the people," did it. America built Miami because Americans wanted Miami. ("America's Miami")

A unique kind of tropicality has been at the heart of what modern America wants from Miami. Given the anti-modernity of the West's imaginary tropics, it may seem odd that a city like Miami, founded in 1898 and first flourishing in the 1920s, could so successfully present itself as a tropical locale.[4] Modern cities are not, by definition, primitive sites, but Miami gave tropical primitivism a selective expression. The tropics of early-modern Miami were largely matters of comfortable weather, lush vegetation, youthful vitality, and balmy leisure. In this way the city made use of Florida's established reputation for healthful climate. (For decades Miami's most popular ploy was to stress the health-giving effects of tropical air and sunshine.) Giving tropicality an exclusively sunny face, Miami presented itself from the beginning as a natural, youthful, magical, and "truly tropical" garden, a place of ripe tropical fruit, warm breezes, and rejuvenating pleasures. Miami was not the ambiguous, primitive tropics so much as a limited variation on the theme "tropical paradise."

Of course, Miami was not a natural "tropical paradise" accidentally discovered down south.[5] There was never anything paradisal about the land with its tropical diseases and its mosquitoes, and there was to be little that was "natural" about the city. Miami owed its existence as much to the technologies of vaccination, pest control, water management, and air-conditioning as to any other sophistication of modern life. Made a tropical paradise, Miami was, in fact, a self-conscious product of driving modernization: In southeast Florida "the almost impenetrable tropical jungle melted away before the weapons of civilization wielded by an army of energetic men" ("The Pursuit of Happiness: The Story of Miami" 8).

Miami was developed as a man-made, high-tech tropical resort, a product that sold very well. During the real estate boom of the mid-twenties, when Miami (and Florida more generally) became the locus of the most frenzied land speculation seen in this century, the average investor bought into a dream that was quite clearly, at least in part, a fabrication, a forerunner of Disney World and Epcot Center, perhaps—never a natural tropical paradise. Miami offered primitive pleasures but was far removed, in its completion, from a primitive condition. The north wanted and manufactured an improved tropics.

Thus, Miami joined the simple allure of an unsophisticated tropics with all the conveniences of modern life.[6] Miami was conceived as a fruitful garden brought to perfection by the northern developer, a beach-side retreat complete with modern amenities and splendid business opportunities.[7] That was the paradoxical mix America created. In becoming, for a time, the premier winter retreat for northeasterners, Miami perfected the modernist tropical resort: mass-produced, bought and sold, a surrogate, unambiguous tropics promising a pleasant escape from the modernity that created and sustained it.

As the most nearly tropical region of the continental United States, however, Miami has both made use of and been embarrassed by what might be called its "tropical exposure." The city boasts warm weather, but it lies exposed to the devastation of tropical hurricanes. This climatic metaphor also has social implications: through Miami we are exposed to each other in forceful ways. Being close to "home" and close to the tropics themselves, Miami forces us to confront our relations to Haiti, Cuba, the Caribbean, and Latin America. Perhaps more unsettling than the hurricanes are the actual people of the tropics—not idealized primitives—who come to Miami, bringing their different languages, customs, problems, and expectations.

In Miami the stark realities of tropical impoverishment become as manifest as the black corpses of drowned Haitians on white South Floridian beaches. The tropical fantasy of Miami breaks down when the Orange Bowl is filled not with fans of the Miami Hurricanes but with refugees from Mariel, Cuba. Ironically, our disturbed sense of being at home in "our" tropical Miami demands the detention in the Everglades of refugees from the tropics. It demands the passage of an "English only" ordinance (repealed in 1994) and an ordinance outlawing the animal sacrifice central to the Afro-Cuban religion of *Santería*. (The ordinance was declared unconstitutional by the U.S. Supreme Court in 1995.) These reactions attest to Miami's tropical exposure, the incursion of disturbing elements of the actual tropics into the national fantasy of the modern tropical resort.

This kind of tropical exposure might well be investigated through attention to various clashes between tropical ideal and reality in Miami: natural bounty/agribusiness, innocent community/political conflict, leisure/unemployment, romance/AIDS, and so on. The remainder of the essay will take up the significance of one element in the tropical incursion, the *balsero* or "rafter." The *balsero* is a tropical border-crosser uniquely associated with Cuban Miami. The term refers to persons who set to sea from the Cuban coast hoping to drift toward Florida. They commonly travel in flimsy rafts made from the inner tubes of truck tires. Rafters carry such provisions of food and water as they can muster, but these are often lost in the waves and winds of the open ocean. In a small vessel the crossing is dangerous at any time, and no one can say how many rafters have perished at sea. A great many rafts are found empty, but it is difficult to know how many occupants such rafts may have carried and whether or not the passengers were previously picked up.

Perhaps half of all rafters survive this grueling experience made possible by geographical happenstance. The proximity of Key West and Cuba, the northerly movement of the Gulf Stream, and the warmth and relative calmness of Caribbean waters combine to make rafting from Cuba to the United States feasible, if very dangerous, and Cubans have fled their homeland by raft since shortly after the revolution of 1959. Their numbers have varied according to the changing politics and economies of Cuba and the United States, but in recent years rafters have come in record numbers. Over twenty-five hundred, on average more that seven per day, were reported to have arrived in Florida in 1992. This stream continued without major change until the summer of 1994, when Fidel Castro announced that rafters would be allowed to leave Cuban shores unhindered. Approximately 30,000 of them set out for Florida before the U.S. government decided, in May 1995, that rafters intercepted at sea would no longer be automatically granted asylum in the United States. Though the rate of exodus dropped off sharply after the change of policy, as of June 1996 the U.S. Coast Guard was continuing to rescue twenty to forty rafters on average every month.[8]

The *Balsero*

In Miami the rafter becomes the preeminent tropical sign of exposure: the most compelling example, on one level, of this "tropical" city's own exposure to the tropics; on another level, of a collective anxiety bound up in the figuration of primitivism itself, the fear of helpless exposure to seemingly chaotic, irrational, and devouring natural forces. When they survive, *balseros* emerge from the tropics in the most primitive condition, presenting a stark parody of the simplicities idealized in tropical primitivism and at the same time exhibiting the consequences of overexposure in the tropics threateningly represented for the West in savagery, riotous jungle, and cannibalism.

The publication in English of J. Joaquín Fraxedas's *The Lonely Crossing of Juan Cabrera* (1993) and of John Sayles's *Los Gusanos* (1991) allows us to explore the ways in which the multiple meanings of *balseros* become textually manifested and transformed in Miami's highly charged tropical atmosphere. Both writers produce tragic accounts of rafters' experiences, and both dwell upon Miami's connection to that experience.

Fraxedas tells of the journey of Juan Cabrera, a professor of Physics at the University of Havana. In the course of the sea voyage Juan's two companions are killed: Raúl, a tough-minded ex-soldier once a worker on the Cabrera plantation, and Andrés, a fifty-five-year-old man who had spent twelve years as a political prisoner on the island. All three men had hoped to rejoin family in Miami. Juan is rescued through the efforts of Alberto, a Cuban exile pilot who dies when his plane crashes shortly after he has reported Juan's location. Having fled contemporary Cuba, Juan is shocked by the degree to which old Havana has been reproduced in Miami. Also important is Vivian, a Cuban-American Coast Guard officer. Educated in Connecticut, Vivian stands at a critical distance from the politics surrounding the rafters. For rafters Miami is the promised land. For her Miami has a curiously unreal tropicality associated with the character of Cuban-American exile, the waiting to return.

Also set in Miami, Sayles's novel weaves several stories together as it documents Marta de la Pena's obsessive, disastrous mission to commemorate her brother's death at the Bay of Pigs by raiding a Cuban power installation in 1981. In Sayles's work Miami is a place of political intrigue, violence, and betrayals where Cubans either decay, kill each other, or plot attacks upon their homeland. The novel's rafting story is told by Serafín, a friend of Marta's and her brother's. Relaxing on Miami Beach, he recalls his experience at the Bay of Pigs, where he was forced to flee the military debacle on a small utility raft with seven other men. He drifted in the Gulf of Mexico for over a week and was the group's only survivor. Member of a futile expedition organized in Miami, he has returned there psychically destroyed.

In telling their rafting stories, both writers are working with materials set in a complex social and historical context. In Miami the rafter has become an essential element of local Cuban and American life and culture. Rafters have been the subject of two television documentaries, at least two Spanish-language theatrical productions, one in English (*Passages*), and hundreds of news articles in the *Miami Herald* and other local papers. Rafts have been put on exhibit at a fine-arts gallery in Coral Gables. There have been fund-raising dinners for rafters and songs dedicated to them. One man collects rafts from the Coast Guard, storing them in his backyard (and in the yards of friends). He hopes to establish a rafters' museum. "Brothers to the Rescue," a voluntary association of Cuban and Latin-American pilots, flies planes into the Florida Straits weekly to look for rafters, often at the request of anxiously waiting relatives. Sighting a raft, pilots call the Coast Guard and circle until a boat arrives. Their small craft have crashed twice, one incident leaving an Argentine pilot paralyzed from the waist down. In early 1996 two of their aircraft were blown out of the sky by the Cuban air force.

Rafters themselves have been rescued by the Coast Guard only to be caught up in chasing a drug runner's speedboat. Some are picked up just off Cuban shores after being at sea only a few hours. One rafter arrived in Miami aboard the Queen Elizabeth II. Many women and children have come by raft. Some rafters arrive in Miami only to be whisked off to Louisville, Kentucky. Some are reunited with friends and relatives, others find no one. Despite this variety of experience, the rafter's story has taken on a certain form as a coherent cultural myth.[9] In its mythic prototype, rafting is seen as both a desperate action and a carefully considered decision. The clandestine assembly, provisioning, transportation, and launching of the raft takes heroic cunning and discipline. Rafting is undertaken by men. (Thus the common use in Spanish of the term "balsero" rather than "balsera.") Rafting is an act of independence and defiance, a risking of death for the sake of liberty. Rafters communicate in code with relatives in Miami. The trip is long and dangerous: one risks capture and imprisonment at any point between the conception of the scheme and arrival in international waters. One can easily drift away from Florida, remaining lost at sea to die of exposure or drown in bad weather. There are also sharks to contend with. If not rescued soon enough, *balseros* may become delirious, drink sea water, and jump into the ocean. Most distressing, *balseros* helplessly watch their friends and families die of thirst and exposure.

Sayles and Fraxedas work carefully with these materials. Miami is not simply a tropical resort for any of the characters they develop. Instead, the city becomes, for Sayles (an Anglo-American writer), a scene of relentless political violence, for Fraxedas (a Cuban-American who published the novel simultaneously in Spanish), the location where a community uncertainly salvages itself. For both writers the rafter as powerful tropical sign brings tropical realities to bear upon the ideal of the resort city. Furthermore, the rafter is presented as a complex, essential element of local Cuban society and culture while remaining a more broadly western symbol of tropical primitiveness, one suggesting that fear of the primitive involves recognition of a certain fundamental human helplessness and self-destructiveness.

For Sayles, the rafter exists within a more generally drawn primitivism. Echoing the rhetoric of the Euro-American primitivist tradition, Sayles characterizes an American CIA informer in the Dominican Republic as afflicted with a mysterious tropical disease that produces chronic diarrhea. Seeking help, the advice this character receives alludes comically to *Heart of Darkness*: "The German ex-patriot doctor in Puerta Plata, who ran the seafood restaurant, went into a long Conradian dirge about the maladies of the Western soul in tropical climates and told him to eat a lot of cheese" (Sayles 162).

Training in Guatemala for the invasion of Cuba, Marta's martyred brother, the poet Ambrosio, writes of an environment that is hellish tropical fantasy. He tells his sister of a jungle in which everything rots while it is still alive, of a "heat that slides its arms around you and sucks the breath from your lungs with a hot, wet kiss of decay" (264). This decay is aggressive. It reaches out and overwhelms. Soldiers must cut through bleeding vines as thick as men's arms. Fences put up against the jungle are overgrown days later. The insects indigenous to this tropics are monsters, the Indians "one step up from the mud they are covered with" (265). As Sayles's characters see them, the tropics are grounded in a horror of nature ill-defined and out of control, the land and its primitives melding into one riotous organic morass that stinks of mental and bodily corruption.

For Fraxedas the tropics impose the natural conditions that define the rafter's experience. The tropics make the sea voyage possible and they also strip the voyager down to primitive essentials. As the wind "strokes the warm surface of the tropical Atlantic" it generates the Gulf Stream in which rafters ride north (front matter). The same Caribbean wind, "warmed by the tropic sea," becomes a hurricane that afflicts the rafters on their way, destroying all their provisions (Fraxedas 33). The Gulf Stream carries the beautiful, rose-colored fish that Juan and Raúl are able to catch for refreshment, but it also brings the shark that continues the destruction of the group, tearing one raft apart and devouring Raúl.

These rafters are overexposed to the elements, exhausted by "too much sea, too much sky, too much sun" (Sayles 144). They fear predators. Re-duced to the most primitive of circumstances, desperate for shelter, food, and water, they can make only modest attempts at controlling their situation. Juan navigates by the stars, but he can't do anything about the raft's direc-tion. Serafín tries unsuccessfully to fish with a companion's dog tags. The rafters improvise a sunshade out of their shirts or use a shredded raft to catch rain water. They eat the crabs found in patches of floating seaweed. Raúl suc-cessfully fashions a fish net out of eight feet of rope. Nevertheless, he feels fundamentally adrift. "[W]ithout anything to do and without a tool to do any-thing," he feels for the first time "truly lost" (52). Here primitiveness be-comes near-helplessness within deadly surroundings, and the rafters' help-lessness culminates in watching each other die. When Andrés is shot by the crewmen of a Cuban gunboat, Raúl and Juan, who are hiding behind the raft, can only reflect in terror that there is nothing to be done about it, "¡Nada! ¡Nada! ¡Nada!" (23). Later, Juan looks on powerlessly as Raúl is torn apart by a tiger shark. He expects the creature to come after him as well. By chance it does not.

There is a special violence to the deaths recounted in these two narratives that goes beyond the mechanics of being killed. It links tropical exposure to the terror of the breaking apart of the self. Sayles follows in detail the physiol-ogy of death by dehydration. Fraxedas provides gruesome details of the shark attack. When Raúl's body is bitten in half we are told of the sound of the bones crunching. (Juan did not think the sound could be so loud.) When Andrés is shot we see the "red and white splatter" as the bullet smashes the skull (23). Serafín awakens one morning to find a companion's gangrenous foot being picked at by small fish. His friend Chiste is being eaten alive as his body grad-ually rots away. (Serafín catches some of the fish, which are later shared and eaten by the men on board.) In both accounts there is recurrent attention to bodies coming apart, an attention that goes to telling extremes. Juan imagines the devoured Raúl as round clumps of shark excrement breaking up in the water (134). Serafín and his companions talk of cannibalism. Is it cannibalism, they wonder, to eat an animal that has eaten a man? Chiste warns his companions that if they cannibalize him they will be cursed to return after death to the raft and spend eternity there. It is as if cannibalization brings the destructive exposure of the tropics full circle. Men become their own devourers and thus their punishment is to remain on the tropical raft in which they are relentlessly taken apart and consumed.

This is a hell of entrapment that parallels the rafter's own helplessness, for there is nothing the rafters can do about the degradation they undergo. Much as they may talk amongst themselves, tell jokes, or encourage each other, their cooperation or self-sacrifice can do little to change their condition. Thus the rafter's experience for Sayles and Fraxedas inevitably comes down to a personal meditation on death and surrender. Serafín gives himself up to lie on the raft and let the sun take him. He imagines his body baking in the sun and transforming "into a fossil of cured black leather" (146). Both Juan and Serafín finally attempt self-destruction but their bodies take on independent animation, forcing themselves back onto the rafts.

Serafín and Juan cannot end their own lives because their physical decay is accompanied by the collapse of conscious will and rationality. In their final delirium both men are reconciled to their deaths, but they no longer have any real control over themselves. Death is finally something they must simply wait for, and in so doing they complete their drift from any semblance of modernity. Lost at sea, they survive under the most minimal conditions possible. Their society is not that of a modern metropolis, but of a handful of others. They do no science, governing, or business on the raft. The rafter has almost no material resources, few tools, and, though his condition is desperate, there is little he can do about it. Unempirical and unobjective, the rafter is sentimental and introspective. His thoughts move inevitably toward delirium, not rationality. He meditates upon death. The rafter is cut off from the larger human world, left at the mercy of the natural world.

While the modern is associated with a dispassionate, methodical pursuit of various ends, with empiricism and technological advance, the *balsero* desperately seeks one end and hazards the riskiest of methods. While Modernity is progressive, the rafter lives in a seemingly endless present with little to do but wait for death or rescue. Modernity is largely directed at convenience in the conquest of nature and death. The rafter suffers in having no control over nature or death.[10] Having reached the extremes of endurance, the rafters of Sayles's and Fraxedas's creations unexpectedly adopt a "primitive" form of thought, poetic and associative: Serafín imagines living at the bottom of a cold lake with his deceased uncle, a fisherman. Juan speaks to his dead father, whom he denied knowing in the years after the revolution because his father was a despised *latifundista* (plantation owner).

Both rafters come to the point of delirious recognition, but here the two accounts differ in their significance. Along with everything else that has dropped away Juan sloughs off the fear and shame that overcame him the day revolutionaries took his father. Serafín is rescued by an embarrassed U.S. military that does not wish to advertise his existence. He remembers most acutely that the Cuban island tried to swallow him. He thought he might have been another Antonio Maceo, a Cuban revolutionary hero of the nineteenth century, but now his life has lost direction. As if still drifting on a raft, he lets life take him "where it wants" (137). He is unable to maintain relationships. Juan, on the contrary, discovers consolation in thinking of others. When he thinks of the wind, it is a force connecting him with friends and relatives, no matter the distance. In his suffering there is atonement, whereas for Serafín there is only disillusionment and scarring.

That our narratives take such turns is especially revealing because both accounts are self-consciously reworked versions of the rafter story. They are interventions in *balsero* culture. Serafín begins his recollections when a friend on the beach relates the fanciful tale of a Cuban couple, both athletes, who trained themselves for the escape to Miami. When their raft broke apart they pushed it the remainder of the way to Key West. (Just before despairing, fireworks from a 4th of July celebration show them how close they are to land and freedom.) Serafín's memory of his escape from the Bay of Pigs disaster sets the first story in ironic contrast. The fireworks he remembers are of deadly shelling on the Cuban beach. While waiting for Juan in Miami, relatives recall tales of rafters who have survived hurricanes. Vivian remembers growing up reading tales of rafters in Spanish (80). She remembers the story of a man who strapped flippers to a horse and tried to ride it to Miami. She remembers the first raft she ever found. The upper torso of a man remained tied to it, the rest of the body having been eaten away. Alberto searches for rafters because of the hundreds of stories he has heard about them. Though he has never found a rafter, until Juan, the stories are "the reason he kept looking" (107).

Choosing among many possible stories, then, Sayles tells one of betrayal and futility. In contrast, fully half of Fraxedas's novel is occupied with the thoughts of persons in Miami involved with the rescue of rafters. Human relations in *The Lonely Crossing* are reassuring, a consolation for exposure and death at sea, and Fraxedas's novel seems full of embraces: A Coast Guardsman carrying a rafter child, Raúl gripping Juan during the hurricane, Juan embracing his wife in Miami, Raúl's brother gripping Juan close upon hearing of Raúl's death. The reinforcing relations in Fraxedas's novel extend to the community. The concluding tone of *The Lonely Crossing* is set by Alberto's funeral. Hundreds of strangers appear to pay their respects to him at a Chapel for La Virgen del Cobre, the patron saint of Cuba. That chapel brings the group together. It is "a symbol and a gathering place of the Cuban exile community in Miami" (161). In searching for Juan, Alberto has a sense of peace and communion. Now the community shares that in grieving for him. For Serafín in Sayles's Miami, none of these community-oriented consolations seem possible.

For Sayles Miami is the place where a failed Cuban-American assault on Castro was plotted. There Americans try to cover up the humiliating remains of the fiasco while Cubans relive and recreate their tragedy. Sayles's rafter, Serafín, returns unwanted to Miami. When he sits by Miami's famous tropical beaches his thoughts turn to violence and the dead. He remembers viciously fighting with Cuban boys to sell Pepsi to American tourists on Cuban beaches—beaches in which he was not allowed to swim. Looking past the crowd of bathers on Miami Beach, he sees a man fully dressed in a suit. The Haitian man tells Serafín that he comes to the beach to look out over the water where his wife drowned when her boat capsized. The chapter in which Serafín recounts his rafting experience ends here with a mutual, mute commemoration that undercuts the otherwise comfortable beach scene.

In the end, Fraxedas's novel presents a number of different accounts of a Miami that is transformed by the rafters' experience. Cuban Miami gratefully accepts Juan as a rafter, and for him Miami appears as an amazingly vital and exact recreation of old Havana. It seems as if the Gulf Stream had torn away a chunk of Cuba and deposited it on Floridian shores, much as tornadoes are said to now and then throw a house into the air and miraculously set it down with the china intact. The Gulf Stream has brought "all the colors, all the flavors" of a Cuba that no longer exists (165).

For Alberto, the rescue pilot, Miami had become, instead, an unsettling measure of normalcy. He reflects that for a Cuban exile it is possible to go about one's life there giving little thought to the stories of *balseros*. The rafters are reminders, but reminders that can be ignored. There is at the same time a falsification in that denial, because one remains spiritually linked to Cubans left on the island: "It is very strange to be a Cuban exile in the United States, having gone through what you have gone through and knowing what you know . . . and hearing the stories you hear every day, and still go on living a normal everyday life as if nothing were happening around you, he thought" (100). For Alberto Miami is a place in which Cubans live with a sense of something unresolved.

Vivian also sees in Miami, and in the United States more generally, her measure of normalcy. The more American she becomes, the more normal her life can be. Americanness is an escape, a kind of relief from what she regards as the "o muerte" (. . . or death) extremism of Cubans. Socialism or Death, Country or Death, Freedom or Death. Why can't Cubans be more like Americans? she

"Soy balsero y trabajo por comida. Ayúdame." Yo llegué aquí el 14 de noviembre. Un hombre ahí me dijo que eso era un mal ejemplo para Los cubanos porque yo estaba pidiendo trabajo por comida. Yo le dije que yo no sé hacer otra cosa. Yo no sé robar. No sé quitarle la cartera a una vieja. No sé vender drogas. En Cuba yo trabajaba en abono químico. Soy de Regla y no tengo familia. Allá yo no podía vivir porque el régimen está muy malo. ["I came in a raft and I work for food. Please help me." I got here on November 14th. Some guy told me that I was giving Cubans a bad name by asking for food in exchange for work. I told him that I didn't know how to do anything else. I don't know how to steal. I wouldn't know how to snatch a purse from an old woman. I don't know how to sell drugs. In Cuba I worked with chemical fertilizers. I'm from Regla and I have no family. I couldn't live over there because the regime is very bad.]
— Julio Ramírez Marques, unemployed. Miami, Florida, 1993.
(Photo © Eduardo Aparicio, 1994)

wonders. Miami is not paradise because paradise remains back in the vague memory of old Cuba. Miami is a place of solemn and inescapable waiting: "an air of vigil hung over the city like the fragrance of a million tropical blossoms, as it had for the past thirty years. And if you were a Cuban living in Miami, there was no place you could escape from it" (122–23). That vigil gives the city an unreal aspect. Normalcy conflicts with the constant reminders the *balseros* bring of connections to the Cuban island and of desperate conditions there. Miami, in its normalcy, appears a bizarre fantasy, its tropicality a shifting illusion: "What an insane, impermanent city! How insubstantial, she thought. Everything is as liquid as a dream. A warm, balmy tropical dream where things appear out of the darkness only to vanish again in the mists" (123).

The Sophisticated Tropics

Miami's tropical exposure, the incursion of disturbing elements of the actual tropics into the national fantasy of the modern tropical resort, has given rise to a whole series of meanings and associations. Looking forward, what may the cultural fate of the *balsero* as a tropical sign be? Will the presence of the rafter in Miami simply become one of many contradictory elements subsumed by the city's contemporary cosmopolitanism?

Like the primitive, the rafter provides a clear vantage "outside" of modernity, but in a postmodern era such a position may no longer be useful or tenable. Postmodernity confuses inside and outside, the natural and the artificial, the non-human and the human. It encompasses contradictions as it gives up making sense of the world. This can be seen in Miami's contemporary situation. Given the bad publicity the city received throughout the eighties and early nineties, Miami could hardly continue to present itself as an improved tropical paradise. During the early nineties, in the wake of urban riots and as the numbers of Haitian refugees and Cuban rafters began to soar, the city adopted a new marketing slogan: "Miami, the Sophisticated Tropics."[11]

In a long history of tropical self-representation, Miami had adopted various labels, but they have always involved an element of Tropicality itself. Not so this new one. Sophistication has nothing to do with the tropics. As much as the tropics have been an essential part of modern Euro-American world views, within the scope of those visions the tropics have never been places of sophistication. In offering a "Sophisticated Tropics," however, the city recasts its image for a postmodern time. At one level the sophistication of Miami's Tropicality points to the sophistry and fantasy at the root of the idea of the modern Tropical Resort; at another it represents the city as a place of cosmopolitanism with a (wealthy) Latin feel, an inter-American market place, a cultured free-trade zone.

Most importantly, perhaps, sophistication in its worldly knowledgeability transcends rather than ignores (or addresses) the tropical conditions Miami is exposed to. Postmodern sophistication does not share in the Positivist aspirations of the modernist project. It is informed but playful, variously aware but self-centered, always self-conscious but never committed. It is skeptical and narcissistic. In adopting sophistication as its label, Miami addressed its own postmodernity, its movement beyond the allures and boundaries of the resort to the attractions of the transactional city of the future. The sophisticated tropics are the imaginary places where Miami can credibly be presented as the "Capital of Latin America."[12] It is a place where national tropical exposure is neither an embarrassment nor a provocation to change, because fantasy and reality are no longer capable of truly contradicting each other.

Notes

1. The sun "turns" at a point in the sky marked by the two Tropics.
2. See Michael Adas's *Machines as the Measure of Men* for an intriguing study of the ways in which religious and technological differences between cultures have led Euro-Americans to denigrate others.
3. See Wilber and Jameson's *The Political Economy of Development and Underdevelopment*.
4. Miami in this way adopted for itself the image of Florida as a tropical Eden, a rejuvenating natural locale. This representation was well-established by the turn of the century.
5. The city did make much of its location in Florida's famously healthy tropical climate, but even here there were conflicting versions of Tropicality: that of Paradise Found, and that of "PARADISE MADE" (from the city's tax office's stationery, 1912). Both mythic types can be traced back through Florida's literature and history, and traced further to alternative accounts of Paradise in *Genesis*. See *The Florida Reader* for an elaboration of this thesis and a representative collection of the literature of Florida from 1530 to the present.
6. The cruise ship, a first-world floating hotel, epitomized that development, and Miami became the cruise-ship capital of the world.
7. Although Miami has flourished as a business capital only in recent years, the city has been marketing itself as a Latin American business center since its beginnings. Here are two representative examples from city publications: "Captains of industry discover here new worlds to conquer" ("Miami by the Sea," 1924); "'Mid-City of the Americas' Closer to Yucatan than to Atlanta—closer to South America than to Chicago or New York" ("This is Greater Miami," 1947).
8. These figures are drawn from accounts in the *Miami Herald*, 1992–96.
9. Fraxedas addresses the mythic nature of the *balsero*'s experience when he begins *The Lonely Crossing* by invoking Homer:

> You shall not stay here grieving . . .
> go, cut some beams of wood, and make
> yourself a large raft with an upper
> deck that it may carry you safely over
> the sea. (front matter)

10. I am considering modernity here as it is often regarded in its distinguishing features: positivistic, technocratic, hierarchical, and rationalistic, a phenomenon of factories and cities, of mass communication, mass transport, mass culture, and mass consumption (Harvey 9, 23).
11. From April 1990 to January 1992 Miami's standard tourist information brochure bore this slogan.
12. See "Latin America's Newest Capital City: Miami."

Works Cited

Adas, Michael. *Machines as the Measure of Men: Science, Technology, and Ideologies of Western Dominance*. Ithaca: Cornell University Press, 1989.

"America's Miami." Miami Chamber of Commerce. South Florida Historical Museum. File: 1940–1949.

De George, Gail, and Antonio N. Fins, with Irene Recio. "Latin America's Newest Capital City: Miami." "Foreign Investors are Flocking in—and Business is Booming." *Business Week*, Sept. 30, 1991: 120–22.

Fraxedas, J. Joaquín. *The Lonely Crossing of Juan Cabrera*. New York: St. Martin's Press, 1993.

Harvey, David. *The Condition of Postmodernity: An Inquiry into the Conditions of Cultural Change*. Oxford: Basil Blackwell, 1989.

"Miami by the Sea: The Land of Palms and Sunshine," Winter Tourist Season. (St. Augustine: The Record Co., 1924) South Florida Historical Museum. File: "Miami, Florida-Description, 1920–1924. Pamphlets."

"Miami: Florida's Magic City." Miami Board of Trade. South Florida Historical Museum. File: 1910–1919.

Montaigne, Michel. *The Essays of Montaigne*. Translated by E. J. Trechmann. London: Oxford, 1927.

"The Pursuit of Happiness: The Story of Miami." Official Booklet. City of Miami. Miami: Graydon E. Bevis, 1937. South Florida Historical Museum.

Sayles, John. *Los Gusanos*. New York: Harper/Collins, 1991.

"This is Greater Miami: Metropolis of the Tropics." Miami: Arthur E. Curtis, 1947. South Florida Historical Museum.

Wilson, Charles K., and Kenneth P. Jameson. *The Political Economy of Development and Underdevelopment*. Fifth edition. New York: McGraw-Hill, 1992.

Contributors

Frances R. Aparicio is Arthur F. Thurnau Professor and Associate Professor of Spanish and American Culture at the University of Michigan, Ann Arbor, where she has also directed the Latino/a Studies Program. She teaches courses in Latin American and U.S. Latino/a literatures and cultures and has published widely on popular culture and music, poetry, and the politics of language and bilingualism. She is the author of *Versiones, Interpretaciones, Creaciones* (1991) and *Listening to Salsa* (1997).

Stephen Benz is Associate Professor in the department of English and Foreign Languages at Barry University in Miami. The University of Texas Press has published *Guatemalan Journey,* his account of two years as a Fullbright Scholar in Guatemala. He has also co-edited a volume of essays on Nobel Peace Prize winner Rigoberta Menchú (*Teaching and Testimony,* SUNY Press, 1996).

Debra A. Castillo is Professor of Romance Studies and Comparative Literature at Cornell University, where she specializes in contemporary Hispanic literature, women's studies, and postcolonial literary theory. She is author of *The Translated World: A Postmodern Tour of Libraries in Literature* (Tallahassee: Florida State University Press, 1984), and *Talking Back: Strategies for a Latin American Feminist Literary Criticism* (Ithaca: Cornell University Press, 1992), and translator of Federico Campbell's *Tijuana: Stories on the Border* (Berkeley: University of California Press, 1994). She has published numerous essays on contemporary Latin American, Spanish, U.S. Latino/a, and British commonwealth fiction. She is a member of the *Diacritics* editorial board and book-review editor of *Letras femeninas.*

Susana Chávez-Silverman is Associate Professor of Spanish in the department of Romance Languages and Literatures at Pomona College in Claremont, California, where she teaches courses on Latin American and U.S. Latino/a literature and culture. She specializes in gender studies and postcolonial literary theory and has published essays on contemporary Latin American and U.S. Latino/a literature.

Juan Flores is Professor of Latin American and Caribbean Studies at the City University of New York and cultural studies at CUNY Graduate Center, as well as Director of the Centro de Estudios Puertorriqueños of CUNY. He has published widely in Latino/a and Cultural Studies. He is the editor, with George Yúdice and Jean Franco, of *On Edge: The Crisis of Contemporary Latin American Culture* (Minneapolis and London University of Minnesota Press, 1992). A collection of essays, *Divided Borders,* was published in 1993 by Arte Público Press.

Juan León is Visiting Foreign Lecturer in English at Kyoto University, Japan. He is a literary and cultural historian who has written on the relations between Caribbean and U.S. cultures and on the influence of twentieth-century technology on modern literature.

María Teresa Marrero was born in Cuba and grew up in Redondo Beach, California. She has published her fiction in *Bridges to Cuba/Puentes a Cuba* (Ann Arbor: University of Michigan Press, 1995). She has also published on cultural studies and performance. Currently she teaches Latin American literature at the University of North Texas in Denton.

David Román is Assistant Professor of English at the University of Southern California. He is the author of *Acts of Intervention: Performance, Gay Men, and AIDS* (Indiana University Press, forthcoming). His essays on theater and performance have been published in *Theatre Journal, TDR: A Journal of Performance Studies, American Literature,* and various anthologies.

Silvia Spitta is Associate Professor of Spanish and Comparative Literature at Dartmouth College. She has published *Between Two Waters: Narratives of Transculturation in Latin America* (Rice University Press, 1996) and is currently working on an edition of *Theories of Colonialism in/of the Americas.*

Beatriz Urraca is Assistant Professor in the department of Modern Languages and Literatures at Swarthmore College and Lecturer in Spanish at the University of Pennsylvania. She has published on Latin American and Peninsular cultural studies and literature.

UNIVERSITY PRESS OF NEW ENGLAND publishes books under its own imprint and is the publisher for Brandeis University Press, Dartmouth College, Middlebury College Press, University of New Hampshire, Tufts University, and Wesleyan University Press.

LIBRARY OF CONGRESS CATALOGING-IN-PUBLICATION DATA
Tropicalizations : transcultural representations of latinidad / edited by Frances R. Aparicio and Susana Chávez-Silverman.

   p.   cm. — (Reencounters with colonialism—new perspectives on the Americas)
     Includes bibliographical references.
     ISBN 0–87451–816–4 (cl : alk. paper). — ISBN 0–87451–817–2 (Pa : alk. paper)
     1. Ethnicity—Latin America.   2. Latin Americans—Ethnic identity.
3. Latin Americans—Cultural assimilation.   4. Acculturation—Latin America.
5. Tropics.   I. Aparicio, Frances R.   II. Chávez-Silverman, Susana.   III. Series.
GN564.L29T76   1997
303.48'27308—dc21   97-558